HB&W·HB&W·HB&W·HB&W·HB&W·HB&W·HB&W·HB&W·HB&W·HB&W·HB&W·HB&W·HB&W·HB&

Examination Copy

PRICE POLICY AND PROCEDURE

*W*e are pleased to send you
this book, with our compliments,
so that you may have an
opportunity to review it for
possible class use. We hope you
will enjoy examining it.

Price $3.95

HARCOURT, BRACE & WORLD, INC.

757 Third Avenue, New York, New York 10017
7555 Caldwell Avenue, Chicago, Illinois 60648
1855 Rollins Road, Burlingame, California 94010

HB&W·HB&W·HB&W·HB&W·HB&W·HB&W·HB&W·HB&W·HB&W·HB&W·HB&W·HB&W·HB&W·HB&

PRICE POLICY
and
PROCEDURE

DONALD V. HARPER
University of Minnesota

Under the General Editorship of
WILLIAM F. MASSY
Stanford University

Harcourt, Brace & World, Inc.
New York / *Chicago* / *Burlingame*

TO BETTY

FOREWORD

Among the most difficult problems facing business managers are those of price policy and procedure. At the same time, such problems are the touchstone for workers in the fields of both theoretical and applied microeconomics. Questions of price policy are often paramount in public investigations of industry practice, monopoly power, and so on. No student of business can afford to ignore the far-ranging implications of price policies and procedures.

Books on pricing tend to fall into one of two categories: books for price makers and books about price makers. The former deal—usually in very "practical" terms—with materials designed to help people charged with setting and administering a firm's pricing policies make better decisions. The second kind of book concentrates on the theoretical aspects of pricing and examines the decision-making processes of price makers, analyzing their policies from the point of view of economic efficiency and social welfare.

Price Policy and Procedure is aimed at bridging the gap between these two approaches while retaining the management point of view. Recognizing that theoretical and welfare considerations are (or ought to be) of prime importance to the price maker, Professor Harper integrates materials on these subjects with "practical considerations" throughout the book. While economic theories naturally receive the most attention, his treatment includes behavioral-science, quantitative, and of course marketing theories as well. The book begins with a review of different kinds of pricing problems. Then the characteristics of the internal and external environments of the price maker, which determine his freedom of action, are considered. Building upon this groundwork, the author reexamines pricing problems in a variety of different institutional settings. This multiple approach is necessary if the market conditions, legal constraints, ethical considerations, and operational problems that make up the internal and external environments are to be placed in the proper perspective. Finally, the book includes a chapter devoted exclusively to the application of modern quantitative methods to problems of price setting and control.

Professor Harper's conception of the pricing process, his pedagogical objectives, and his clear and authoritative style have produced a textbook that will make a significant contribution to the advancement of "new look" business education at both the undergraduate and graduate levels.

WILLIAM F. MASSY

PREFACE

Most business firms in the United States have the right and the responsibility to set prices for their products and services. The quality of such pricing decisions can be an important determinant of the success or failure of a firm.

There are two basic kinds of pricing decisions a firm must make. The first is what price *policy* to adopt—that is, what guidelines or rules to follow in pricing. The second is what price *procedure* to establish—that is, the setting of specific prices for specific products or services in accordance with those guidelines or rules.

Although pricing is of interest to persons in several phases of a firm's operations, it is of particular interest and importance to the people responsible for marketing the firm's products or services. In fact, pricing is often considered to be a marketing function, and pricing decisions are often made by marketing executives or after consultation with marketing executives. Pricing can certainly have a great impact on the effectiveness of a firm's marketing effort; indeed, some of the more difficult decisions marketing managers must make involve pricing. Some reasons for this are the lack of information on which to base a pricing decision, the lack in the past in many firms of any systematic approach to pricing problems, and the large role that judgment must play.

This book attempts to provide a comprehensive treatment of the general subject of price policy and procedure from the point of view of the marketing executive. It deals with the various internal and external factors that must be considered in pricing, the kinds of pricing problem the marketing executive faces, the kinds of decision he must make, and the manner in which pricing problems are and should be handled.

This book is intended for students who have completed an introductory course in marketing and are now studying price policy or other marketing courses, such as marketing management, in which the subject of pricing plays a major part. However, it is hoped that practitioners of marketing will also read the book to advantage.

The author is grateful to those who have helped in the preparation of *Price Policy and Procedure*. He extends his thanks to Professors Richard K. Gaumnitz, Nicholas A. Glaskowsky, Jr., and George Seltzer, all of the University of Minnesota, for their encouragement and cooperation, and to Professor William F. Massy of Stanford University for the many suggestions he made to improve the book. The author also thanks the hundreds of undergraduate and graduate students enrolled in his price policy classes in the past ten years who, through class discussion and research papers, have contributed both ideas and facts to the writing of this book. Finally, the author extends his thanks to Mrs. Nancy Breitbarth and Miss Jean Bartelt for their efficient assistance in the typing of the manuscript.

DONALD V. HARPER

CONTENTS

ix

1

THE NATURE OF PRICES

AND PRICING

DEFINITION OF PRICE

Prices determine how resources are to be used. They are also the means by which products and services that are in limited supply are rationed among buyers. The price system of the United States is a very complex network composed of the prices of all the products bought and sold in the economy as well as those of a myriad of services, including labor, professional, transportation, and public-utility services, and others ranging from dry cleaning to lawn-mower repair. The interrelationships of all these prices make up the "system" of prices. The price of any particular product or service is not an isolated thing. Each price is linked to a broad, complicated system of prices in which everything seems to depend more or less upon everything else. In this book we will examine the pricing of both products and services.

If one were to ask a group of randomly selected individuals to define "price," many would reply that price is an amount of money paid by the buyer to the seller of a product or service or, in other words, that price is the money value of a product or service as agreed upon in a market transaction. This definition is, of course, valid as far as it goes. For a complete understanding of a price in any particular transaction, much more than the amount of money involved must be known. Both the buyer and the seller should be familiar with not only the money amount, but with the amount and quality of the product or service to be exchanged, the time and place at which the exchange will take place and payment will be made, the form of money to be used, the credit terms and discounts that apply to the transaction, guarantees on the product or service, delivery terms, return privileges, and other factors. In other words, both buyer and seller should be fully aware of all the factors that comprise the total "package" being exchanged for the asked-for amount of money in order that they may evaluate a given price.

The "true" price of a product or service changes whenever any of the associated elements in the package change, as well as when the money amount to be exchanged is altered. For example, if a department store discontinues return privileges on certain articles, or if a manufacturer of industrial machinery reduces the period during which interest will not be charged on credit transactions, the true price has been changed. The money price has not changed, but the package has.

This tends to complicate comparisons of prices on specific products or services over time. The difficulty lies in the frequency with which the conditions or factors change. For example, for many products changes in quality have been substantial over time, thereby rendering any price comparisons somewhat meaningless. Home appliances and automobiles fall into this classification.

Another source of difficulty in comparing prices over time is the fact that the "published," "quoted," "announced," or "list," price of a product or service may, in reality, not be the price actually paid. Various kinds of concealed price concessions may be given to some or all buyers. In such cases, the quoted price is not the "true" price.[1]

THE CONTRIBUTION OF ECONOMIC THEORY
TO PRICE MAKING

WHAT IS PRICE THEORY?

A large proportion of the literature on economic theory is devoted to explaining the pricing mechanism. Price theory, or microeconom-

---

[1] For a discussion of departures from list prices, see "Discounts That Don't Show," *Business Week,* March 2, 1963, p. 23.

ics, is concerned with the economic activities of individual economic units, such as consumers, resource owners, and business firms. It deals with the flow of products and services from business firms to consumers, the composition of the flow, and the evaluation or pricing of the component parts of the flow. Similarly, it examines the flow of productive resources (or their services) from resource owners to business firms, their evaluation, and their allocation among alternative uses.[2] In short, one of the main objectives of price theory is to explain by means of abstract analysis how prices are determined under various kinds of market structures.

Students of marketing and practitioners in the field should be familiar with the basic elements of price theory and its usefulness in the price-making process, but a brief review of price theory and its contribution to price making may be helpful.

COST AND DEMAND CONCEPTS

In order to discuss price theory it is essential that we have a clear understanding of the definitions of certain basic concepts of cost and demand.

Thus, to review briefly, *average total cost* (ATC) is the average cost per unit and is derived by dividing total costs (which include a "normal" return on invested capital) by the number of units of product or service sold.

Marginal cost (MC), in contrast, is the change in total costs that results from producing an additional unit of product or service. In other words, it is the extra or additional cost incurred in the production of another unit.

Average revenue (AR) is the average revenue per unit sold and is derived by dividing total revenue by the number of units of product or service sold.

Marginal revenue (MR) is the change in total revenue that results from the sale of an additional unit of product or service. In other words, it is the additional revenue received from the sale of another unit.

Price elasticity of demand is a measure of the responsiveness of the quantity sold to price changes. Specifically, it is the ratio of the per-

[2] Richard H. Leftwich, *The Price System and Resource Allocation,* rev. ed. (New York: Holt, Rinehart and Winston, 1963), p. 8.

centage response of the quantity sold to a percentage change in price. The demand for a product or service is said to be *elastic* if the total revenue increases as the price is reduced. Demand is *inelastic* if the total revenue decreases when the price is reduced. If there is no change in the total revenue when prices are changed, demand is said to display *unitary elasticity*. Thus, the more sensitive that the quantity demanded is to price changes, the more elastic is the demand for the offering. In graphic terms, a perfectly elastic demand is illustrated by a perfectly horizontal line, a perfectly inelastic demand is illustrated by a perfectly vertical line.

KINDS OF MARKET STRUCTURES

Several kinds of market structures have been isolated by economists in an attempt to explain how prices are determined in a free enterprise economy. The market structure in which a firm operates is determined by three basic elements: the number of firms in the industry, the size of the firms in the industry, and the nature of the product or service sold, in terms of the degree of product differentiation. In discussing these market structures, the economist assumes that the business firm attempts to maximize profits and that the business executive knows what the firm's cost and demand characteristics are.

Pricing under pure competition   In a situation of pure competition the following assumptions apply:

1. There is a large number of buyers and sellers, each of whom enjoys so small a share of the market that no single individual or firm has any influence on price.
2. There is complete freedom to enter and leave the industry.
3. The products and services sold are homogeneous (or standardized), so that the offerings of one seller of a given product or service are identical to those of all other sellers of that product or service.
4. There is full knowledge on the part of both buyers and sellers as to the terms and conditions of sale.
5. All factors of production in the economy are fully employed.

Under such circumstances, a firm has no need for a price policy; it sells at a price over which it has no control. The market itself fixes a price that equates the quantities sellers are willing to sell with the

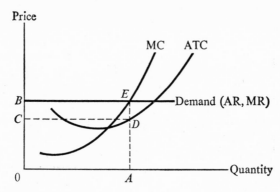

Figure 1   Pure Competition—
Short Run

quantities buyers are willing to buy. As a consequence, the demand
for the output of any particular firm is perfectly elastic; if the firm
raised the price on its product above the established price, it would
reduce demand to zero, whereas it can sell any amount of the product
at the market-determined price. These factors produce a perfectly
horizontal demand curve as shown in Figure 1. (Notice that in pure
competition the demand curve is also the average-revenue [AR]
curve and the marginal-revenue [MR] curve.) The only decisions required of a firm under such circumstances are whether to sell at all
and, if so, how much to produce. The firm would maximize its profits
by producing the quantity at which marginal cost (MC) is equal to
marginal revenue or price. Up to that point, an increase in output
adds more to revenue than to cost; beyond that point, an increase in
output adds more to cost than to revenue.

Thus in Figure 1, the firm would maximize profits by producing a
quantity 0A, the price of which would be 0B. Here the firm is earning
excess profits, that is, profits in excess of a normal return on invested
capital or in excess of what the capital would earn in an alternative
use. Such excess profits are equal to the rectangle CDEB—the difference between price and average total cost (ATC). Excess profits can
exist in the short run, but, under pure competition, in the long run excess profits attract additional firms into the industry and encourage existing firms to expand, thereby causing a downward pressure on price.
Therefore, in the long run, price tends to be equal to the minimum
average cost of each firm. This produces equilibrium, in which there
is no incentive for firms to enter or leave the industry—neither excess

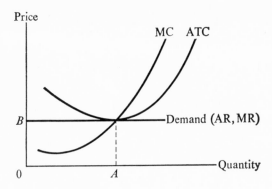

Figure 2 Pure Competition—
Long Run

profits nor losses are being incurred. Figure 2 illustrates a typical long-run equilibrium situation for the individual firm.

Pricing under pure monopoly Pure monopoly is the reverse of pure competition. In a pure monopoly, the seller has complete control over the output of a product for which there is no substitute so similar that the monopolist's sales are affected by price changes in the substitute product. Consequently, the demand curve for the monopolist's product is equivalent to the demand curve for the entire industry. This, in turn, means that as the monopolist lowers prices he will sell more units of his product or service, and that as he raises prices he will sell fewer units. The demand curve slopes downward to the right, unlike the perfectly horizontal demand curve faced by the seller under pure competition. Hence, the monopolist looks for a combination of price and output that provides him with the greatest total difference between cost and revenue, or the greatest total profit.

In both the short run and the long run the monopolist can maximize profits by equating marginal cost and marginal revenue. In Figure 3, for example, the firm would maximize profits at output $0A$ and price $0B,$ for this is the point at which marginal cost equals marginal revenue. The basic kind of adjustment that the pure monopolist needs to make to maintain the profit-maximizing position in the long run is that of changing the scale of plant.

Pricing under monopolistic competition In monopolistic competition, it is also assumed that there is a large number of buyers and sellers, but, unlike pure competition, there is product differentiation; that is, the offerings of competing firms are not identical in the eyes of

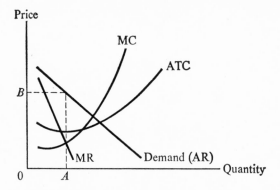

Figure 3 Pure Monopoly

the buyer. However, in monopolistic competition, as in pure competition, the actions of one seller have no perceptible effect upon the other sellers because there is a large number of competitors. Product differentiation accounts for the fact that the demand curve faced by a firm under monopolistic competition is not perfectly elastic but, instead, is somewhat inelastic and slopes downward to the right. Furthermore, because of the competition from close substitutes, the demand curve will not usually have a very steep slope. The short-run pricing situation faced by a firm under monopolistic competiton is depicted in Figure 4.

Here we see that in the short run the firm will produce 0A units and sell at price 0B, thus earning a total excess profit of *CDEB*. With

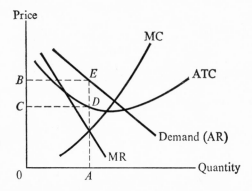

Figure 4 Monopolistic Competition—
Short Run

marginal cost equal to marginal revenue at this point, profits are being maximized for the firm. Notice that this does not mean that all firms in the industry will be charging identical prices if they are all maximizing profits since, by definition, firms in monopolistic competition do not produce homogeneous products or services, and each firm attempts to equate its own marginal cost and marginal revenue. However, the competition from many close substitutes may cause the prices to be relatively close together.

As in pure competition, the presence of excess profits in the short run will attract new competitors and cause existing competitors to expand, thereby producing a long-run tendency for excess profits to diminish. The resultant shift of the demand curve facing the firm, downward and to the left, may eliminate the excess profits, as shown in Figure 5. The theory of monopolistic competition recognizes that the demand curve may not be pushed to actual tangency with the average-total-cost curve, however, since special advantages of branding, trademarks, and patents cannot be removed completely by competition because perfect substitutes cannot be produced. Thus it is possible that the demand curve will not be tangent to the average-total-cost curve in the long run. In any event, in both the short run and the long run, to maximize profits the firm under monopolistic competition attempts to equate marginal cost and marginal revenue.

Pricing under oligopoly   Another departure from pure competition is called oligopoly. It exists when there are so few sellers of a particular product or service that the market activities (including pricing) of one seller have an important effect on the other sellers. In such a situation each seller is aware that the competing firms in the industry are interdependent and that in changing his prices or engaging in other market activities he must take into account the probable reactions of the other sellers. Under pure competition, pure monopoly, and monopolistic competition, the seller faces a definite predictable demand situation that can be identified by the firm, at least conceptually. This is not true in an oligopoly situation, however, as long as there is no collusion between the competing sellers. An independent price change by one seller may be expected to lead to a chain of repercussions that have no definite or predictable outcome. Thus the oligopolist often cannot be sure what will happen if he decides to initiate a unilateral price or output change.

Because there are many different kinds of oligopolies, it is impossible to construct a general theory that will adequately explain all conceivable oligopolistic situations. Consequently, the analysis of oligop-

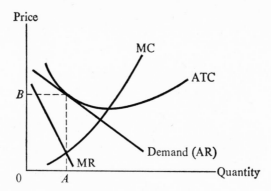

Figure 5   Monopolistic Competition—
Long Run

oly tends to be less specific than that of other market structures. Some of the characteristics that vary from case to case in an oligopoly, and that make generalizations difficult, are the degree of product differentiation, the ease of entry into the industry, and the ability of a firm to predict with certainty what competing firms will do, particularly their reaction to an action that it proposes to take in the market place. To some extent this last characteristic is a function of the presence or lack of collusion.

In an oligopoly, as in the other competitive situations we have discussed, a firm will attempt to equate marginal cost and marginal revenue in order to maximize profits. A thorough survey of the various theories of oligopoly may be found in any text on microeconomic theory. It may be helpful, however, to make a distinction between two kinds of oligopolistic situations. The first is referred to as *pure* or *homogeneous oligopoly* and the second as *differentiated oligopoly*.

In a pure or homogeneous oligopoly there is a small number of firms in the industry, and they sell a homogeneous product or service. All sellers generally are compelled to ask the same price since the purchase decision is predominantly influenced by price when a homogeneous product or service is involved. Furthermore, because there are only a few sellers, each seller must consider what effect his prices will have on pricing by competitors, and each must expect retaliation if he reduces prices. Thus, a firm in an oligopoly will reduce prices only if it thinks it can benefit from the decrease even though competitors should match the lower price.

By way of contrast, in a differentiated oligopoly a seller is not compelled to price at the same level as his competitors since, in the

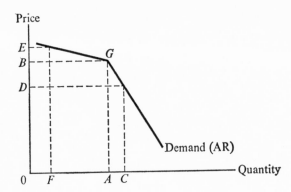

Figure 6   Oligopoly—
Kinked Demand Curve

eyes of the purchaser, there is some real or imagined product differentiation. Hence prices vary among firms in the oligopoly, and they vary in direct proportion to the differences in the degree of product differentiation among the offerings of the competing firms.

Short-run price behavior in oligopolistic industries is sometimes depicted by a "kinked" demand curve, which can be used to describe either pure oligopoly or differentiated oligopoly, although it is more appropriate for the former. Basically, the kinked demand curve is used to describe a situation in which (1) an acceptable price or cluster of prices has been well established in the industry; (2) if one firm lowers its price, other firms will follow that price or undercut the new price in order to retain their market shares, so that a unilateral price reduction by one firm has the effect of leaving market-share distribution about where it was before or reducing it for the firm that initiated the price reduction; and (3) if one firm increases its price, competing firms will not follow the price increase, thereby causing customers of the firm to shift their patronage to other firms that offer lower prices and causing the firm that initiated the price increase to lose all or part of its share of the market. Such a kinked demand curve is shown in Figure 6.

In Figure 6 we assume that the established price for the firm is $0B$. If the firm should adjust price downward to $0D$, the other firms will probably follow. As a result, the firm succeeds only in keeping the same share of the market that it had before (or possibly losing some of that share) while decreasing its total revenue. If the firm should increase price to $0E$, other firms will probably not follow the price change, and as a consequence the firm will lose a considerable share of the market to other firms. For this reason the demand curve above point *G* is shown to be considerably more elastic than it is below point *G*.

Given the situation described by the kinked demand curve, the firm tends to avoid price changes in either direction since downward adjustments only decrease total revenue, and upward adjustments reduce market share substantially or eliminate it entirely.

It must be kept in mind, of course, that the kinked demand curve is only one of several possible situations that can exist under oligopoly and is appropriate only when the situation in question possesses characteristics similar to those listed above.

USEFULNESS OF PRICE THEORY TO THE PRICE MAKER

Bridging the gap between price theory and the practice of setting prices is difficult. The basic problem is that, to a great extent, conventional price theory does not describe the "real world" in that the assumptions upon which it rests are unrealistic.

One common assumption underlying all traditional theories of price is that the entrepreneur, or businessman, carefully weighs and measures the gains and losses that accrue as a result of price decisions that he makes. In theory the price maker is assumed to be a rational person who is capable of analyzing the implications of his decisions and deciding accordingly. This is not a realistic assumption, however, because human beings are not as rational in their economic behavior as it supposes and because information concerning costs and demand is often not available to them in the form or to the degree that is assumed in price theory. There is, in fact, a great deal of uncertainty regarding both costs and demand in the real world.

Another assumption common to all types of price theory is that the firm and the price maker attempt to maximize profits. In practice, however, as we shall discuss in the next chapter, price makers and other business executives may be guided, at least in the short run, by motives other than, or in addition to, profit maximization.

Price theory is also limited in its usefulness in that it assumes that the firm is a single-product or a single-service firm. In the real world, most firms are involved in selling several different products or services, and, as is discussed in Chapters 6 and 7, the fact that a firm has a multiproduct line has a great impact on its pricing decisions.

Because of these restrictive assumptions, theories of price are simplifications. The following considerations are contrary to the special assumptions that underlie the theory of pure competition.

1. Many industries have a limited number of buyers or sellers, some of whom are quite large in size.
2. Large capital requirements often make it difficult to enter an industry, and the fixed nature of some investments sometimes makes it difficult to leave an industry.
3. Products are rarely homogeneous—instead, product differentiation is the rule, whether these differences are based solely on brand names or whether there are substantial physical differences as well in the products and services offered by competing sellers.
4. Full knowledge is generally lacking, especially on the buyers' side.
5. Many industries, furthermore, often do not operate at full capacity.

Because of these considerations pure competition, as rigorously defined in theory, has never existed in practice, and it never will.

Another problem encountered in attempting to apply price theory is that in practice some market situations contain a number of rival sellers that is neither large nor small, but somewhere in between. In such cases sellers are sometimes concerned about the actions of competitors and sometimes not. This means that in theoretical terms it is impossible to designate such industries as either oligopolies or as examples of monopolistic competition. They simply do not fit into a neat theoretical category.

Thus it is apparent that in practice business decisions involve much more than a mechanical equating of marginal cost and marginal revenue for the purpose of determining production levels and prices, as price theory may seem to suggest. Of course it is impossible for price theory to take into account all the economic factors and data in the real world. Abstract theory must single out what appear to be the most important or most relevant variables, and from these build a general theory of how the price system operates. If this were not the case, theoretical analysis would not be manageable or meaningful.

Price theory has been developed primarily for use in the analysis of the effects of broad economic changes and the evaluation of social controls. It is too much to expect that the tools that are useful for social economics would also be useful in the same degree for the price maker.[3]

Nevertheless, in the analysis of how an individual firm sets its prices, price theory is helpful to the extent that it sets forth the general forces that affect pricing and offers some explanation of why these forces affect pricing. In addition, price theory permits the isolation of separate influences on prices where there are many influences operating simultaneously, and it brings to light a number of questions that the price maker should take into account.

Price theory also provides a useful standardized terminology for the discussion of cost and demand concepts. Furthermore, the several kinds of market situations described by price theory, although they are themselves somewhat unrealistic, provide a benchmark against which a "real" pricing situation may be compared. In this regard, for example, price theory points up the necessity of considering the degree of product differentiation and the number of sellers in an industry in any pricing decision.[4]

Finally, price theory is relevant for price making in that it points out some broad social and economic implications of different pricing policies. Such implications are important not only to government officials and others concerned with public policy matters but to the price maker as well.

For these reasons, price theory is basic to an understanding of price policy and price procedure and, in fact, to most marketing activities. Certainly, no marketing executive should attempt to assume the responsibilities of price making without first having a sound knowledge of the basic elements of price theory.

KINDS OF PRICES AND PRICE MAKING

It is possible to make use of the terminology and the various market structures set forth in traditional price theory when describing the

[3] William W. Haynes, *Managerial Economics: Analysis and Cases* (Homewood, Ill.: Dorsey Press, 1963), p. 347.

[4] Edward R. Hawkins relates the theory of monopolistic competition to marketing price policies in "Price Policies and Theory," *Journal of Marketing*, January, 1954. He states on p. 233 that most pricing behavior is quite consistent with the general theory of monopolistic competition.

several kinds of price making practiced in the economy of the United States today. These types of price making have been described by Jules Backman as market pricing, administered or business-controlled pricing, and government-controlled pricing.[5]

MARKET PRICING

According to Backman, market pricing exists whenever the seller has no control over the price he receives in the market place. In such a situation price is determined solely by the free play of the forces of supply and demand. The seller either accepts the price determined by this mechanism or he refuses to sell. He cannot sell at a price higher than that established in the market. Notice that market pricing conforms closely to the model of pure competition. Obviously, where there is market pricing the seller makes no price decisions and needs no price policy.

Examples of true market pricing are very rare and are confined mainly to the organized commodity exchanges (such as those where grain, cotton, and other products are traded), some other agricultural markets, and the security exchanges.

ADMINISTERED OR BUSINESS-CONTROLLED PRICING [6]

Administered, or business-controlled, prices are prices that are established by business firms at their own discretion. The seller sets the price and buyers buy or do not buy as they wish. Here prices are not fixed automatically by the impersonal forces of the market place but rather are the result of policies and decisions made by sellers. The free play of the forces of supply and demand, along with other factors, are important in influencing pricing decisions, but they do not actually establish the price, as in market pricing. Administered pricing,

---

[5] *Price Practices and Price Policies* (New York: Ronald Press, 1953), pp. 3–4.

[6] Some confusion surrounds the term "administered pricing." In this text the term is being used to denote all situations in which prices are established by business firms at their own discretion. Some writers have used it to designate a kind of price behavior (usually undesirable) rather than a method of arriving at or determining a price. Other writers use the term to identify price making in heavily concentrated industries only. The confusion surrounding the term accounts for part of the criticism of administered pricing.

then, is a broad concept that embraces any situation in which there is some degree of inelasticity in the firm's demand curve, such as under monopolistic competition, oligopoly, and pure monopoly.

Because the seller takes the initiative in price making instead of receiving a price from the market, administered pricing is sometimes referred to as reversed or "inverted" price making. Where there is administered pricing, pricing decisions and a price policy are obviously required. As Roland S. Vaile, E. T. Grether, and Reavis Cox have pointed out:

> Price policy and administered pricing assume that there is some discretionary latitude in pricing, within which meaningful decisions are made by the enterprise individually or by groups of enterprises. In almost all business pricing, except for some segments of the primary industries, there is at least a narrow zone of choice among alternatives. Even when sellers are numerous, product differentiation and heterogeneity and the chain linking of products and of types of enterprises may create conditions favorable to and opportunities for the exercise of discretion in pricing by individual firms.[7]

Most prices in the American economy are administered prices in this sense of the term, and they are found in all areas of business activity from the corner grocery store to United States Steel or Du Pont. The degree of discretion, or the amount of control, that the seller has over the price of his product or service varies considerably, basically because of variations in the degree of product differentiation and also because of differences in the size of the firm and the number of competitors in the industry. Administered pricing is found in many market-structure situations; there may be a large number of sellers and very little product differentiation, or there may be only two or three firms in an industry and high product differentiation. For example, the manager of gasoline service station A, who sells a "major" brand of gasoline, exercises administrative control over the prices he charges. He sets a price, and potential buyers either pay it or not. However, because gasoline (at least within the broad categories of "major" and "independent" brands) is considered by many, if not most, purchasers of gasoline to be a homogeneous or standardized product (except for the brand-name differences), many buyers of gasoline are quite sensitive to price differences. Thus, if station manager B reduces his price by several cents per gallon while his competi-

---

[7] *Marketing in the American Economy* (New York: Ronald Press, 1952), p. 403.

tors who also sell major brands do not, he will enjoy increased business because many buyers feel that "gasoline is gasoline" and will patronize the station with the lowest price. Manager A, if he is a competitor of B, then must either suffer a reduction in sales volume or lower his price to be competitive with manager B. If he decides to lower his price, as is often the case, another gasoline price war may begin.[8] Such price wars tend to occur in industries where a product lacks differentiation in the eyes of many buyers, thereby making price the most important factor in the purchase decision. This means that the demand curve faced by the individual seller is highly elastic. For this reason, although the manager of a gasoline service station may exercise administrative control over the prices he charges, his degree of discretion is very much limited by the forces of competition and the nature of demand for the product he sells—barring collusive activity among the gasoline retailers.

In contrast, a seller of a highly differentiated product, such as a manufacturer of a camera that has an exclusive picture-developing feature or a musical instrument with an established, prestigious reputation, is not so limited as to the price at which he can sell his product, nor does he find it so necessary to maintain the same prices as his competitors. Since there is substantial product differentiation, price loses some of its significance to the buyer, and seller A does not have to charge the same price as seller B in order to remain in business. Because his product or service is different from that of his competitors, and because it offers certain features that are not offered by competing products or services, a certain number of buyers may be willing to pay prices above those asked by competitors in order to obtain these unique product features. In such a situation the demand curve faced by the individual seller is to some degree inelastic. The greater the product differentiation is—whether physical, or psychological, or both—the more control the seller has over the price.

Other important factors that influence the amount of control the seller has over the price of his product or service are the size of the firm and the number of competing sellers. Thus, there are some in-

---

[8] Price competition in gasoline at the retail level is complicated by the existence of "major" and "independent" brands and the accepted differential in price between the two categories. In other words, price warfare in the above example may be not only between retailers of major brands but also between them and those who sell independent brands.

dustries, such as steel manufacturing, where despite the fact that the product is essentially homogeneous, or standardized (except for brand names), the largest firm has been able to exercise a considerable amount of control over price. In this case the other firms in the industry, which is composed of a relatively small number of firms, have been willing to follow its lead, for a number of reasons. This industry approaches pure oligopoly.[9]

Other industries are characterized by considerable product differentiation and are composed of a small number of large firms, as in differentiated oligopoly. The automobile industry is an example. Here the ability to control price is relatively great although, of course, individual firms do not enjoy anything like complete freedom to set prices without regard for the nature of competition and demand, as is pointed out in later chapters.

Thus, the term "administered pricing" is used to designate a catchall category that includes most pricing environments in the United States and many different degrees of control over price. In fact, one could theoretically set up a scale of values for this category in which industries or firms with very little control over their prices are listed at one end and industries or firms with near monopoly power over prices are shown at the other end.

GOVERNMENT-CONTROLLED PRICING

The prices of some goods and services produced by private business are set directly by government—federal, state, or local. Consider, for example, government regulation of the rates or prices in the transportation and public-utilities industries, agricultural price programs, and wartime or other emergency price controls. In such cases public administration of prices has replaced or works in conjunction with privately administered prices or market prices. In the case of the traditionally regulated industries—transportation and public utilities— the usual practice is for the regulated companies to make use of their administrative authority to set prices with the understanding that such prices are subject to review and possible adjustment or rejection by the government regulatory agency involved. Thus, in industries such

[9] Price leadership is discussed more fully in Chapter 3.

as these public administration works with and on occasion replaces private administration of prices. In the case of emergency price controls, such as those imposed in wartime, price fixing is done entirely by the government.

In addition to the situations in which government regulates pricing in private industry by means of a formal system of regulation, it should be noted that government is playing an increasingly important role in price making in other ways as well. For example, government participation in price making by private business is found in the defense industry and other industries where private business firms supply goods or services to government. In such cases government influences price just as any buyer would. Sometimes government is the only possible buyer (monopsony), and it then exerts a decisive influence on pricing decisions.

Governments also set prices on products or services they provide to the public, such as postal rates, rates for electric power sold by the Tennessee Valley Authority, water rates set by municipally owned companies, and charges for street, sewer, and other improvements made by local governments (monopoly situations).

The scope of government participation in the pricing process of American business is not limited to such overt examples as those cited above. Much of the pricing in the private sector of the economy is subject to influence by government as exerted through pressures from high government officials and Congressional committees (nonstatutory influences) or through legislation such as the Sherman Act, the Robinson-Patman Act, the Federal Trade Commission Act, patent laws, tariff laws, and resale price maintenance laws.

KIND OF PRICING TO BE DISCUSSED

In this text we shall be concerned chiefly with administered or business-controlled pricing since the vast majority of pricing decisions in the American economy falls into this category. Because market pricing occurs relatively infrequently and involves no price decisions or price policies, it will not be considered further. The role of government in pricing will be discussed in Chapter 4, primarily in connection with the legal environment in which pricing decisions are made and with some nonstatutory government influences on pricing.

Direct government regulation of pricing, such as that found in transportation and some other industries, is not covered in this text.[10]

CRITICISMS OF ADMINISTERED PRICING

Administered pricing has been subjected to criticism from various sources and has been investigated by the federal government. The criticisms are that there is a lack of competition in administered pricing, that administered prices are those of big business, that they are too inflexible, and that they contribute to inflation.

LACK OF COMPETITION IN ADMINISTERED PRICING

One criticism that is sometimes made of administered pricing is that there is much less competition in an industry in which administered pricing exists than would be the case if market pricing prevailed. It has been said that administered prices are "noncompetitive" or "monopoly" prices since the forces of supply and demand do not determine prices, as would be the case under market pricing. It is charged that under administered pricing competition is reduced or eliminated and that the price maker has considerable power to charge the price that will be most profitable for his firm.[11]

As we have seen, however, actual examples of market pricing are hard to find in the American economy. The reason for the general absence of market pricing is simple—the conditions necessary for its existence are usually not found in the real world. Market pricing, as we have defined it, approximates pure competition, yet as we pointed out

[10] There is extensive literature available on direct government regulation of pricing in the traditionally regulated industries such as transportation and public utilities. For example, an excellent source of information on government regulation of pricing in the transportation industry is D. Philip Locklin, *Economics of Transportation,* 6th ed. (Homewood, Ill.: Irwin, 1966).

[11] For example, the following statement has been attributed to the late Senator Estes Kefauver: "Administered prices are those which, in contrast to competitive prices determined by market supply and demand, are arbitrarily set and held constant, or on occasion even increased despite a fall in demand." See "The Fruits of Price Investigation," *The Progressive,* July, 1961, p. 12.

earlier in this chapter, very few market structures in the real world approach the theoretical concept of pure competition in every respect.[12] Instead of pure competition we find various forms of monopolistic competition or oligopoly, which are characterized by product differentiation, small numbers of sellers in some industries, large firms as well as small firms, and lack of complete knowledge.

Despite these elementary flaws in their arguments, critics of administered pricing insist on comparing administered pricing with market pricing or, in other words, pure competition. They imply that any departure from the concept of pure competition is undesirable. Indeed, the very terms "monopolistic competition" and "imperfect competition" that have been used to designate such departures in price theory seem to imply that there is something unnatural about these forms of competition. It is true, of course, that pure competition, if it existed, would in the long run result in prices equal to minimum average costs and that there would be no sales promotion expenditures and no profits for firms beyond the minimum required to keep them in the business. This is partially responsible for its attractiveness as a standard. Another important reason is that economic theory prior to the 1930's put heavy emphasis on pure competition, so that as new theories developed in later years, they tended to be looked upon as departures from the "norm" of pure competition.

As we have seen, pure competition is generally unattainable in the real world because of its artificial, unrealistic assumptions. Therefore, it is unreasonable to use pure competition as a standard by which to judge the existing competitive system. The theory of pure competition provides a useful model that illustrates in simplified form the general pressures or forces that influence prices. Nonetheless, pure competition, as it is rigorously defined, has never existed and never will exist, although there are isolated examples, such as commodity exchanges, that closely approximate it. Furthermore, it is interesting to note that we probably would not like pure competition even if we could have it. It is doubtful that we would want a situation in which all products of a given type were identical even though they were produced by different firms all of which were small.

What, then, is the role of competition in the real world of administered pricing and less than perfect markets? Is competition any more

[12] For a discussion of this point, see Backman, *op. cit.,* pp. 4–6, and *Pricing: Policies and Practices* (New York: National Industrial Conference Board, 1961), pp. 9–12.

or less an effective force than would be the case under market pricing or pure competition? It is, of course, difficult to make a general statement as to the role that competition plays in the business world today, since, as we have mentioned, such a wide variety of industries is involved. Competition is certainly more potent in some than in others. It is impossible to measure objectively the degree of competition that exists in any given industry, however. Under administered pricing, competition can be and often is very vigorous. This competition usually revolves around a number of factors in addition to (sometimes instead of) price. These are the host of variables, including personal selling effort, advertising, product development, delivery services, and credit terms, which are referred to as nonprice competition. Certainly, in many industries competition is keen although the industries are characterized by administered pricing. In such cases the price maker does not merely set a price for his product or service arbitrarily. Instead, there are a number of factors that he must take into account, of which competition and competitors' prices are among the more important. He must also consider the nature of demand, costs, the characteristics of the product or service, and various legal aspects. In short, administered pricing is not clearly inconsistent with active competition.[13]

To summarize, administered pricing may in some cases be associated with situations in which active competition does not exist to any great degree, but it is also associated with countless situations in which competition is very active. Properly defined, the term refers to a method of price making, which in itself does not indicate a lack of vigorous competition.

ADMINISTERED PRICES—THE PRICES OF BIG BUSINESS

The claim is sometimes made that administered prices are the prices of "big business" and that small business firms use some other

---

[13] Joel Dean points out that the same set of facts can indicate to some people that a competitive situation exists and to others that a competitive situation does not exist. See "Competition As Seen by the Businessman and the Economist," in Harvey W. Huegy, ed., *The Role and Nature of Competition in Our Marketing Economy* (Urbana, Ill.: Bureau of Economic and Business Research, University of Illinois, 1954).

kind of price making. This is, of course, false since, as we have seen, most prices in the United States are administered, and all kinds and sizes of industries and firms make use of administered pricing. The small retailer, wholesaler, or manufacturer practices price administration just as surely as does Standard Oil of New Jersey or General Motors. Indeed, even when the American economy was characterized chiefly by small business firms, administered pricing prevailed as it does today.

INFLEXIBILITY OF ADMINISTERED PRICES

Market prices are usually thought to be highly flexible in nature; that is, they change very often, perhaps every few seconds, in response to changes in the forces affecting them. Administered prices, on the other hand, are said to be more inflexible in that the seller arbitrarily holds them at some given level for some length of time. Actually, whether or not a given price is flexible depends not so much on whether it is a market price or an administered price, but rather on a number of factors that affect the behavior of prices over time. These would include the characteristics of the product or service, the nature of demand for the product or service, the nature of costs in the firm or industry, various legal considerations, the structure of the industry, custom and habit, and many other factors.[14] Today the economic effect of so-called inflexible administered prices is of much less concern than was the case in the 1930's.[15]

One criticism that was prevalent in the 1930's was that inflexible administered prices tended to prevent prices from adjusting automatically to changes in market and production conditions, so that when a recession or depression occurred the failure of inflexible administered prices to be lowered with sufficient speed to adjust to the new conditions resulted in a sharper reduction in sales volume than would have been the case if the adjustment had been made more rapidly. Thus, it was said, the downswing of the 1930's was worse in that production fell further than it would have if automatic price adjust-

---

[14] The causes of inflexibility are discussed by Backman in *Price Practices and Price Policies*, Chapter 3, and by Dean in *Managerial Economics* (Englewood Cliffs, N.J.: Prentice-Hall, 1951), pp. 458–60.

[15] The term "inflexible" in itself carries a bad connotation. There perhaps would be a different reaction to inflexibility of prices if, instead of the terms "inflexible" and "flexible," the terms "stable" and "unstable" were used.

ments had been made. The chief proponent of the idea was Gardner C. Means.[16] Indeed, it is not surprising that Means' definition of an administered price is closely related to the idea of inflexibility since it was he who coined the term originally to mean a price that is set by administrative action and held constant for a period of time.

A number of studies have been made on the topic since then, and all seem to refute the idea that inflexible administered prices actually increased unemployment and reduced production in the depressed 1930's. These studies and those of later recessions indicate that inflexible administered prices are not necessarily accompanied by drastically reduced production during an economic downswing.[17] They indicate that while price is often an important factor, other factors must also be considered in order to explain the changes in production that occur in such periods. However, although the studies provide no factual support for the generalization that declining production and rising unemployment during a recession or depression are attributable to price administration, it should be kept in mind that price comparisons over time can be misleading because of qualitative changes in the product and changes in the conditions surrounding the sale of the product.

It is probably true that price inflexibility *can* in *some* instances contribute to low production and high unemployment although, as we have said, such an effect of price inflexibility has been very much exaggerated. Today this problem is thought to be of only minor importance. Commenting on the controversy surrounding administered prices in the 1930's, George J. Stigler remarked: "Toward the end of the decade the literature on rigid prices displayed growing anemia; it

[16] See his *Industrial Prices and Their Relative Inflexibility,* 74th Cong., 1st sess., Senate Document 13 (Washington, D.C.: U.S. Government Printing Office, 1935).

[17] See Backman, "Price Inflexibility and Changes in Production," *American Economic Review,* September, 1939; "Price Flexibility and Changes in Production," *Conference Board Bulletin* (New York: National Industrial Conference Board, 1939); "Administered Prices," in United States Steel Corporation, *Steel and Inflation: Fact vs. Fiction* (New York: United States Steel Corporation, 1958), pp. 234–54; Backman and Marvin Levine, "Price and Production Behavior in Recession," *Current Economic Comment,* August, 1958; Ernest M. Doblin, "Some Aspects of Price Flexibility," *Review of Economic Statistics,* November, 1940; Alfred C. Neal, *Industrial Concentration and Price Inflexibility* (Washington, D.C.: Public Affairs Press, 1942); Saul Nelson and Walter G. Keim, "Price Behavior and Business Policy," *TNEC Monograph 1* (Washington, D.C.: Temporary National Economic Committee, 1940); and Willard J. Thorpe and Walter F. Crowder, "The Structure of Industry," *TNEC Monograph 27* (Washington, D.C.: Temporary National Economic Committee, 1941).

is fair to say that economists abandoned the close study of the subject, less because its lack of scientific import was established than because it had become boring." [18]

ADMINISTERED PRICES AND INFLATION

In more recent times administered pricing, particularly in concentrated industries, has been accused of having contributed to inflation in the United States.[19] The Senate Subcommittee on Antitrust and Monopoly, under the chairmanship of the late Senator Estes Kefauver, was very much concerned with this question. Testimony before this subcommittee by Means and others to the effect that administered prices were a major cause of the inflation of the 1950's led to various proposals for federal legislation, all of which were unsuccessful.[20]

The charge that price administration has contributed to inflation has been refuted by various studies made of price movements in the 1950's. Backman's analysis of price changes between 1955 and 1957,[21] for example, illustrates that there is no simple or certain relationship between concentration of production capacity and market share in the hands of a few firms and price administration, on the one hand, and the direction or magnitude of price change on the other. Backman found that some of the products sold by concentrated industries bore administered prices and had larger than average price increases, but he also found that in many concentrated industries ad-

[18] "Administered Prices and Oligopolistic Inflation," *The Journal of Business,* January, 1962, p. 1.

[19] Thus we have the rather strange situation in which the same kind of pricing is accused of causing depression (deflation) on the one hand and inflation on the other.

[20] In a recent book in which Means attacks administered pricing power in concentrated industries, he argues that such pricing is inflationary. See *Pricing Power and the Public Interest* (New York: Harper & Bros., 1962). For a critical discussion of Means' book, see William H. Peterson, "Divergent Views on Pricing Policy," *Harvard Business Review,* March–April, 1963. In a discussion of the problem of concentrated economic power, Carl A. Auerbach concludes that some form of statutory price and wage regulation is needed to attain high employment, steadily increasing output, and stable prices. See "Administered Prices and Concentration of Economic Power," *Minnesota Law Review,* December, 1962.

[21] "Administered Prices," *op. cit.,* pp. 216–28, and "Administered Prices: Their Nature and Behavior," *Current Economic Comment,* November, 1957.

ministered prices showed only small changes. Prices in industries with low concentration and administered prices showed similar disparity. Backman concluded that it is difficult to understand how price administration *per se* could be held responsible for the general price rise from 1955 to 1957. Where other conditions, particularly those affecting demand or costs, either favored or compelled the price rise, administered prices rose. Where these conditions did not favor or compel a price rise, administered prices failed to rise. Market-determined prices, he pointed out, exhibited similar responsiveness. Thus, for Backman: "The primary pressures and responsibilities for price behavior, therefore, are found in these factors [those affecting demand or cost], not in the fact of price administration." [22] Stigler comes to the same conclusion: "The attribution of inflation to monopoly power of enterprises is . . . lacking both a theoretical rationale and an empirical basis." [23]

Thus, despite the difficulties in making price comparisons over time, one must conclude that price administration does not necessarily contribute to inflation. Many administered prices have not increased; in fact, many have declined, while the general price level has risen. It is true that some administered prices have increased along with the increase in the general level of prices and that some of these administered prices have increased at a more rapid rate than the average of all other prices. But some market prices have also increased more than the general price level. In short, empirical evidence shows that it is impossible to generalize on the topic by saying that administered prices do or do not contribute to inflation.

CONCLUSIONS ON CRITICISMS
OF ADMINISTERED PRICING

Properly defined, the term "administered pricing" describes a *method* of price making. It implies nothing about whether the prices

[22] "Administered Prices," *op. cit.,* p. 228.
[23] Stigler, *op. cit.,* p. 9. Criticisms of the idea that administered prices contribute to inflation are also found in Horace J. DePodwin and Richard T. Selden, "Business Pricing Policies and Inflation," *Journal of Political Economy,* April, 1963, and in the testimony of Walter D. Fackler and Padraic P. Frucht in the Kefauver hearings. See *Hearings before the Senate Subcommittee on Antitrust and Monopoly,* Part II (Washington, D.C.: U.S. Government Printing Office, 1959), pp. 5221–342.

set through administrative action are too high or too low, too flexible or too inflexible, whether competition exists or does not exist, or whether such prices contribute to depression or to inflation.

Price administration, or the power of business firms to set a price on their products or services, has been the natural result of the characteristics of the American economy and is found today in all sectors of American economic life. Although it has sometimes been abused, this general method of price making could not be eliminated without drastically changing the entire economic system—probably for the worse. Thus, we must accept the fact that administered pricing exists and that the term "administered pricing" does not *per se* imply criticism of the pricing process.

PLAN OF THE BOOK

The topic of pricing may be approached in several different ways. The economist looks at the way in which business firms set prices on their products as an outsider interested in analyzing and evaluating the process. Within business firms themselves those persons who are chiefly interested in the financial aspects of the business look upon prices as an indicator of revenue earned or to be earned. Production people, on the other hand, tend to look upon prices as some kind of a constraint within which they must produce the product or service in question, and marketing people envisage prices as a tool with which to develop the market for the output of the firm.

In the following chapters, we will examine price making in the American economy from the point of view of the marketing executive. We will consider some of the kinds of pricing problems that the marketing executive faces, the kinds of decisions he must make, and the manner in which pricing problems are and should be handled. Chapters 2 and 3 are devoted to some internal and external considerations that have a bearing on pricing decisions; Chapter 4 deals with the legal and ethical aspects of pricing; Chapter 5 discusses some normative pricing models; Chapter 6 examines the special pricing problems of manufacturers; Chapter 7 does the same for distributors (wholesalers and retailers); and in Chapter 8 we will consider several different pricing policies and attempt to draw some conclusions relative to price policy and procedure.

Selected References

There are many excellent publications that deal with price theory, ranging from books on principles of economics to highly advanced and technical books and articles. One of the best current intermediate-level treatments of price theory is found in Richard H. Leftwich, *The Price System and Resource Allocation,* rev. ed. (New York: Holt, Rinehart and Winston, 1963).

Price theory as applied to management decision making is discussed in the several books on managerial economics such as Joel Dean, *Managerial Economics* (Englewood Cliffs, N.J.: Prentice-Hall, 1951), and William W. Haynes, *Managerial Economics: Analysis and Cases* (Homewood, Ill.: Dorsey Press, 1963).

The nature of price making and the price system are discussed by Jules Backman in *Price Practices and Price Policies* (New York: Ronald Press, 1953), particularly Chapters 1, 2, and 3, and in *Pricing: Policies and Practices* (New York: National Industrial Conference Board, 1961), pp. 7–15. An excellent article that describes the price-making process is Harvey W. Huegy, "Price Decisions and Marketing Policies," in Hugh G. Wales, ed., *Changing Perspectives in Marketing* (Urbana, Ill.: University of Illinois Press, 1951).

In addition to the many references cited in the footnotes relative to criticisms and evaluation of administered pricing, a discussion of the controversy surrounding administered prices and the studies that have been made of the subject (up to mid-1960) is found in William E. Strevig, "Administered Prices: A Review and Appraisal," *Southwestern Social Science Quarterly,* September, 1961. The relationship between administered prices and inflation is examined in Gardner Ackley, "Administered Prices and the Inflationary Process," *American Economic Review,* May, 1959, and in Henry W. Briefs, *Pricing Power and "Administered" Inflation—Concepts, Facts, and Policy Implications* (Washington, D.C.: American Enterprise Institute for Public Policy Research, 1962). An article that deals with pricing in the steel industry and inflation is M. A. Adelman, "Steel, Administered Prices and Inflation," *Quarterly Journal of Economics,* February, 1961. The behavior of administered prices in oligopolistic industries is discussed by John M. Blair in "Administered Prices: A Phenomenon in Search of a Theory," *American Economic Review,* May, 1959.

2

INTERNAL CONSIDERATIONS

IN DEVELOPING A PRICE POLICY

In the preceding chapter we saw that the dominant form of price making in the American economy is administered, or business-controlled, pricing, in which the business firm has the right and the responsibility to set prices for its products or services. This being the case, the vast majority of business firms have need of a price policy.

Although there are important exceptions, the need for a price policy is generally more important in manufacturing than in other types of enterprises since manufacturers generally have more discretionary power in pricing than do wholesalers, retailers, or producers of raw-material, or primary, products. The reason for this greater discretionary power is that there are greater product differentiation and a more limited number of sellers in many manufacturing industries than in the other activities.

THE NATURE OF PRICE POLICIES

A price policy is an overall guide to action in pricing. It involves general principles or rules that a firm endeavors to follow in making everyday pricing decisions. For example, a broad range of price policies is available to a firm; it may make any of the following decisions:

1. Never to sell any units of output at prices below its full costs.
2. Always to attempt to price its products below the prices of competitors.
3. To "follow the market," that is, to copy competitors' prices.
4. To price above competitors' prices in order to appeal to a "prestige" market.
5. To attempt to build large volume through low prices regardless of what its competitors do.
6. To follow the prices of a particular competitor.
7. To price in order to provide the firm with a given percentage return on investment.
8. To price in such a way as to discourage price cutting in the industry and to deemphasize price as an element in the purchase decision.
9. To price in such a way as to discourage competitors from entering the market.
10. To price in order to maximize profits for all products and services offered by the firm as a group, rather than to maximize profits on each individual product or service separately.

There are still other possible price policies.[1]

Price policies, once adopted, may be followed for long periods of time, or they may be changed frequently. Many practitioners feel that a flexible approach to pricing that can be adjusted easily to meet changing conditions is advantageous. In any case, price policies, like other marketing policies, should be reviewed frequently in order to ensure that they are suited to present conditions.

A firm may find that more than one price policy is required to fit the different kinds of products or services that it offers.[2] A firm is

[1] A. D. H. Kaplan, Joel B. Dirlam, and Robert F. Lanzillotti list five pricing policies of the firms they include in their study of twenty large corporations, designed to: achieve a target return on investment, achieve stabilization of price and margin, maintain or improve market position, meet or follow competition, and remain subordinated to product differentiation. See their *Pricing in Big Business* (Washington, D.C.: Brookings Institution, 1958), p. 128.

[2] Some business firms have the problem of pricing goods and services which are exchanged between separate divisions of the firm. Such pricing, which is referred to as "intracompany," "interdivisional," and "transfer" pricing, is not covered in this book. A number of articles have appeared on the subject. They include Paul W. Cook, Jr., "Decentralization and the Transfer-Price Problem," *Journal of Business,* April, 1955; Joel Dean, "Decentralization and Intra-company Pricing," *Harvard Business Review,* July–August, 1955; Forrest L. Heuser, "Organizing for Effective Intra-Firm Pricing," *N.A.C.A. Bulletin,* May, 1956;

particularly likely to have more than one price policy if it is a multi-product or multiservice firm. Routine daily pricing decisions and procedures should conform to these policies. Thus, if a firm has decided as a matter of policy that it will follow the prices of a certain competitor, its routine pricing procedure will be simply to change prices whenever the competitor's prices change. A more involved routine pricing mechanism is required when a firm's policy is to try to obtain a given percentage return on investment or to build up large volume through low prices.

The willingness and the ability to establish price policies varies considerably from firm to firm. In fact, although pricing constitutes one of the more important marketing decisions that must be made in many firms, it is often done in a haphazard way. Many firms have nothing that even vaguely resembles a price policy. According to Joel Dean, ". . . pricing decisions remain a patchwork of *ad hoc* decisions. In otherwise well-managed firms, price policy has been dealt with on a crisis basis. This kind of price management by catastrophe discourages the kind of systematic analysis needed for clear-cut pricing policies." [3] Kaplan, Dirlam, and Lanzillotti, in their study of twenty large corporations, concluded that in some cases, there was an almost complete absence of anything that could be cited as the price policy of the company, other than that of following a market.[4] There seems to be more interest in the establishment of a price policy when new products are involved. Thus, results of a survey among 146 firms showed that seven out of ten of the firms studied indicated that

J. Hirshleiber, "Economics of Transfer Pricing," *Journal of Business,* July, 1956; Paul W. Cook, Jr., "New Techniques for Intra-Company Pricing," *Harvard Business Review,* July–August, 1957; John Dearden, "Interdivisional Pricing," *Harvard Business Review,* January–February, 1960; Robert W. Murray, "Where Out-of-Pocket Costs Make the Best Transfer Price," *N.A.A. Bulletin,* August, 1961; Howard C. Greer, "Divisional Profit Calculation—Notes on the 'Transfer Price' Problem," *N.A.A. Bulletin,* July, 1962; Willard E. Stone, "Legal Implications of Intracompany Pricing," *Accounting Review,* January, 1964; and John Dearden, "The Case of the Disputing Divisions," *Harvard Business Review,* May–June, 1964.

[3] *Managerial Economics* (Englewood Cliffs, N.J.: Prentice-Hall, 1951), p. 401. Another student of the topic remarked: "Too often, pricing is an ill-considered decision, made without regard to the effect it has on purchasing, manufacturing, marketing—or precedent. When pricing becomes a mere concession to cost or competition, the product line (or the whole company) suffers later, if not sooner." "Take Guesswork out of Pricing Decisions," *Business Management,* May, 1963, p. 48.

[4] *Op. cit.,* p. 127.

the major factors governing the pricing of new products are embodied in formal policy statements.[5] It should also be noted that the announced price policy of a given firm may not be followed consistently over time, and sometimes the price policy of a firm is not made known to price makers because of lack of good communication or lack of interest on the part of management. Factors such as these may bring about a wide divergence between price policy and pricing practice.

Although many business firms have neglected the task of establishing a price policy and others have failed to put into practice the price policies they supposedly have adopted, the fact remains that in many firms pricing is one of the key decisions in successful operation of the business. Whether or not pricing is highly important to a firm depends on a number of factors, such as the degree to which buyers of the product or service are influenced by price, the difficulty in determining the "right" price, the degree of discretion the seller has in setting price, the position the seller occupies in the industry in relation to other firms, and the degree of product differentiation that exists.[6]

In firms where pricing does, in fact, have an important impact on sales, a price policy is as necessary as an advertising policy, a product-development policy, a channel-of-distribution policy, or any other marketing policy. Without a price policy a firm that is confronted by such a market will enjoy a far lower degree of success than if it had a sound approach to its pricing problems.

No matter what kind of business a firm is engaged in, and regardless of whether the firm's output is a physical product or a service, certain basic factors should be considered in developing price policies for the firm. Some of these factors are internal to the firm; others are external. Internal factors are, of course, more easily identified and also more easily controlled than are factors that are external to the firm. An understanding of the various internal and external influences on pricing is required before intelligent decisions concerning pricing can be made.

In this chapter we will examine a few of the internal factors that a firm must consider in establishing a price policy. These include the

[5] See G. Clark Thompson and Morgan B. MacDonald, Jr., "Pricing New Products," *Conference Board Record,* January, 1964, pp. 9–10.

[6] That pricing in some firms is a less important competitive factor than some nonprice factors such as product research and development and sales research and sales planning is discussed in an article by Jon G. Udell, "How Important Is Pricing in Competitive Strategy?" *Journal of Marketing,* January, 1964.

objectives of pricing, the organization for pricing, the role of price in the marketing program, the characteristics of the product or service, and costs. In the following chapter we will consider certain external factors. Specific problems and decisions peculiar to manufacturers and distributors are discussed in later chapters.

THE OBJECTIVES OF PRICING

An intelligent approach to developing a price policy begins with a clarification of the basic objectives of the firm. The overall objectives of the firm should be synonymous with its pricing objectives. The simplest approach is to assume that the firm's basic objective is to maximize profits, as is done in price theory. However, in any firm, particularly where the active managers have little or no ownership in the firm, various other objectives may exist—at least in the short run —instead of, or in addition to, the objective of maximizing profits. Examples of company objectives that differ in important respects from the objective of profit maximization include:

1. The firm wants to get its products to its customers at reasonable cost.
2. The firm wants to avoid charges of monopolizing an industry and other legal prosecution.
3. The firm may be interested in increasing its market share or its rate of growth, even at the expense of immediate profits.
4. The firm may fear that it would incur adverse public relations as a consequence of attempting to maximize profits.
5. The firm may feel that ethical considerations prevent it from operating in such a way as to maximize profits.
6. The firm may be interested only in some fixed amount of profit as its goal, rather than "maximum" profits.
7. The firm may be interested only in immediate survival.
8. The firm may be particularly anxious to maintain good relations with labor.
9. The firm may be interested in maximizing prestige, rather than profits.

Some of the objectives listed above may contribute to long-run profit maximization, but in varying degrees they represent qualifications to the assumption that in the short run the firm wants to maximize profits. Some of the other objectives listed indicate that, even in the long run, a firm could conceivably be satisfied with some level of profits that is less than maximum.

It would be difficult, if not impossible, to find a firm that has one overall objective. Usually, a firm has several objectives and in some cases these objectives may conflict with one another. (It should also be noted that some firms have never formulated any overall objectives!)

It is the task of top management to make sure that all those who hold responsible positions in the firm are aware of its overall objectives and understand them. This is the only way in which the firm can begin to achieve consistency in any of the policy areas of its operations.

In addition to the overall objectives of the firm, the hired managers of the firm have personal objectives of their own, such as a desire for promotion, higher salary, greater security, prestige in the firm, and the avoidance of legal trouble. These personal objectives may conflict on occasion with the overall objectives of the firm.[7]

Although its importance varies from firm to firm, pricing is one of the tools that a firm has at its disposal in its attempt to reach the stated objectives. In order to be meaningful and effective, the price policy or policies adopted clearly must be consistent with the overall objectives of the firm. Thus, a firm whose overall goals include increasing market share may adopt a price policy of always charging prices that are below those of competitors in order to expand its market share. Sometimes, in fact, a price policy is identical with an overall company objective, such as when the company objective and price policy are both to achieve a given target rate of return on investment.

ORGANIZATION FOR PRICING

There are two basic kinds of pricing decisions. The first is to decide on the price policy or policies the firm is to follow, and the second is

---

[7] The problems associated with reducing conflicts between personal and company objectives are beyond the scope of this book.

to price specific products or services in accordance with the policy or policies. This latter decision may be referred to as the pricing procedure, or mechanics, as distinct from price policy.

RESPONSIBILITY FOR PRICE POLICY

In any type of firm the way to ensure maximum effectiveness in pricing is to delegate the responsibility for price policy to some specific executive or to some committee of top executives. Very often, in fact, the conference method is used, although no committee has been formally established for the purpose. For example, in some firms the board of directors has the final say on price policy. In general, since price policy is so closely related to the company's overall goals, it should be handled by those who are in the best position to know and understand those goals and who possess the authority to establish a policy and have it carried out. One would rarely find an executive, however, whose *only* function was to develop the price policy of the firm. Usually this is just one of the activities for which the executive is responsible.

Since pricing is of such vital importance in the marketing program of a firm, it is essential that marketing implications be given adequate consideration in developing the company price policies. In fact, a strong case can be made for delegating the responsibility for the establishment of price policy to a marketing executive or at least to a committee that includes one or more marketing people.

RESPONSIBILITY FOR THE MECHANICS OF PRICING

In contrast, the mechanics of pricing, that is, the business of setting a specific price, need not be performed at the top of the management ladder. Indeed, in some situations, the mechanics of pricing may be performed at relatively low levels in a firm's organizational structure, as when salesmen are allowed to adjust prices.

The way in which the responsibility for routine pricing decisions is delegated is especially important in very large firms. In such cases, strong arguments can be offered in favor of both centralized and decentralized control. The advantages of centralized price making are that the firm maintains better control over pricing and that it is more likely to follow a consistent approach to pricing. On the other hand, decentralized control over pricing has the advantage of placing the responsibility for price making in the hands of those who are closest to the problems concerning the product or service involved.

The organizational level at which the mechanics of pricing should be performed is, to a great extent, a function of the difficulty in performing the task, and also of the frequency and speed with which pricing decisions must be made. In terms of difficulty, for example, if a firm has established a price policy whereby a given percentage markup is taken over fully distributed costs on each unit of output, the mechanics of setting a price are much simpler than if the firm's policy is to price in such a way as to discourage competition from entering the industry. In other words, the more the price-setting task is routinized in accordance with fixed formulas or procedures of some kind, such as a predetermined markup on full costs or "following the market," the easier it is to delegate price-making authority and the lower on the organizational scale it can go.

When a firm has to make a large number of pricing decisions quite frequently or must make pricing decisions rapidly, it may be necessary to delegate the pricing function to lower levels in the firm. In such a case, it is best to try to routinize the function as much as possible.

In their study of large business firms, Kaplan, Dirlam, and Lanzillotti found that a wide variety of pricing arrangements were practiced, ranging from closely held power over every price change at the top-management level to instances of almost complete delegation of pricing authority to product sales managers and salesmen.[8] Firms in which little or no pricing authority was delegated to sales managers or department heads tended to be those that sold a major durable product or a group of related products that accounted for the bulk of their sales and for which price quotations were issued at regular intervals rather than at short and irregular intervals. Firms in which there was a large degree of delegation of price-making responsibility to divisional sales managers and department heads tended to be in industries in which there was keen competition, characterized by frequent short-term price changes, or they were companies that sold many products in many different kinds of markets.[9] In small firms, because of the

[8] *Op. cit.*, p. 220.
[9] *Ibid.*, pp. 245–47.

lack of specialization and size, top management has to concern itself not only with establishing price policy but also with the everyday procedure of pricing specific products.

With regard to the delegation of pricing responsibility to individuals or to committees it should be noted that, as Alfred R. Oxenfeldt points out, the committee arrangement lacks clear centralization of responsibility and ordinarily results in delay and confusion. Thus, as a general rule, it is most effective to charge one person with pricing responsibility for a given item or line of products or services so that everyone will know to whom to turn when a price decision is required.[10]

The size of the organization needed to support the person or committee charged with pricing responsibility should vary with the characteristics of the firm and the complexities of its pricing problems. For example, Oxenfeldt lists eight factors that, in his opinion, influence the size and type of organization that a firm should create to carry out the pricing function:

1. The range of discretion over price that is possessed by the firm.
2. The speed with which price decisions must be made.
3. The number of products for which prices must be set.
4. The number of separate markets—primarily geographic areas or industry groupings—for which prices can be handled individually.
5. The caliber of personnel available to perform the pricing function.
6. The resources and effort that top management is prepared to devote to the pricing function.
7. The amount and complexity of information that can be brought to bear on the price decision.
8. The level of authority required to gain the assistance of and information from other members of the firm.[11]

This suggests that in some firms very few people need be directly concerned with pricing, whereas in other firms large staffs of statisticians, researchers, accountants, and economists will be needed on a full-time basis to assist in making price decisions. Furthermore, firms

[10] *Pricing for Marketing Executives* (San Francisco: Wadsworth, 1961), p. 61.
[11] *Ibid.*, p. 62.

of similar size, which manufacture the same type of product, may take entirely different approaches to the problem of organizing for pricing, and of course any particular firm may find it necessary to change its approach over time.

INTRAFIRM COOPERATION NEEDED

Those who are assigned responsibility for price policy and execution cannot act independently. Within the marketing area of the firm, prices cannot be set without the benefit of discussions concerning channels of distribution, advertising, and other aspects of the marketing program. Prices also have an effect on the financial condition of the firm, the production needed to serve a given market, and other nonmarketing segments of the firm's operation.

Thus a number of persons and departments in the firm may be able to offer valuable assistance in arriving at the right price policy or the right price. Within the marketing area, the sales department may relay information on customer reaction to prices, and the marketing research department may provide data on price trends in the industry and other matters of interest to those responsible for pricing. Outside the marketing area, cost accountants, company economists, production managers, purchasing agents, and others can also provide essential information for the pricing process. Thus, price making actually requires the cooperation of many individuals within the firm, although few of them are formally recognized as being involved in the pricing process.

THE ROLE OF PRICE IN THE MARKETING PROGRAM

Price is one of the elements in the "marketing mix," which also includes personal selling, advertising, packaging, branding, product development, physical distribution, and the channels of distribution. All the elements in the marketing mix are sales-producing tools available to the firm, and it is up to the marketing manager to combine them in the most effective way possible in light of his firm's particular objectives.[12] The marketing manager must determine the specific role of each of the several elements in the mix. As he does so, he must necessarily consider the relationship between the elements. Price can contribute positively to the sales effort only if it coordinates properly with the other elements of the marketing mix. The combined impact of these elements creates an impression of the product or service and of the firm itself in the mind of the potential customer, and if that impression is to be favorable, they must blend together as a "team" or "package."

The effect of changes in one of the elements in the mix on the other elements must also be considered. Thus, in terms of price, if advertising expenditures are reduced, must prices be reduced as well to "move" the product? Or if significant physical improvements are introduced in a product, should price be increased? Or if the price of a consumer product is changed substantially, is it also necessary to change the kind of retailers who distribute the product? Or if price is raised, must the advertising and personal selling effort be increased as well? Thus, for our purposes, price decisions cannot be made effectively without due consideration of the role price is to play in the total marketing effort and of the relationship between price and the other elements in the marketing program.

The most obvious and direct way in which price may be used as a sales-producing tool is through low prices and price cutting. This will be an effective strategy, however, only if the demand for the product or service involved is fairly elastic, that is, sensitive to price changes. "Price cutting can be an effective part of the marketing mix but it must be used with care—only after analysis of demand and cost." [13]

---

[12] Price is sometimes not considered to be part of a firm's promotional mix, as can be seen in the following statement of Brian Dixon in *Price Discrimination and Marketing Management,* Michigan Business Studies, Vol. 15, No. 1 (Ann Arbor, Mich.: Bureau of Business Research, University of Michigan, 1960), p. 27: "The term 'promotional mix' is used ordinarily to refer to the combination of advertising, personal selling, and dealer cooperation appropriate to a given sales circumstance. The promotional role of price is not considered. Price, along with design and performance, is treated as a fixed or semifixed sales influence—lacking the continual flexibility of the 'promotional mix' items. This view ignores the actively promotional element in price policy."

[13] E. Jerome McCarthy, *Basic Marketing, A Managerial Approach,* rev. ed. (Homewood, Ill.: Irwin, 1964), p. 863.

It is a particularly dangerous device when retaliation from competitors can be expected.[14]

Nonetheless, in some firms and industries, low prices are emphasized as an important selling point. Among consumer goods, one may find many examples in the retail field of firms that rely heavily on low prices. This is certainly true of discount houses, for example, and, to a lesser degree, of food chain stores and retail mail-order houses. Certain segments of the clothing industry, the paperback book industry, and the private label segment of the home appliance industry are a few of the many instances in which manufacturers of consumer goods have profited by an emphasis on minimal prices.

Price can be used as an element of the sales effort in less obvious ways as well, however. For example, various forms of psychological pricing are used by many sellers. Thus we have "prestige" pricing in which a high price is used to add prestige to the product or service. In such cases the price is as important as the product or service itself in attracting the prestige market. Evidence of the fact that relatively high prices can be effective in producing sales is found in the many cases in which price reductions have been accompanied by declining sales volume. Here it would seem that customers felt that the lower prices indicated lower quality. Tibor Scitovsky finds that, more often than not, people judge quality by price, that the word "cheap" usually connotes inferior quality, and that the word "expensive" is in the process of becoming a synonym for superior quality.[15]

Prestige pricing situations, then, are characterized by a backward sloping demand curve, as is shown in Figure 7, which indicates that as price is lowered quantity demanded declines.

[14] Note in this regard the use of price "deals" (temporary price reductions) for consumer goods as discussed in an article by Charles L. Hinkle entitled "The Strategy of Price Deals," *Harvard Business Review,* July–August, 1965. See p. 84 for a discussion of some objectives of such price "deals."

[15] "Some Consequences of the Habit of Judging Quality by Price," *Review of Economic Studies,* 1944–45, Vol. 12 (2), No. 32, reprinted in Perry Bliss, *Marketing and the Behavioral Sciences* (Boston: Allyn and Bacon, 1963), p. 478. That consumers sometimes react positively to a high price is discussed by Harold J. Leavitt in "A Note on Some Experimental Findings About the Meaning of Price," *Journal of Business,* July, 1954. See also D. S. Tull, R. A. Boring, and M. H. Gonsier, "A Note on the Relationship of Price and Imputed Quality," *Journal of Business,* April, 1964. The example of Paper-Mate ball-point pens being successfully introduced at a relatively high price is given by E. Heath van Duzel in "Is the Wrong Price Hurting Your Sales?" *Sales Management,* September 6, 1963, p. 59.

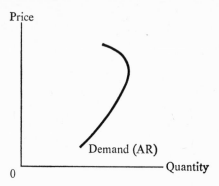

Figure 7 Prestige Pricing

Even if a product or service does not fall into the "prestige" category, to the degree that price is used to "classify" a product or service in the minds of buyers, price can still play an effective sales-producing role. To do so, the price attached to a product or service must accord with the brand "image" it presents to the potential customer.[16]

Sometimes firms attempt to downgrade the importance of price in the marketing mix. For example, manufacturers of some consumer goods attempt to discourage the use of price as a competitive weapon through various schemes designed to prevent price competition among retailers. Effective price leadership also cuts down on price competition. In still other situations competing firms have attempted to eliminate price as a competitive factor by entering into collusive agreements on prices. In such cases the sales effort is channeled into the so-called nonprice factors.

CHARACTERISTICS OF THE PRODUCT OR SERVICE

DEGREE OF PRODUCT DIFFERENTIATION

One of the more important factors that determines the amount of discretion that a firm has in setting prices is the degree to which its prod-

---

[16] The relationship between price and brand image is discussed in Alfred Oxenfeldt, David Miller, Abraham Shuchman, and Charles Winick, *Insights into Pricing* (Belmont, Cal.: Wadsworth, 1961), Chapter 4.

ucts or services are differentiated from competing products or services in the eyes of buyers. Barring the presence of factors such as effective price leadership, a very small number of firms in the industry, or monopsony on the buying side, the more product differentiation a firm enjoys, the more independent it can be in its price-making activities.[17]

Product differentiation itself may consist of actual physical differences in the offerings of competing sellers, or it may consist of so-called psychological differences based on advertising, brand reputation, colors of packages, and various other intangible emotional factors.

In addition, product differentiation often involves delivery terms, credit terms, guarantees, availability of service on a product, and the other elements that comprise the total package being purchased. In fact, in many industries where competing products or services are very similar, any differentiation that exists is based almost entirely upon these other elements.

Sometimes it is more effective to concentrate on differentiating the firm instead of, or in addition to, differentiating the offerings of the firm. This is particularly true in retailing where differentiation of the firm is based on location, lines of merchandise carried, services offered to customers, various public-service activities of the firm, and other factors. In retailing, successful firm differentiation is perhaps more important than the differentiation attached to any one product such a firm might handle. In manufacturing, some firms have been able to differentiate themselves significantly from competing firms in the eyes of the public through consistently high-quality products, good service, honest dealings with the public, or good labor relations; in such a case the favorable reputation of the firm itself spills over onto the products or services it produces.

Competition in the American economy consists to a great extent of the efforts of firms to differentiate their offerings or themselves in the eyes of the public by stressing what is unique about themselves or the products or services they offer. Wroe Alderson has referred to this rivalry as "competition for differential advantage." [18] Because of the

---

[17] Product differentiation is just one element in the total market structure in which a firm operates. The other elements in this structure are discussed in Chapter 3.

[18] *Marketing Behavior and Executive Action* (Homewood, Ill.: Irwin, 1957), pp. 101–29.

varied tastes and needs that exist in both the consumer and industrial markets, a firm has ample opportunity to set itself apart from the competition for certain segments of the market.

If a firm enjoys little product or firm differentiation, it can attempt to improve its position by adjusting various elements that comprise the overall product package, such as product characteristics, services, or guarantees, or it can attempt to develop differentiation through various sales-promotional devices, particularly advertising. Actually, nonprice competition of this sort is often preferred by businessmen to price competition for the following reasons: (1) They feel that competitors find it more difficult to duplicate nonprice innovations than price adjustments. (2) It is a "safer" approach than price competition because the risks of serious errors in pricing and of price wars are avoided. (3) They feel that the beneficial effects of successful nonprice competition on the attitude of the customer toward the firm are more lasting than are the effects of price adjustments.

The less product or firm differentiation a company enjoys, the less effectively it is able to use price manipulation as a tool of marketing strategy. This is not to say, however, that a firm that, because of differentiation, can price its products or services independently necessarily sets prices that from the buyers' standpoint are unjustifiably high. It merely means that the firm can use prices more effectively as a marketing tool. High prices may or may not be selected by the firm, depending upon its marketing strategy.

It should also be noted that independence in price making based on product differentiation is seldom, if ever, permanent; existing competitors may introduce important changes in their offerings, or new competitors with new products or services may enter the industry. Thus, it has been said: "Undue reliance upon supposed but questionable product advantages will almost surely lead to faulty pricing." [19]

INDUSTRIAL OR CONSUMER GOOD

Whether the product or service of the company under consideration is being sold in the industrial-goods market or in the consumer-goods market has some bearing on the approach it takes to pricing.[20]

---

[19] D. Maynard Phelps and J. Howard Westing, *Marketing Management,* rev. ed. (Homewood, Ill.: Irwin, 1960), p. 270.

[20] *Industrial goods,* in this context, are understood to include goods and services used in producing other goods and services, such as machinery, raw mater-

Similarly, there are several basic types of goods produced in the industrial-goods market, including raw materials and various kinds of manufactured or processed products, such as parts, operating supplies, installations, and various kinds of equipment.[21] The pricing problem is often significantly different for each of these types of industrial goods. The same may be said of different types of consumer goods. Let us first examine the major differences that exist between industrial goods as a group and consumer goods as a group, and the pricing implications of these differences.

Derived demand   Industrial goods are purchased in order to produce other goods or services. They are said to have a "derived" demand because the buyers of industrial goods base their purchase decisions primarily on the condition of the market for the products or services that are to be produced. In such a situation, it is clear that price will not be a very effective means of producing sales if the market for the goods or services to be produced is not "good."

The importance of any particular industrial good, in terms of the total product or service being produced, may be great or small. The less vital a role the industrial good plays in the manufacture of the product in question, the less effective price adjustments by the producer of the industrial good will be, since the impact of such price adjustments on the costs of the manufacturer of the final good will be slight. Thus, a seller of an essentially homogeneous, or standardized, industrial good that is of minor importance in the manufacture of the final product or service produced by a major customer will be reluctant to adjust prices downward since such adjustments probably have little effect on the total demand for the industrial good. It may be that he can temporarily steal demand away from other producers of the same industrial good, but if the product is essentially homogeneous, it will merely result in uniform price reductions throughout the industry with no increase in the total demand for the industrial good in question. On the other hand, if some product differentiation exists in the industry, an individual seller may be able to increase his sales permanently through price manipulation as well

---

ials, electricity, etc. *Consumer goods* are understood to include goods or services purchased for personal or household consumption.

[21] For a detailed description of the nature of industrial goods, see any of the many books on the fundamentals or principles of marketing or one of the books on industrial marketing, such as Ralph S. Alexander, James S. Cross, and Ross M. Cunningham, *Industrial Marketing*, rev. ed. (Homewood, Ill.: Irwin, 1961), pp. 6–13.

as through product differentiation, even though the total demand for the product or service involved cannot be expanded. In such a case an increase in one seller's sales causes a decrease in the sales of other sellers.

On occasion, however, a particular industrial good plays a crucial role in the manufacture of a given final product or service. In such a case, price adjustments made by the producer of the industrial good may influence prices of the final product or service it is used to produce and hence affect demand for the industrial good itself. Here price can be an extremely effective sales tool.

The arguments concerning derived demand presented above are essentially short-run arguments. In the long run a price adjustment downward on even an industrial good that is relatively unimportant to the final product could encourage industrial buyers to substitute that good for others, and an upward price adjustment could have the reverse effect.

Nature of the buyer   Since the buyers of industrial goods are thought to be more "rational" in their approach to purchasing decisions than are consumers, and because they are more familiar with the market, they are more likely to be price-conscious, or at least more capable of judging the "correctness" of a price. Therefore, in general it would appear that price is more effective here than in the consumer-goods market. This seems particularly true in those industrial buying situations in which several persons or departments in the firm participate in the purchase decision. These factors also suggest that the producer's costs are more important in the pricing of industrial goods than is the case in the consumer-goods market since the industrial buyer is usually more aware of the relationship between the producer's costs and his prices.

Another implication of the difference between industrial buyers and consumers is that the effect of sales promotion that is not based on "real," measurable product advantages is usually less significant in the industrial-goods market. Because the industrial buyer is a professional, he has greater expertness in the art of buying and a more detailed knowledge of the products under consideration. As a consequence sales promotion, except when based on provable claims, exercises less influence on demand than is the case with consumer goods. "It is the job of the industrial buyer to buy and not to be sold." [22] This also means that price tends to play a greater role in the

---

[22] *Ibid.,* p. 342.

marketing mix of a firm operating in the industrial-goods market than it does in the consumer-goods market.

Delayed use of product Another factor that tends to strengthen the importance of price to the industrial buyer is that he views the value of an industrial product as being equal to its worth at the time he uses it. Since he generally uses it some time after he commits himself to its purchase, his conception of the present value of the good is influenced by what he imagines prices will be in the future. A decline in price, therefore, may suggest that prices will continue to drop in the future, and this may lead him to adopt a waiting policy. Thus, in the industrial market a drop in price may have the immediate effect of reducing demand instead of increasing it. When an increase in price occurs, on the other hand, the industrial buyer may conclude that the increase is the beginning of a general advance, and he may increase his immediate purchases in order to avoid paying higher prices later. The result of such reactions on the part of industrial buyers is that the demand for industrial products over short periods of time may show a reverse elasticity. When price declines, sales may decline. When price rises, sales may rise. The same tendencies may also appear in the consumer-goods market but to a lesser degree because consumers are not experienced professional buyers and unlike industrial buyers do not consider most of their purchases important enough to warrant a very elastic response to price changes.

Discounts Because industrial goods are often purchased in large volumes, quantity discounts are frequently given. They have a very important influence on the purchase decision. In the consumer-goods market middlemen often receive quantity discounts from manufacturers, but rarely does the final consumer receive such discounts.

Number and importance of buyers The number of potential buyers of any industrial good is usually less than the number of potential ultimate buyers of a consumer good. As a result, an individual industrial buyer is usually much more important to the seller than is any individual ultimate consumer in the consumer-goods market, and hence the influence of an industrial buyer over price making is greater. The fact that industrial buyers typically buy in larger volume than consumers do also makes individual industrial customers more important to the seller and more influential in matters of pricing.

It must be pointed out, however, that although the number of ultimate buyers of a consumer good is large, and any one consumer is relatively unimportant to the manufacturer in terms of his ability to influence price, consumer goods are usually distributed through a limited number of middlemen. The number of very large middlemen, such as retail chain-store companies, is very small. This type of middleman is extremely important to a manufacturer of consumer goods and may exert considerable influence over price making as administered by manufacturers of such products.

Another important distinction between consumer goods and industrial goods is that many industrial goods are purchased very infrequently and involve very large outlays of money. This is the case, for example, with the purchase of various pieces of capital-equipment items, such as generators. In such cases, the importance of pricing for any individual sale greatly exceeds the importance of pricing for any individual sale in the consumer-goods market. A related characteristic of industrial goods is that they are sometimes custom-made for a single customer. As a consequence, the price of the custom-made product is tailored to that one customer, whereas the prices of consumer goods must apply to hundreds, thousands, even millions of ultimate consumers. One might conclude that the problem of arriving at the "right" price is easier to solve in the industrial-goods market.

Fluctuation in sales volume   Industrial goods exhibit a greater degree of fluctuation in sales volume over the stages of the business cycle than do consumer goods. The main reason, as we have mentioned before, is that the purchase of industrial goods tends to be postponed as much as possible in a downswing of the cycle because at such times the markets for the products or services produced by industrial goods are weak, while in an upswing there is a rush to supply expanding markets and hence a rush to purchase industrial goods. This is particularly true of durable machinery or other equipment. Cuts in prices of such industrial goods during the slack periods probably have very little, if any, effect on sales volume because potential purchasers feel that there is no point in making purchases of such goods no matter how attractive the price may be when the demand for their own products or services is down. As a consequence, despite the greater fluctuation in sales, prices of these industrial goods tend to fluctuate less than those of many consumer goods. Therefore, during the busy periods, industrial goods must be priced in such a way that they will produce sufficient revenue to cover operations throughout all stages of the business cycle.

In the consumer-goods market, on the other hand, sales volume is not as sensitive to changes in the business cycle, that is, there is less fluctuation over the stages of the business cycle than in some industrial goods. The need for certain consumer goods continues despite the stage of the cycle. This is especially true of nondurable necessities like food and clothing. As a consequence, price adjustments downward by any one firm may prove to be an effective means of increasing sales during downswings since consumers are especially price conscious at such times. Furthermore, since sales volume does not fluctuate as much over the cycle, pricing in "good" periods does not have to "carry" the firm through the "bad" periods and can therefore be more flexible.

Bids and negotiation Another distinguishing feature of pricing in the industrial-goods market is bid pricing. Many buyers of industrial goods, including government agencies, often require that potential suppliers file competitive bids before awarding the business.[23] On other industrial-goods sales, much price negotiation may occur between sellers and buyers, particularly if the product or service was designed specifically for the buyer in question. This type of price negotiation is rare in the consumer-goods field at the retail level, although examples can be found.[24]

Control of prices Because the channels of distribution are usually shorter for industrial goods than they are for consumer goods, producers of industrial goods have greater control over resale prices, as the goods move through the channels to the ultimate user, than does the manufacturer of consumer goods. To remedy this imbalance resale price maintenance laws and other devices have been developed to aid the manufacturer of consumer goods in controlling the prices that distributors charge for his product.

A related distinction between the pricing of industrial goods and the pricing of consumer goods is that in the industrial-goods field price changes are easier to administer because the channels of distribution are shorter and the number of buyers is smaller. Furthermore, there is usually no large-scale advertising or other promotion to be changed. All that is necessary is to change price lists and the information contained in the salesmen's sales presentation.

Pricing research Another important difference is that research related to pricing is more productive in the industrial-goods area because information given by industrial buyers in a research study is likely to be more reliable than that given by consumers. Sampling

[23] See Chapter 5 for a discussion of competitive bidding.
[24] Some negotiation takes place in the consumer-goods field at levels above the retail level, such as between manufacturers and large retailers.

problems are also easier to solve because of the smaller number of customers in the market.

Price leadership   Finally, price leadership is probably more common in the industrial-goods market than in the consumer-goods market because price leadership is often a characteristic in industries in which a relatively small number of competing firms are selling a product that is nearly homogeneous, or standardized, in terms of quality.[25]

KIND OF CONSUMER GOOD

In traditional marketing literature, consumer goods are usually grouped into three classes—convenience, shopping, and specialty goods. *Convenience goods* are low in price or value, and are purchased frequently in small quantities. The consumer is unwilling to expend much time or effort in making such a purchase. Examples include cigarettes and loaves of bread. *Shopping goods* are higher in price or value, are purchased less frequently, and consumers will exert some effort in order to purchase them; in fact, consumers like to compare the offerings of different manufacturers or distributors, and hence "shop" for them. Many articles of clothing and furniture are shopping goods, for example. *Specialty goods* are usually, although not necessarily, relatively high in price or value, and are generally purchased infrequently. When buying such goods, the consumer is willing to exert considerable effort to locate the product, but he does not attempt to make comparisons with other products in the shopping-goods sense. This is because the consumer insists on the special qualities in the specialty good. Prestige brands of clothing, some electronic equipment, and certain brands of tobacco fall into this category.

Although there are definite limitations to the usefulness of these classifications, they are at least helpful in developing an approach to pricing. For example, product differentiation and brand loyalty are usually not very important in the market for convenience goods, and prices of competing products tend to be very similar or identical.

In the case of shopping goods, product differentiation can be important. Price differences between competing products are possible, and perhaps desirable, to the degree that consumers associate price

---

[25] Price leadership is discussed in Chapter 3.

with quality when making comparisons. A technique known as "price lining" is often employed for shopping goods, wherein a seller offers products designed to "fit" a limited number of price categories or price lines. In product areas where price lining is common, manufacturers and retailers usually become associated with certain price lines in the eyes of consumers.

Maximum retail distribution is not essential for shopping goods since the consumer is willing to come to the retailer, or at least to exert some effort in purchasing shopping goods. Manufacturers should set prices that will attract the kind of retailers who, in their opinion, are needed to do an effective marketing job. In some cases, this involves setting up systems of very limited distribution for the product.

Specialty goods are the kind of consumer goods that allow the price maker the greatest independence in price making, since there is substantial product differentiation and since consumers are willing to exert considerable effort to buy the product or service and are not very sensitive to price. In fact, for some specialty goods, high prices are actually preferable to low prices in terms of their effect upon sales volume. Specialty goods that fall into this category are prestige items, or even luxury goods, such as expensive automobiles, fur coats, and jewelry. Specialty goods are normally sold through a very limited number of retailers, and pricing should be designed to attract the kind of retailers who are best suited to the overall character or image of the product. Thus, it may be necessary to provide relatively high margins in order to attract high quality, "exclusive" retailers to handle a prestige type of specialty product.

COSTS

THE RELATIONSHIP BETWEEN COSTS AND PRICES

The importance of the role of costs in pricing is often exaggerated. Cost is only one of a number of factors that are considered in pricing. In certain circumstances, some of the other factors are far more important than costs. The main reason for this exaggerated conception of the importance of costs as a factor in pricing is that economic theory and common logic tell us that prices should equal, or cover, costs. This in turn seems to imply that costs are the *chief* determinant of prices. It is true that prices tend to cover costs in the *long run,* as adjustments in supply of a product or service and adjustments in price tend to equate prices with costs (costs being defined to include a "necessary" or "normal" profit, or return to capital). However, there may be departures from this pattern in the *short run,* because of factors other than costs that are important in most pricing decisions.

Another misconception associated with the relationship between prices and costs is that costs are always a *price-determining* factor. In practice, prices are often a *cost-determining* factor. Often the firm first tries to find out what prices it can reasonably expect to get for its products or services in the market place, given the nature of demand, the nature of competition, the degree of product differentiation, and other factors, and then it works backward to design or purchase a product or service that is suited to such a price. In this fashion, price often determines the costs of production (or purchasing) and marketing. To some extent, the closeness of this relationship may be said to vary with economic conditions. When business conditions are poor, businessmen tend to think that they are forced to adjust costs in order to conform to reduced prices. When business conditions are improving, they are inclined to think that prices must be raised to conform to higher costs.[26]

In short, the relationship between costs and prices is very complex and more difficult to understand than oversimplifications such as "prices must cover costs" or "costs determine prices" would seem to suggest. In most industries, there is much more to pricing than merely determining costs and then adding a margin for profit.

IDENTIFYING AND MEASURING COSTS

Another problem associated with determining the role of costs in pricing is the fact that costs are often very difficult to identify and measure. This problem is complicated by the fact that many firms are

---

[26] This point is mentioned by Jules Backman in *Price Practices and Price Policies* (New York: Ronald Press, 1953), p. 126; in "How Noncost Forces Shape Price Policy," *Nation's Business,* June, 1958, p. 70; and in *Pricing: Policies and Practices* (New York: National Industrial Conference Board, 1961), pp. 34–35.

multiproduct or multiservice companies and, under such circumstances, allocation of joint or common costs to specific products or services is often difficult. Furthermore, cost information that is appropriate for accounting purposes is often inappropriate for pricing purposes.

COST CONCEPTS

Many different concepts of cost can be used for pricing purposes. One aspect of costs is time, for example. Clearly future costs are the most important type of costs in pricing. Past costs have little relevance in a pricing decision unless costs tend to be stable over time. The same is true of current costs. In general, estimated future costs, provided they are reliable, are more useful in pricing decisions than past or current costs.

There are many other different concepts of cost.[27] Three of these, which are basic to pricing, are *fixed costs, variable costs,* and *incremental costs.* Fixed costs, or overhead costs, are those that do not vary with output, such as property taxes, interest payments, or rental fees. Variable costs, on the other hand, vary with changes in the rate of output. Examples are direct labor costs, fuel costs, and raw-materials costs. Average variable cost, or unit variable cost, is determined by dividing the total variable cost by the number of units at any level of output.[28] One may also isolate a third category of costs called incremental costs, which may be defined as the added costs of a change in the level or nature of activity, such as the cost of adding a new product, or a new geographic market, or the cost of changing distri-

[27] Joel Dean defines several cost concepts, which include variable costs, out-of-pocket costs, incremental costs, opportunity costs, past costs, short-run costs, traceable costs, escapable costs, controllable costs, and replacement costs. *Op. cit.,* pp. 257–72. Milton H. Spencer and Louis Siegelman list the following costs: absolute and alternative; direct and indirect; fixed and variable; short-run and long-run; differential, incremental, and residual; sunk, shutdown, and abandonment; urgent and postponable; escapable and unescapable; controllable and uncontrollable; and replacement and original. See their *Managerial Economics,* rev. ed. (Homewood, Ill.: Irwin, 1964), pp. 302–09.

[28] Marginal cost is the change in *total* cost (the added cost) that results from producing an additional unit of a product or service. Average variable cost and marginal cost are thus two quite different concepts. However, average variable cost may sometimes be roughly equal to marginal cost over a small range of output. This would be the case when average variable cost is constant. In other words, the increments to total cost (increments are variable costs) are constant.

bution channels. Not all incremental costs are necessarily variable.

For purposes of pricing, the most important are variable costs and incremental costs, both of which deal with added costs. In the following discussion, the term "variable costs" is used to designate the added costs involved in changing a firm's volume of output, whether the purpose be to add new customers for existing products or services in existing markets, to add a new product or service, to expand into different markets, or some other purpose. In short, we will use the term "variable" to denote additional costs that are incurred as a result of a management decision that causes a change in the firm's volume of output.

FULL-COST PRICING

The concept of costs used by businessmen in pricing decisions varies. Often they are speaking of full costs, that is, the fully allocated costs, both fixed and variable, associated with the product or service in question. The popularity of full-cost or "cost-plus" pricing—fully allocated costs *plus* a fixed or variable profit margin—has been frequently noted in the literature on pricing.[29] However, a recent study of pricing by eighty-eight small firms indicates that most of these firms do not confine themselves to determining costs and then adding a predetermined *fixed* margin although many of the firms studied use full cost plus a *variable* or *flexible* margin. The study also showed that most small firms that said they based their prices solely on full costs, in fact, seemed to take demand into account as well.[30]

Despite studies of this sort, which suggest that the popularity of full-cost pricing has been exaggerated, this approach is still widely practiced across the country. One reason is that many businessmen

[29] An example is a study by R. L. Hall and C. J. Hitch reported in "Price Theory and Business Behavior," *Oxford Economic Papers,* No. 2, May, 1939.

[30] W. Warren Haynes, *Pricing Decisions in Small Business* (Lexington, Ky.: University of Kentucky Press, 1962), pp. 25–29. See also his "Pricing Practices in Small Firms," *Southern Economic Journal,* April, 1964. See also I. F. Pearce, "A Study in Price Policy," *Economica,* May, 1956, in which the author points out that, although cost plus a margin of profit may be the stated price policy of a firm, in practice an estimated selling price is arrived at in this way, but a higher or lower price may actually be the one used in the sale. The question of whether full-cost or marginal-cost pricing is followed by businessmen is discussed in John Haldi, "Pricing Behavior: Economic Theory and Business Practice," *Current Economic Comment,* November, 1958.

feel that any price below full costs will result in loss to the firm. Other businessmen argue that it is proper to use full-cost pricing because they are entitled to a "fair" profit. Another reason for the popularity of full-cost pricing is that prices based on full costs are easier for buyers to understand than are prices that have been influenced by demand or competition. As a consequence, price increases based on cost changes are more likely to be acceptable to buyers.

Full-cost, or cost-plus, pricing is a convenient and expeditious method of pricing and can be a proper approach if competitors follow suit. The major limitation of full-cost pricing, assuming that full costs can be accurately determined, is that such pricing often does not take account of demand considerations, such as the buyers' needs and their ability and willingness to pay. It also tends to ignore the activities of competitors in the market place. When demand and competitive factors are neglected, only by accident would full-cost pricing produce a price that maximized profit for the firm.[31]

THE PROPER ROLE OF COSTS

Approached in the proper manner, costs should be used to establish a floor below which a firm will not price its products. "The proper function of cost is to set the lower limits on the initial price charged for a product, while value to consumers sets the upper limit. The job of the pricing executive is to pick the space between these two extremes that will best serve his purposes." [32] The costs that are of crucial importance in a pricing decision are the variable costs associated with producing or distributing additional amounts of a product or service or adding a new product or service. Unless the firm is operating at full capacity, fixed costs can usually be ignored in pricing products or services. If it has excess capacity and nothing better to do with it, the firm can sell its output profitably at any price that more than covers variable costs. Such prices make at least some contribution to fixed costs and are therefore profitable in the sense that if the product or service had not been sold at the low price, there would have been no contribution to fixed costs at all. However, al-

---

[31] Many writers agree that the forces in the market place are more important than costs in pricing. See, for example, Lawrence C. Lockley, "Theories of Pricing in Marketing," *Journal of Marketing,* January, 1949, p. 366.

[32] Phelps and Westing, *op. cit.,* p. 278.

though it is not always desirable to price products so that both fixed and variable costs are completely covered, it must be remembered that in terms of the firm's overall operations in the long run, all costs must be covered by prices.

Thus, in the short run for the firm's overall operations, or in the long run for certain items in the firm's product or service line, prices can be profitable even though they do not cover full costs. For example, in the *short run,* it may be profitable to sell the firm's *entire* offerings at prices below full costs provided that (1) prices are high enough to cover variable costs and, preferably, that they make some contribution to the fixed expenses of the business; (2) it is *necessary* to charge such low prices in order to sell the product or service; and (3) there is no better use for the facilities involved. Of course, if a product is priced so that receipts do not cover variable costs, then every unit of the product or service sold results in a loss. Only in rare circumstances would such a policy be a wise one, such as, for example, a short-term emergency situation in which prices are unusually depressed and the firm sells at such low prices in order to keep its labor force intact or to keep machinery in operation. No firm should voluntarily charge prices below full costs unless such a policy appears necessary. In other words, unless market conditions, competition, or other factors require that less-than-full-cost prices be charged, it is unwise to do so in terms of company profits. Only when there is no better use for the facilities involved are less-than-full-cost prices proper from the standpoint of profits.[33]

The same three considerations apply when considering whether or not to charge prices that do not cover full costs on individual items in the product or service line as a *long-run* approach to pricing. The prices must ordinarily cover variable expenses, be required in order to sell the item under consideration or be required for other reasons, and there should be unused capacity.

There are several reasons for wanting to price an item below full cost over a long period of time. For example, an item at the "low end" of the product line (the item of smallest size or poorest quality and lowest price) may be priced low either to fight competition without lowering prices on other items in the line or to encourage trial

[33] When a firm prices its products so that prices on its entire offerings are not covering full costs, the firm can encounter a cash shortage, that is, it may find that it is unable to pay salaries and other fixed cash requirements out of operating revenue.

purchases by buyers in the hope that they will then trade up to more expensive items in the line at a later time. Another reason for pricing below full cost is that the firm may want to encourage the purchase of some complementary product. This is the reason, for example, a manufacturer places a low price on a copying machine; he is trying to develop a market for the copying paper that he also manufactures and that must be used with the machine. Clearly, none of the reasons given above is valid unless the firm has some excess capacity. If the firm were operating at full capacity, it would be difficult to justify prices that do not cover the full costs of the firm.

Indeed, the very fact that excess capacity exists can itself be a reason for pricing below full cost. For example, manufacturers who produce their own brands sometimes also produce private brands [34] for mail-order houses or other distributors in order to make use of excess capacity. Even though the prices charged for the private brands may be below full cost, any contribution a firm receives toward the fixed expenses of the business is profitable as long as no sale could be made at higher prices and there is idle equipment available.

The fact that the prices of one or more items in the firm's line do not cover the full cost incurred in their production does not necessarily mean that the cost burden on other items in the firm's line is increased. The low-price items are not subsidized by the other items *provided* that the low prices cover variable expenses and that it is necessary to charge such low prices in order to sell the item. In such a case, any contribution the low-price items make toward the fixed expenses of the business actually *decrease* the cost burden on the other items since there would be no contribution from the sale of these items without the less-than-full-cost prices. However, if it is not necessary to charge the low price in order to sell the item, that is, if other reasons have led to the decision to adopt a low price, then it is possible that the cost burden on the other items in the line is being increased and that, in effect, the other items in the line are subsidizing the low-price item.

In practice, a policy of variable-cost pricing for some portion of the total firm output and full-cost pricing for others can be employed only when markets can be separated from one another, that is, when demand prices for different products or services produced, for differ-

---

[34] Private brands are products that bear the trademark, brand, or label of a wholesaler or retailer, in contrast to those products that carry the brand names of manufacturers.

ent outputs of the same product or service, or for the same product or service in different geographic markets are separate from one another. Businessmen often feel that variable-cost pricing is not a sound approach to pricing because they are afraid a low variable-cost price for one segment of the firm's output will force them to lower prices on the rest of the firm's output as well, with the result that there is little or no contribution toward fixed expenses. However, as we have seen, this will not happen if markets are separated from one another.[35]

Another important objection to variable-cost pricing is that it is sometimes very difficult to identify and measure the variable costs that should be assigned to a given product or service. This means that certain somewhat artificial formulas must be used. Actually, however, the problem is no more serious than that ordinarily encountered in full-cost pricing where, in addition to the assignment of variable costs to specific products or services, a share of fixed expenses must also be arbitrarily allocated among the firm's products or services.

Some costs should not be considered at all in pricing decisions. For example, "sunk" costs, expenses already incurred that cannot be revoked or changed, fall into this category. They are the result of decisions made in the past which cannot now be reversed, such as expenditures on research and development, or on specialized machines that become obsolete before their useful life has ended. As Oxenfeldt points out, if a firm has invested a large sum of money in research and development, for example, in the hope of improving its product but has produced no discovery of value, it would be unwise to increase its prices to cover its research and development expenditures. If, on the other hand, the research and development program introduced an extremely valuable improvement in production methods or in the product, the price that a firm could ask for these discoveries should in no way be affected by the research and development outlays. Indeed the firm should set a price that literally ignores sunk costs.[36]

In sum, costs are just one of several factors to be considered in a pricing decision, and for pricing purposes costs are best regarded as a floor. The important costs are the variable costs involved in producing and/or marketing the product or service. To attempt to base all

---

[35] Sometimes it is not possible to have separation of markets. In other cases it is occasionally difficult to tell if markets are, in fact, separated or if they will remain separated.

[36] Oxenfeldt, *op. cit.*, pp. 42–43.

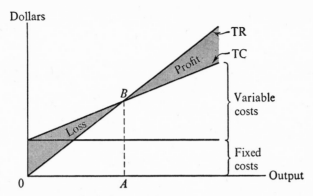

Figure 8   Break-even Analysis

prices on full costs without regard to demand and competitive conditions is a narrow and one-sided approach to pricing, which only by accident could result in the best prices for the firm. The needs and desires of the buyer are neglected in such an approach. The buyer ordinarily does not know or care much about the seller's costs, except perhaps in the industrial-goods market. Consequently, unless the price that covers full costs is one that buyers are willing to pay, there will be no sale.

There are several methods a firm might use in measuring and predicting profits. Two methods of profit measurement and forecasting that relate costs and prices are break-even analysis and contribution analysis. These methods are also of some use in price making.

BREAK-EVEN ANALYSIS

Break-even analysis is an attempt to relate the firm's total costs (TC) and total revenue (TR) to quantity sold for the purpose of determining the probable effects on profits of alternative courses of action, including price adjustments. Such analysis makes use of a break-even chart like that shown in Figure 8.

The chart is designed to show how profitable each level of output (quantity sold) is. The break-even point lies at the intersection, *B*, of the total-revenue and total-cost curves, and occurs at output 0*A*. The area labeled "profits" represents net profit at the various outputs beyond the break-even point; outputs less than 0*A* result in losses, as indicated.

The fact that the total-revenue and total-cost curves are linear indicates that an implicit assumption in break-even analysis is that additional units of the product in question can be sold at the assumed price. Thus, quantity demanded is not affected by prices in the break-even chart, that is, the chart shows only what the revenue will be at the given price *if* an unlimited amount of the product can be sold at that price. (The firm would have a perfectly horizontal demand curve.) The assumption that an unlimited amount can be sold without changing price is not valid over wide ranges of output, although it may be true that over short periods of time (small ranges of output) prices need not be changed. The decision maker using break-even analysis must make a judgment as to whether or not the quantity that can *actually* be sold at the given price is greater or less than that required to break even. The break-even chart itself does not provide this information. Another drawback to break-even analysis is that detailed information on fixed and variable costs is frequently unavailable for individual products. These and other problems associated with break-even analysis are discussed in detail in texts on managerial economics and in some general marketing texts.

Since break-even analysis is intended primarily to provide a picture of the outcome of different combinations of prices, costs, and quantities, it is of little help in price *determination,* although it is useful in comparing *alternative* prices in terms of their effect on the break-even point. Furthermore, one must recognize that break-even analysis does not indicate what quantities can actually be sold at alternative prices.

CONTRIBUTION ANALYSIS

As we have mentioned earlier, fixed costs can for the most part be ignored in pricing decisions since the price maker should be concerned primarily with variable costs and the contribution made to fixed costs and profits. Contribution analysis differs from break-even analysis in that, instead of attempting to illustrate the difference between total revenue and total costs so as to measure profits at different levels of output, it attempts to show the difference between total revenue and variable costs (or some similar concept of costs) at different levels of output in order to measure the contribution made to fixed costs and profits. Thus, if a product sells for $1.50 per unit and the variable costs involved are $0.40 per unit, each unit sold covers its variable costs and makes a contribution of $1.10 to the fixed costs

Dollars

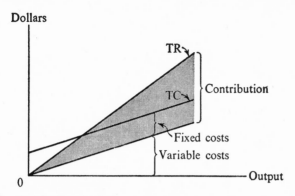

Figure 9 Contribution Analysis

Source Milton H. Spencer and Louis Siegelman, *Managerial Economics,* rev. ed. (Homewood, Ill.: Irwin, 1964), p. 100, by permission.

and profits of the firm. The "contribution" is total revenue minus variable costs.[37] Contribution analysis thus attempts to illustrate the contribution under different combinations of total revenue, variable costs, and output and may be depicted graphically as in Figure 9.

Such analysis enables the price maker to evaluate directly the contribution made to fixed costs and to profits at different levels of output at different prices. Although it does have limitations based on the difficulty of estimating demand and costs, it appears to be more useful to the price maker than traditional break-even analysis in that it focuses on the critical contribution element.

Selected References

The price policies of twenty large corporations are reported on by A. D. H. Kaplan, Joel B. Dirlam, and Robert F. Lanzillotti in *Pricing in Big Business* (Washington, D.C.: Brookings Institution, 1958). See especially Chapters 1 and 2. Price policies of small business firms are discussed in some detail by W. Warren Haynes in *Pricing Decisions in Small Business* (Lexington, Ky.: University of Kentucky Press, 1962) and by Lanzillotti and Gordon

---

[37] Variations of contribution analysis are discussed in depth in A. J. Bergfeld, "The Importance of Cost in Pricing," in American Management Association, *Pricing: The Critical Decision,* AMA Management Report No. 66 (New York: American Management Association, 1961), and in Alfred J. Bergfeld, James S. Earley, and William R. Knobloch, *Pricing for Profit and Growth* (Englewood Cliffs, N.J.: Prentice-Hall, 1962).

O. Parrish in *Pricing, Production, and Marketing Policies of Small Manufacturers* (Pullman, Wash.: Washington State University Press, 1964).

Discussions of various objectives of pricing are found in Lanzillotti, "Pricing Objectives in Large Companies," *American Economic Review,* December, 1958; Kaplan, Dirlam, and Lanzillotti, *Pricing in Big Business,* Chapters 1 and 2; and Alfred R. Oxenfeldt, *Pricing for Marketing Executives* (San Francisco: Wadsworth, 1961), pp. 58–60.

For a very good discussion of organization for pricing, see Oxenfeldt, *Pricing for Marketing Executives,* pp. 60–63. Organization for pricing in large firms is treated by Kaplan, Dirlam, and Lanzillotti in *Pricing in Big Business,* Chapter 3.

An excellent article on the differences between the marketing of industrial goods and consumer goods is Industrial Marketing Committee Review Board, "Fundamental Differences Between Industrial and Consumer Marketing," *Journal of Marketing,* October, 1954.

The role of costs in pricing has been the subject of many publications. For example, see Oxenfeldt, *Pricing for Marketing Executives,* pp. 39–47, for a discussion of the fact that the only relevant costs in pricing are added costs. Various aspects of the relationship between costs and prices are described by Jules Backman in *Price Practices and Price Policies* (New York: Ronald Press, 1953), Chapter 5, and in *Pricing: Policies and Practices* (New York: National Industrial Conference Board, 1961), pp. 28–40. The several books on managerial economics contain some discussion of the relationship between costs and prices. See, for example, Joel Dean, *Managerial Economics* (Englewood Cliffs, N.J.: Prentice-Hall, 1951), Chapter 5 and pp. 444–57, and Milton H. Spencer and Louis Siegelman, *Managerial Economics,* rev. ed. (Homewood, Ill. Irwin, 1964), Chapter 9 and pp. 372–73 and 379–83. The role of costs in pricing by small firms is given extensive treatment by W. Warren Haynes in *Pricing Decisions in Small Business* and is also discussed by Jules E. Anderson and Earl C. Gassenheimer in *Pricing Arithmetic for Small Business Managers,* Management Aids for Small Manufacturers, No. 100 (Washington, D.C.: Small Business Administration, 1959). A good discussion of full-cost and marginal-cost pricing from the point of view of the accountant is found in Morton Backer, "Flexible Costs for Pricing Decisions," *N.A.A. Bulletin,* April, 1964. A recent critical discussion of full-cost pricing may be found in Theodore E. Wentz, "Realism in Pricing Analysis," *Journal of Marketing,* April, 1966.

3

EXTERNAL CONSIDERATIONS

IN DEVELOPING A PRICE POLICY

In the previous chapter we discussed some of the important internal factors that must be considered in developing a price policy. These internal factors are controllable by the firm in that the firm can determine itself the nature of these factors and their influence on pricing. In this chapter we shall examine some of the factors external to the firm that affect price policy, including demand, nature of the industry, suppliers, kinds of buyers, economic conditions, and legal considerations. Unlike the controllable internal factors discussed in Chapter 2, the external factors are largely out of the control of the business firm.

DEMAND

The nature of the demand for the product or service in question is one of the most important considerations in the average pricing decision. This demand is determined by a number of factors, including the price of the offering, the prices and availability of substitutes, the incomes of buyers, the tastes and preferences of buyers, the character of nonprice competition, the characteristics of the product or service offered, the number and size of competitors in the industry, and the number and size of buyers. In short, the demand for a product or service is shaped by many factors, all of which are interdependent. Price is only one of these. The effect of a change in any one of the factors depends to some extent on the behavior of the other factors. For example, if price is lowered, its effect on demand depends partly upon whether incomes of buyers change or remain constant. Or, if price is increased, its effect on demand depends in part on the behavior of prices of substitute products.

It is up to the price maker to determine the precise relationship between changes in prices and demand. This can only be done if he appreciates the effects of simultaneous changes in other demand-influencing factors. In order to make the best decisions concerning price policy and specific price problems, the price maker clearly should endeavor to learn as much as possible about the character of demand and how demand might be affected by adjustments in price in both the short run and the long run.[1] Even firms that have little control over prices need to know whether anticipated changes in prices will affect sales of the industry and the firm.

Thus, essentially the problem is to estimate the price elasticity of demand for the product or service in question, for as we noted in Chapter 1, price elasticity is a measure of the responsiveness of the quantity sold to price changes (assuming all other variables are constant). Specifically, it is a measure representing the ratio of the percentage response of the quantity sold to a percentage change in price. The demand for a product or service is *elastic* if the total revenue increases as the price is reduced. Demand is *inelastic* if the total revenue decreases when the price is reduced. If there is no change in the total revenue when prices are changed, the situation is one of *unitary elasticity*. In other words, the more sensitive the quantity demanded is to price changes, the more elastic is the demand for the offering.[2]

The price maker must really consider two kinds of demand. The first is the nature of demand for the generic product or service (industry demand) as it is affected by industry-wide price changes, such as the nature of demand for bottle caps in general. The second is the nature of demand for the individual brand that the seller is offering, or the output of the particular firm, such as the nature of demand for

[1] For a discussion of the importance of price elasticity of demand when considering a price reduction, see Clare E. Griffin, "When Is Price Reduction Profitable?" *Harvard Business Review,* September–October, 1960.

[2] For a discussion of some factors that tend to make demand for a product insensitive to price changes, see Richard T. Sampson, "Sense and Sensitivity in Pricing," *Harvard Business Review,* November–December, 1964.

brand X bottle caps. The latter kind of demand elasticity is sometimes referred to as "brand elasticity" or "market-share elasticity" to distinguish it from the elasticity of demand for the generic product or service.

The price elasticities of the two kinds of demand can be quite similar, or they can be quite different. In the gasoline industry, for example, they are quite different. The demand for automobile gasoline in general is relatively inelastic in that moderate changes in the price of the product will not cause very significant changes in the quantity of gasoline purchased. Instead, the quantity of gasoline purchased appears to be more a function of the number of automobiles in operation than of the price of gasoline, as long as wide variations in price do not take place. In sharp contrast, the elasticity of demand for individual brands appears to be very high, as evidenced by the fact that small changes in the price of a particular brand can cause very large changes in the quantity of that brand purchased. In terms of our discussion in Chapter 1, the high brand elasticity for gasoline may be attributed primarily to the fact that, on the whole, consumers seem to regard the product as being homogeneous.

In connection with the notion of the price elasticity of demand for the output of an industry, it should be noted that there is often a relationship between the prices in different industries. A general price adjustment in industry A may influence not only the demand for industry A's offerings, but also the demand for the offerings of industry B, if the offerings of the two industries can be substituted for one another. Indeed, a high *cross elasticity* of demand means that the products or services involved are close substitutes for one another.

The prices of one industry may also influence the demand for another industry's products or services when the offerings of the two industries are complementary, that is, when they are used in combination. Sometimes products of this sort are components of the same final product, such as an automobile. In other cases, the complementary products are used together by consumers but do not combine to yield some other final product. Razors and razor blades, baseball bats and baseballs, and electric guitars and amplifiers are examples of this latter type of complementary product.

Despite the fact that the effects on demand of certain price policies and particular prices often represent vital considerations in pricing decisions, many business firms operate with very little knowledge of the nature of the demand for their offerings. To a great extent, this is because of the difficulty in obtaining reliable information about demand. Such firms apparently make certain assumptions about demand and make price adjustments on a strictly intuitive basis, in the sense that subjective judgment is used to predict the effect of such adjustments on demand. In the commercial airline industry, for example, there has been a great deal of controversy and disagreement in recent years concerning passenger fares. Some airline executives have suggested that if the airlines would offer substantial reductions in fares, the increased traffic generated by such reductions would more than offset the reduction in fares, and total revenue of the airline companies would increase as a consequence. Other airline executives, however, insist that substantial reductions in fares would have little effect on the amount of traffic carried and would only result in lower total revenue for the industry as a whole.

This example is not as unusual as it may seem; many firms and industries are highly uncertain about the nature of demand for their offerings.[3] All they are sure of is the quantity being sold at the current price. This, of course, represents only one point on the demand curve of a firm or an industry. It is a rare firm or industry that can draw up a demand schedule that accurately depicts the price elasticity of demand for its offerings. Indeed, if such demand schedules could be drawn up, pricing decisions would be much more routine than they are at present, and much of the uncertainty in pricing would be eliminated. Empirical studies of the price elasticity of demand for the offerings of entire industries or of individual firms under market conditions are rare, although some good studies of the nature of industry demand for certain manufactured products such as automobiles and cigarettes have been made.[4] In addition to problems concerning time

[3] W. Warren Haynes points out in his study of eighty-eight small firms that no firm in the study used any quantitative estimates of price elasticity of demand. See his *Pricing Decisions in Small Business* (Lexington, Ky.: University of Kentucky Press, 1962), p. 44.

[4] See, for example, C. F. Roos and V. von Szelski, *The Dynamics of Automobile Demand* (New York: General Motors Corp., 1939). A number of demand studies are discussed in Werner Z. Hirsch, "On the Phenomenon of Inelastic Demand," *Southern Economic Journal,* July, 1951, and Aaron W. Warner and Victor R. Fuchs, *Concepts and Cases in Economic Analysis* (New York: Harcourt, Brace & World, 1957), pp. 144–69. Textbooks on managerial economics often contain illustrations of studies of demand. See, for example, William W. Haynes, *Managerial Economics: Analysis and Cases* (Homewood, Ill.: Dorsey Press, 1963), Chapters 4, 5, and 6, and Marshall R. Colberg, Dascomb R. Forbush, and Gilbert R. Whitaker, Jr., *Business Economics: Principles and Cases,* 3rd. ed. (Homewood, Ill.: Irwin, 1964), Chapter 3.

and cost, the chief reason for the lack of adequate empirical studies of the subject is the extreme difficulty encountered in relating demand to price, given the number of uncontrollable variables that affect demand, such as changes in buyers' tastes and incomes, and changes in the offerings and prices of competitors. Because of the severe difficulties inherent in such analysis, relatively little of it has been done by business firms. Although there are sophisticated statistical methods available with which data concerning the relationship between prices and quantity demanded can be analyzed, they are of little use if the necessary data is not available.

DEMAND ANALYSIS

Although little has been done in practice to analyze the relationship between price and sales volume, especially for particular brands and firms, there are some methods available for the collection of data on this topic.

Experimentation In recent years, experimentation of one kind or another has become increasingly popular in marketing. Experimentation is an attempt to measure, under controlled conditions, the effect of changes in certain variables on selected marketing factor(s). As in any scientific experiment, by controlling, or holding constant, or eliminating variables other than the one(s) being tested, it is hoped that any changes that occur can be attributed to the variable(s) being tested. (In controlled experiments involving price, for example, price is the variable being tested and an attempt is made to hold the other factors constant.) Much of this marketing experimentation has been in the area of consumer behavior and has concentrated on variables such as advertising, salesmanship, package design, and price, all of which are thought to have an effect on consumer purchasing decisions.

Experimentation in marketing can take the form of laboratory experiments, which may be conducted in an experimental laboratory or under controlled conditions in some other location. In laboratory experiments subjects are exposed to situations in which they are asked to make decisions that will reflect the importance to them of price or some other marketing variable in the purchase decision.[5]

[5] Examples of this kind of experimental method involving price are given in three works by Edgar A. Pessemier: "A New Way to Determine Buying

The subjects in such an experiment are sometimes asked to assume the role of buyers—a device called "role playing"—and attempt to project themselves into a buying situation, such as a simulated shopping trip. The subjects may actually be given money in advance, some of which they may choose to spend on the products being used in the experiment.

There are two cardinal features of such behavior research: duplication of the market situation in the laboratory, variation being permitted only in the feature, price, product line, or promotion technique the effects of which are under investigation; and observation of the reactions of the experimental subjects.[6] Advocates of the controlled laboratory-experiment method note in this regard that the experimental conditions should be *psychologically* equivalent to the market, not necessarily *physically* identical. As long as the experimental situation is made "real" to the subject by duplicating those aspects of the market that influence his actions, then the experimental results will closely parallel the decisions made by buyers under similar conditions in everyday life.[7]

Laboratory experimentation solves some of the tremendous problems associated with trying to determine the effects of price on demand by examining isolated variables of the actual market situation. Although laboratory experimentation appears to offer considerable promise for the future, the fact that at present the subjects are asked to make purchase decisions under highly structured circumstances limits somewhat the practical application of these findings.

Other kinds of pricing experimentation can be performed in the field instead of in a laboratory. Unlike the laboratory-experiment method, field experiments of this sort attempt to measure the effect of price on sales volume in "real" shopping situations. Field experiments are sometimes conducted in retail stores by manufacturers of

---

Decisions," *Journal of Marketing,* October, 1959; "An Experimental Method for Estimating Demand," *Journal of Business,* October, 1960; and *Experimental Methods for Analyzing Demand for Branded Consumer Goods with Applications to Problems of Marketing Strategy* (Pullman, Wash.: Washington State University Press, 1963). See also Jack Abrams, "A New Method for Testing Pricing Decisions," *Journal of Marketing,* July, 1964.

[6] Alderson and Sessions, "Basic Research Report on Consumer Behavior," in Ronald E. Frank, Alfred A. Kuehn, and William F. Massy, *Quantitative Techniques in Marketing Analysis* (Homewood, Ill.: Irwin, 1962), p. 130.

[7] Pessemier, "An Experimental Method for Estimating Demand," *Journal of Business,* October, 1960, p. 374.

consumer goods. In such a case, a "control" store, or group of stores, is usually compared with an "experimental" store, or stores, in which price is being manipulated.[8] Prices are usually manipulated in the experimental store(s) and held constant in the control store(s). Since the only factor being varied by the experimenter is price, a comparison of sales volumes will reveal what results may be expected from changes in price. The stores used in such an experiment may be in the same community or in different communities, depending upon the objectives of the study and the time and expense considerations involved.

An important factor in field experimentation is that the stores being compared must be very similar in size, merchandise assortment, and kind of neighborhood and clientele served to ensure that differences noted in sales volume can safely be attributed to differences in price. The same applies to the communities involved; they must be similar in economic characteristics and other factors to ensure that differences in local characteristics do not distort the findings. It is also important that the experimental situation be such that the results of the experiment can be projected to the total market.

Field experimentation can also be performed by sellers who distribute their products through the mail, rather than through retail stores. In fact, since variability between stores is eliminated as a possible problem, price experimentation conducted with catalogs and other mailing pieces is likely to yield more reliable results.

Trial-and-error pricing is a rather crude variation of field experimentation, whereby various prices are tried out in the market place before final price decisions are made. As a rule no attempt is made in such experiments to define control stores, or areas, and experimental stores, or areas. This simple method is often used with new products for which there is little available information about pricing and other marketing factors.

There are several problems involved in any type of field experimentation, two of the most basic of which are that they are often expensive and time consuming and that it is sometimes difficult to maintain control over factors other than the experimenter's own price. For example, a labor strike in one of the control or experimental cities

---

[8] Several examples of field pricing experiments are described by Joel Dean in *Managerial Economics* (Englewood Cliffs, N.J.: Prentice-Hall, 1951), pp. 181–83, and by Edward R. Hawkins in "Methods of Estimating Demand," *Journal of Marketing,* April, 1957.

can distort all of the findings obtained by the study. Prices of competing products cannot be controlled either. If a major competitor decides to make significant price adjustments during the period of the experiment, the results of the experiment will almost surely be distorted. In fact, firms sometimes deliberately manipulate their prices in an abnormal manner in order to invalidate the results when they learn that a competitor is conducting a field experiment of this sort. Furthermore, if it is customary for competitors to adjust prices when the experimenting firm adjusts its prices, then what should be tested is the overall effect of *both* changes on the sales volume of the experimenting firm, since in such a case it would be unrealistic to test the firm's own price changes alone. It is sometimes possible in this regard to persuade retailers to manipulate the prices of competing products along with the prices of the products of the experimenting firm.

Survey of buyers   Still another method of estimating the elasticity of demand for a product or service is to ask, by means of a survey conducted by personal interview, mail, or telephone, buyers of the product or service what their reaction is, or would be, to certain price changes. Surveys of this sort usually include questions such as, "How much would you be willing to pay for _____?" or "Of the following prices, which would you be willing to pay for _____?"

Actually, the survey method (sometimes referred to as the questionnaire method) is a relatively ineffective way of determining the degree to which demand is sensitive to price. Its primary weakness lies in the fact that the buyer is asked to give his or her reaction to prices without being placed in an actual, or even simulated, buying decision situation. Experience indicates that buyers find it extremely difficult to predict what they would do in a given situation, even when they are very sincere and honest in trying to answer the questions. As a consequence, the results of such surveys are often of little value.

The difficulties associated with the survey method are more pronounced when surveys are taken among buyers of consumer goods than when they are taken among buyers in the industrial-goods market. This is because, on the average, the buyer of industrial goods tends to be a more rational, better informed buyer who may have knowledge of substitute products and who is better able to judge a price and predict his own behavior. However, it is impossible to say how much more reliable the survey method is among industrial buyers.

Historical statistical analysis   Price elasticity of demand for a product or service can also be estimated on the basis of company and industry records, which show past changes in price and sales volume. Estimating the probable effect of past price changes, the analyst can extrapolate and make an intelligent guess concerning price elasticity of demand in the future. Often, however, what seems to be a simple cause-and-effect relationship is not really there. Thus, if price adjustments correlate with changes in demand, it is difficult to determine whether the price changes caused the changes in demand, or whether some other factor that happened to change at the same time caused demand to shift. It is equally difficult to say whether changes in demand caused the changes in price, or the reverse. Furthermore, what happened in the past may not be repeated in the future, since both conditions of demand and supply may be changing over time. Finally, historical records showing prices of the firm and prices of competitors along with sales volumes for the firm and for the industry may not be available. Sometimes data is not available in sufficient detail because of improper record-keeping, or because the firm, or the industry, is too new to have had much experience. Lack of good records can also occur when price changes in the past have been too infrequent or too small to establish a clear relationship between price changes and quantities sold.

Clearly, the research techniques presently available for determining customer reaction to prices have several important drawbacks. This partially accounts for the fact that the executives responsible for pricing decisions often know very little about the nature of the demand for the offerings of their firms. Firms are showing an increasing interest in the subject, however. About one fourth of the 146 firms participating in a National Industrial Conference Board study reported that they customarily pretest pricing decisions involving new products. The "test-market method" is the technique most widely used. Other methods are surveys of prospective customers concerning prices for new products and "general marketing and economic research investigations," including "price-demand analysis." [9]

Of course, the importance of knowing something about the nature of the demand for one's product varies from firm to firm. Even firms that have little control over the prices they charge are anxious to

[9] G. Clark Thompson and Morgan B. MacDonald, Jr., "Pricing New Products," *Conference Board Record,* January, 1964, pp. 11–13. It should be noted that the term "test-market method" is sometimes used to describe field experimentation and on other occasions involves no more than trial-and-error pricing.

know whether anticipated changes in prices will affect their sales volume, however. A firm that operates under conditions approaching market pricing, or in an oligopolistic industry in which deviations from current prices are highly undesirable, does not find it as important to know the nature of the demand for its output as does a firm that has considerable discretion in setting prices. Nevertheless, in most pricing situations, almost all firms need to know something about the price elasticity of the demand for their products, and research, particularly of the experimental kind, promises to be of considerable assistance to price makers in the future.

THE NATURE OF THE INDUSTRY

MARKET STRUCTURE AND THE NATURE OF COMPETITION

Another extremely important factor that must be considered in developing a price policy is the nature of the market structure in which a firm operates. It is also one of the more difficult factors to evaluate. Each firm must determine for itself what its market structure is like and how it affects price policy determination. The market structure consists of three basic elements: the number of competitors, size of each competitor, and the degree of product differentiation.[10] Other factors that help determine market structure include the ease of entry into the industry by new competitors, their ability to provide effective competition, and the pricing programs they adopt. Together these elements determine the market structure or, in other words, the nature of competition that a particular firm faces.[11] The market structure is a significant factor not only in pricing decisions but also in determining the nature of demand.

Basic kinds of market structures   As we discussed in Chapter 1,

[10] Product differentiation was discussed in Chapter 2 and is not dealt with in detail in this chapter.

[11] Competition is one of the key factors in pricing decisions and is often the most important factor. In a study of 146 firms, the National Industrial Conference Board found that competition ranked second behind profit and cost considerations as a factor to consider in the pricing of new products. See Thompson and MacDonald, *op. cit.,* pp. 7–9.

traditional price theory isolates four basic kinds of market structure: pure competition, pure monopoly, monopolistic competition, and oligopoly. These four kinds of market structure differ in number of competitors, size of competitors, and degree of product differentiation.

We have said that pure competition in its true form has never existed in the real world. There are, however, some markets that approach the theoretical model of pure competition, thereby making it of some practical value to price makers. In some situations, the demand for the product approaches perfect elasticity and this, in turn, means that the price maker has very little control over price. Examples are industries in which the product is close to being homogeneous and there is a fairly large number of sellers, such as industries that produce certain agricultural or mineral products. Although the firm can sell virtually all that it wants to sell at the established price, it can sell practically nothing at a price that is higher than the established price, since buyers will transfer their patronage to rivals if the firm in question raises its prices unilaterally. In such a market situation, the price maker must "follow the market."

By the same token, pure monopoly is also very rare in the real world. Those few business firms that most closely approximate pure monopoly are found in the public-utility field where power companies and telephone companies are given monopoly rights by the government. Even in such situations, however, a firm is not necessarily completely insulated from competition; there may be competition from substitutes as in the case of natural gas, which faces competition from electricity and coal. Even if there is no direct competition, there are almost always other means for customers to satisfy their wants by substituting other kinds of products or services. Nonetheless, when a firm approximates a monopoly position, the price maker has an opportunity to price with little or no regard to competition. Notice, however, that the price elasticity of demand is still of considerable importance since knowledge of elasticity enables the price maker to forecast the effect of a proposed price on sales volume.

Market situations resembling monopolistic competition are often found in the real world. Many industries are composed of a large number of sellers offering a differentiated product or service. Examples include the retailing of hardware or bakery goods and the manufacture of women's dresses or furniture. As we have seen, in such situations the demand curve slopes downward and to the right, which means that there is room for some degree of price administration. Because of the large number of competitors in a situation resembling monopolistic competition, the price maker need not be overly concerned with the pricing decisions made by any one competing seller, unless there is practically no product differentiation in the industry. If product differentiation is minimal, the demand curve faced by the firm is highly elastic and, as a consequence, the firm is forced to price "at the market" or very close to it. In such situations the prices of competitors are extremely important. As long as some substantial degree of product differentiation exists, however, a firm may price its products differently than competing products.

The fact that there is a large number of competitors in an industry resembling monopolistic competition and that there is some degree of product differentiation also means that the approach to pricing is less consistent among the firms than when the number of firms is small, or when there is little or no product differentiation. As a result, there is a greater variety of prices available to buyers, and price is a more volatile competitive instrument.

Finally, we know that in an oligopoly there are a small number of sellers, each of whom is important enough to affect the decisions of others; the sellers are interdependent. There are a number of industries in the American economy that resemble oligopoly, including steel, automobile, cigarette, and aluminum manufacturing. In price theory a distinction is usually made between pure, or homogeneous, oligopoly and differentiated oligopoly, whereby the former term is used to refer to a small number of firms offering a homogeneous product, and the latter to a small number of firms offering a differentiated product. As we mentioned in Chapter 1, it is more difficult to generalize about oligopoly situations in price theory than is the case with the other three basic market structures because of the interdependence of the demand curves facing each seller. Some general tendencies can be pointed out, however.

In situations that approximate pure oligopoly, the prices of different firms tend to be uniform because any attempt to set prices below those on competing products will lead to immediate retaliation by competitors and hence lower prices for all. Conversely, prices above those of competitors cannot produce sufficient sales volume because the product is very nearly homogeneous in the eyes of buyers. Consequently, under homogeneous oligopoly the price maker usually "follows the market" in his pricing decisions.

On the other hand, in markets that approximate differentiated oligopoly, price uniformity is not required because there is some product differentiation. In such a case the price maker need not "follow the market" but, instead, can pursue a more independent course in pricing.

The size of the competitors relative to the firm in question is a particularly important factor for pricing decisions in oligopoly-type situations. Clearly, if a firm is small relative to its competitors, its approach to pricing will probably be entirely different from what it would be if the firm were large relative to its competitors, or if all firms in the industry were of approximately the same size. In short, whether or not a firm in an oligopolistic industry has much discretion or latitude in pricing is often a function of the relative size of the firm.

Price leadership   Price leadership often exists in oligopolistic situations, whereby one firm, or a small number of firms, dominates the industry in terms of share of the market.[12] Price leadership is said to exist when the prices of one firm, or several firms, are followed by other firms in an industry. The other firms need not follow the leader's prices exactly; often they endeavor to maintain a constant differential between their own prices and the prices of the leader. It should also be noted that the price leader may vary from one geographic area to the next within the same industry and that leadership may change hands over time.[13]

Theoretically, price leadership is most likely to be found in industries in which there is a nearly homogeneous product and a relatively small number of firms (industries that approach pure oligopoly). In practice, however, it is often found in industries in which there is considerable product differentiation.

Although price leadership has sometimes been the result of direct or overt price collusion between competing firms, it may be a natural consequence of the existing conditions in the industry. All that is really necessary for price leadership to exist is that the prices of a firm or firms be consistently acceptable to most of the industry and

[12] Of course price leadership may occur in other kinds of market structures as well.

[13] Specific examples of price leadership are discussed in Edward P. Learned, "Pricing of Gasoline: A Case Study," *Harvard Business Review*, November, 1948; Harry L. Hansen and Powell Niland, "Esso Standard: A Study in Pricing," *Harvard Business Review*, May, 1952; and Jules Backman, *Pricing: Policies and Practices* (New York: National Industrial Conference Board, 1961), Appendix D.

that there is a custom in the industry of following a leader(s). The leader(s) usually accounts for a substantial share of the market; often it is the largest firm in the industry.

Smaller firms might wish to follow the prices of a larger firm or firms for several reasons:

1. The larger firm(s) may have coerced the smaller firms into following its prices by threatening to "dump" the product in the smaller firms' local markets at extremely low prices or to "punish" the smaller firms in other ways. Given the legislation that now exists, particularly at the federal level, such a practice is highly unlikely, however.

2. The small firms may simply assume that the larger firm(s) is capable of setting satisfactory prices and, therefore, that it is wise to follow such prices.

3. The small firms may think that the larger firm(s) is the most efficient firm in the industry and that to be competitive they must follow the prices of the larger firm, at least in a downward direction.

4. Following the prices of the larger firm(s) may be the most convenient form of pricing for smaller firms. By leaving the task of developing prices to the leader(s), they do not need to spend much time or money on it themselves.

5. The prices set by the leader(s) may prove to be very profitable prices for smaller firms, who are happy to take advantage of the "umbrella" the leader(s) is holding over them. This effect is illustrated by the fact that in industries characterized by price leadership the price leader(s) sometimes experiences a declining share of the total market over time. The reason is that the profitable prices established under price leadership encourage the entry of new firms and the expansion of existing firms.

6. The same cost factors may affect all the firms in the industry (for example, an industry-wide labor contract), and if the leader(s) adjusts prices to reflect changes in costs, the other firms follow suit since the same forces are also affecting them.

7. Sometimes smaller firms copy the production methods, distribution methods, and even the products of a larger firm(s). A natural result of this tendency is to copy the prices of the larger firm(s) as well.

8. A smaller firm may be operating at full or at most efficient

capacity. In such a situation there would be no purpose in attempting to price below the prices of the leader(s) since the firm would be unable to handle any increase in its sales volume anyway.

9. Following a price leader is sometimes the "accepted" thing to do, particularly when prices are lowered. Smaller firms feel that the public may wonder why a given firm did not cut prices when other firms did so, even though the firm may not always raise prices when the other firms do.

10. It is good common sense to follow a leader in order to avoid price warfare, which could prove destructive to smaller firms. This factor is particularly important in an industry with a homogeneous-type product.

For reasons such as these price leadership exists in many industries in the United States even though there is no overt collusion.

Whether or not a particular firm is a price leader or a price follower is usually not a matter of choice. Assuming that choice were possible, however, should a firm be a leader or a follower in pricing? The chief advantage in being a leader is that the firm has full control over its own destiny and is not subject to the whims or mistakes of another firm. There are also significant disadvantages in being a price leader, however. For one thing the leader assumes full responsibility for errors in pricing. Therefore, the leader must consider the effect of prices, not only in terms of its own operations but in terms of the operations of other firms in the industry as well. Furthermore, the expenses of research and the other activities associated with pricing must be borne by the leader. Finally, criticisms by government agencies concerning the legal aspects of price leadership tend to focus on the actions of the price leader.

The price followers have no control over their prices if they decide to follow a leader, but there are several advantages in being a follower nonetheless. The follower may take advantage of the talents of the price leader's experts. Furthermore, it is less expensive and very convenient to be a price follower, and it enables the firm to avoid many of the legal problems that price leaders must face.

The prices of the price leader(s) are more likely to be consistently followed by other firms when an industry is prosperous than when it is suffering from a decline in sales and perhaps has a problem of excess capacity. In the steel manufacturing industry, for example, when there is an industry-wide or nation-wide recession, there seems to be a strong tendency for price followers to deviate from the price leader's prices in order to attract business. This may take the form of open price cutting or secret price concessions. In fact, it might be said that in some industries price leadership exists *only* when prices are being raised and that when prices are being lowered the leader(s) becomes a follower. It should also be noted, however, that price leadership may also break down in sharp upward swings in the business cycle as "followers" strive to take advantage of premium prices.[14]

One of the results of price leadership is that it tends to eliminate price competition among the firms in the industry. As a consequence, efforts to maintain or expand sales volume are generally confined to nonprice competition. Heavy expenditures on nonprice factors are common in such situations. The actual level of prices that results from price leadership depends on how consistently the other firms follow the prices of the leader(s) and on the nature of the industry involved. Under perfect price leadership where the leader(s) is followed under all circumstances by all other firms in the industry, the leader(s) is in a pricing position comparable to that enjoyed in theory by the pure monopolist and it might be expected to set prices that would yield maximum profit for itself. In practice, however, other firms are not willing to follow the leader(s) under all circumstances, particularly when sales are falling. As a rule price leaders are followed only so long as they do not depart too much from what followers think prices should be. Price leaders, like any other firms, do not have perfect knowledge of supply and demand conditions and occasionally make what followers regard as pricing mistakes. Lastly, fear of prosecution under the antitrust laws discourages monopolistic behavior on the part of the price leader(s). As a result, price leadership usually does not result in monopoly profits but, instead, has the effect of stabilizing the prices in the industry and, in particular, of preventing price cutting.

Freedom of entry into the industry   Ease of entry into the industry is another factor that has a bearing on the pricing decisions made

[14] With reference to the steel industry, A. D. H. Kaplan, Joel B. Dirlam, and Robert F. Lanzillotti state that "Competitors of the corporation are more likely to take premiums in periods of prosperity, while U.S. Steel appears to demand no more than its published prices. In recession, however, the company has followed the trend toward concessions initiated by competitors." See their *Pricing in Big Business* (Washington, D.C.: Brookings Institution, 1958), p. 19.

by the marketing executive. In some industries there are barriers to entry into the industry that insulate a firm from new competition. This, in turn, influences the nature of the demand for the output of each firm and the price policies they adopt. Generally, the demand curve faced by a firm in such a situation is more inelastic than would otherwise be the case. In other industries it is relatively easy for a new firm to begin operations. This tends to increase the elasticity of demand for the output of an individual firm and acts as a damper or limit on the discretion or control that each firm has over prices. Some of the barriers to entry that might exist, in addition to legal barriers such as licensing requirements or patent rights, include high capital requirements, cost advantages enjoyed by firms that are already in operation, extreme product differentiation, and the fact that existing firms control sources of supply of raw materials.

AGE OF THE INDUSTRY

The age of the industry can also influence the approach that a firm takes, or should take, to pricing. It is best to discuss the pricing implications of the age of the *industry* in conjunction with the pricing implications of the age of the *product* or *service* offered by the industry, however. Since this topic is discussed in depth in Chapter 6, at this point we will simply point out that the price maker in a new industry can expect to encounter more aggressive pricing approaches from his competitors. Prices, in a new industry, tend to be a more volatile marketing instrument than in old and well-established industries because new methods of production and marketing, and improvements in the products or services offered are being developed at a rapid rate, and these changes are reflected in prices. Furthermore, the industry is still in the process of being "shaken out" as weak or inefficient firms are being removed. Another factor that contributes to the use of price as an active marketing tool in a new industry is that the market for the industry's products is still being developed, and as a consequence downward price adjustments can produce significant changes in sales.

On the other hand, in an old, well-established industry stability and status quo are the rule; no one wishes to "rock the boat." New methods of production and marketing, and new changes in the product or service are not being developed at a rapid rate, and the weak or inefficient firms have long since left the industry. Furthermore, the product or service has been well accepted by the market for some time, and, as a rule, the size of the market is stable or perhaps declining.[15]

Therefore, unless there is significant patent protection for the new product or service upon which a new industry is based, a new industry is generally characterized by pricing that is considerably more aggressive than it is in an older industry. Thus, for the price maker in a new industry, price is an important competitive tool, and the importance of the price-making function is greater than it is in an older industry.

SUPPLIERS

Although their influence is usually somewhat indirect, suppliers of raw materials, parts, and other industrial goods can have some effect on pricing decisions made by producers. For example, the prices charged for raw materials and parts may have a great influence on the prices established for the goods or services being produced if the raw materials or parts represent a sizable proportion of the total cost of the firm. Of course, some raw materials and parts may be relatively unimportant in terms of the firm's total costs, and others may be very important. In some cases, the cost of raw materials or parts is unimportant in *total,* being of far less significance in terms of the firm's total costs than other cost items, such as labor. Indeed, suppliers of labor influence pricing in much the same manner as do suppliers of raw materials and parts.

As testimony to the important role that suppliers play in price making, it is occasionally necessary for a firm to attempt to negotiate prices with suppliers for the express purpose of keeping the prices of the goods or services supplied at a level that will permit the firm to price its offerings at a given price.

Sometimes this relationship between the prices of raw materials, parts, and labor, and the prices of the firm's products or services operates in reverse, in that the price a seller charges for a product or service may influence the amount his suppliers will charge him. Thus,

[15] For an interesting discussion of the differences in pricing by the automobile industry in its early years as compared with the current situation, see Clare E. Griffin, *op. cit.*

if the firm sets a high price on its product that improves the profitability of its operations, it may discover that it must pay a higher price for the goods and services supplied.[16]

The prices of goods supplied do, of course, play an extremely important role in pricing by wholesalers and retailers. This is because the prices charged by suppliers represent a very large cost element for such distributors and, to a great extent, the prices charged by suppliers, which represent the cost of goods sold to the distributor, are a starting point for pricing over which the distributor has no control. Since distributors sometimes mark up merchandise by well-established, customary percentage amounts, the prices of suppliers can, in such cases, directly determine the prices of distributors. As a consequence, the prices charged by suppliers of merchandise are often determined by working backward from prices that the supplier would like to have the distributors charge. In some cases, such as in the retailing of consumer goods, suppliers effectively establish the retail prices themselves by means of resale price maintenance laws and other methods.[17]

BUYERS

The type of people and firms that buy the product or service a company offers for sale should also help shape its price policy. The number of buyers in the market for a given product or service and their size vary considerably from industry to industry. At one extreme is the cigarette industry in which thousands of retailers handle the product and millions of consumers use it. At the opposite extreme are monopsony situations in which there is only one buyer as, for example, the federal government in the case of national defense items. Even within the same industry, firms may sell their products or services in several different kinds of markets in which the number and size of buyers vary considerably.

As a rule, the more buyers there are in the market place, and the smaller each is, the less influence any individual buyer will have on

---

[16] Alfred R. Oxenfeldt, *Pricing for Marketing Executives* (San Francisco: Wadsworth, 1961), p. 34.

[17] Pricing by distributors is discussed in Chapter 7.

price. Conversely, the fewer the buyers in the market place, and the larger they are, the greater the influence that an individual buyer has on price (unless, of course, there are also very few sellers or few who can adequately serve the buyer). If the buyers are strong enough or large enough to produce the item in question themselves, they wield a great deal of influence on price. In such cases buyers can gain price advantages from sellers. However, this power is held in check to some extent by the existence of the Robinson-Patman Act, which we will discuss in Chapter 4.

To illustrate the varying importance of the buyer in pricing decisions, let us look briefly at the aluminum manufacturing industry. One kind of market for aluminum is the major container manufacturers. Aluminum is also sold to manufacturers of hardware items, which represent a totally different kind of market. In the first case, the buyers are large and few and they purchase aluminum in enormous quantities. In other words, individually, they are extremely important to the aluminum manufacturers, and this gives them the power to influence aluminum prices. On the other hand, there are many small manufacturers of hardware items, no one of which is very important to the aluminum companies. In this market the aluminum producers enjoy much more independence in pricing.

Another example of an industry with multiple markets is the manufacturers of automobile batteries. The several kinds of markets served by such manufacturers include the original equipment market, which consists of manufacturers of automobiles, and the replacement market, which consists of various independent dealers such as gasoline service stations, fleet owners of one kind or another, and distributors who purchase private label batteries. In each of these markets the relationship between seller and buyer is different.

Many industries are involved in selling the same or similar products or services to several different kinds of markets. Clearly a single price policy cannot be used for all markets served. In the case of aluminum producers, for example, the approach to pricing that is appropriate for aluminum companies in the container market is probably inappropriate in the hardware market. The same can be said when comparing the pricing approach that an automobile battery manufacturer uses in the original equipment market and the approach he uses in the gasoline service-station market. Therefore, a firm often needs several price policies and procedures.

An additional point to remember concerning the number of buyers in a firm's market is that the ability of the seller to "know" the market, in the sense of being alert to the trends taking place in buyer preferences and the changes in attitudes toward certain brands, varies with the number of buyers in the market. In general, the more buyers there are, the less frequent and intense is the contact between the seller and individual buyers, and consequently the less able is the seller to gauge the market.[18]

ECONOMIC CONDITIONS IN THE MARKET

The economic conditions in the market(s) served by a firm are also important in pricing. For those sellers whose product or service is purchased over a very large geographic area economic conditions may vary considerably from area to area. As a consequence, the firm may wish to use different approaches to pricing in the different areas.

PRICING IN A RISING MARKET

In the upward swing of the business cycle, the demand for a product or service will probably increase. This in turn often means that a firm can exercise more independence in pricing and that its usual pricing practices can be followed. Certainly, the pricing task is easier in such times than it is when the market is declining. The mere fact that the market is rising, however, does not mean that a firm can enjoy complete independence in pricing. Markets can be rising and still be very competitive at the same time. In fact, rising markets often encourage competitors to enter the industry or to expand their capacities. The 1960's provide an excellent illustration of a highly competitive boom period in which prosperity is accompanied by a definite buyers' market, increasing competition, and lower profit margins in many industries.

[18] Not only do distributors (wholesalers and retailers) influence pricing by producers to the extent that they constitute a type of market as indicated above (in terms of their size and number), but they also influence pricing by producers in their capacity as distributors. This topic is discussed in Chapter 6, which deals with pricing by manufacturers.

With regard to pricing, the principal problem that occurs during an upswing in business activity is that costs may be rising along with the market for the product or service that is being sold. Hence, at such times, it is particularly important that costs be watched carefully to ensure that they are playing their proper role as a floor in pricing. There is a tendency, which we noted in Chapter 2, for businessmen to attribute more importance to costs as a determinant of prices when business conditions are good. In fact, most price increases are justified to the public by business firms as being price adjustments that were necessitated by rising costs. Nonetheless, *unit* costs may actually decline during boom periods since overhead or fixed costs can be spread over more units. Hence, before raising prices to compensate for what are thought to be higher costs in a rising market, it is wise to check that the cost figures used are accurate and to determine the specific reason for a decline in profits. The firm may be able to produce the product or service at a lower cost. Alternatively, perhaps the firm can avoid a price increase by giving customers a little less for their money without affecting the performance of the product or service in any important way.[19]

If inflation should accompany an upswing in business activity, the government may take a more active interest in pricing in the hope of countering such inflationary tendencies. Problems of this sort are discussed in Chapter 4.

PRICING IN A DECLINING MARKET

When the business cycle turns downward, many industries and firms are faced with declining sales volumes. At such times the pricing function takes on particular importance because of the pressure to "do something" and because buyers become especially price-conscious at such times.

In fact, a downswing of the cycle may call for a change in the overall objectives of a firm. If one considers the upswing of the cycle to be "normal" and if objectives are ordinarily geared to such conditions, then it follows that a change in objectives and in price policy may be in order during a downswing, particularly if it is severe. Alfred R.

---

[19] See statements by Thomas H. Barton in "Take Guesswork out of Pricing Decisions," *Business Management,* May, 1963, p. 49.

Oxenfeldt discusses pricing in a declining market in some detail and suggests that in such situations appropriate long-run objectives and actions might include drastic price reductions that are designed to rid the industry of marginal operators, or the maintenance of the existing price level in order to impress upon customers the fact that the industry stands for stable prices in the face of ups and downs in demand. Short-run objectives could include such things as sheer survival, raising cash to meet bills as they come due, discouraging major customers from entering into the production of the item in question themselves, beating a price-cutting competitor to the punch, and helping out a customer industry that is having price difficulties. Oxenfeldt says that a medium-run objective should be to restore the market to a stable and profitable condition as soon as possible and to eliminate customers' hopes and expectations of sizable price reductions.[20]

Thus, the price policy a firm should follow during a business downturn depends upon which specific objectives are important at the time. Oxenfeldt lists eight possible approaches. First, the firm might just "stand pat," no matter what the others do. Second, it might elect to lead the industry by initiating price adjustments. Third, it might elect to follow a particular firm in the industry. Fourth, it might elect to alter prices only as its costs change. Fifth, it might reduce its markup but otherwise continue to base its prices on cost. Sixth, it might attempt to forecast what its competitors would do and do the same thing before they do it. Seventh, it might add "stripped-down" models to its line, which would sell for less than its current offerings, without altering current prices on other products. Finally, it might pursue an intuitive pricing policy.[21]

Theoretically, if costs should decline along with the decline in business activity, then price decreases might be in order. In practice, however, at such times businessmen tend to think more in terms of trying to reduce costs in order to conform with lower prices, as we mentioned in Chapter 2. However, notice that *unit* costs may actually rise during recession or depression, since when sales decline fixed costs must be spread over a smaller output. Therefore, if a firm follows a full-cost pricing policy, the result of such cost changes is likely to be that prices will be raised during business downturns and lowered during upswings. Clearly, such an approach to pricing can only serve to accentuate the decline in sales during a downswing. Instead,

[20] Oxenfeldt, *op. cit.,* p. 85.
[21] *Ibid.,* pp. 85–86.

a firm that is faced with declining sales volume may be best advised to price below full costs either on all of its offerings or on just a few items, for reasons discussed in Chapter 2.

It might also be noted that for durable goods price reductions made during a downturn—whether or not they are based on changes in costs—may have little effect on sales volume since the demand for durables is postponable. This applies particularly to industrial durable goods. Since in a cyclical downswing there is usually little demand for the products or services that are produced by the industrial good in question, it is not likely that price reductions will stimulate sales.

LEGAL CONSIDERATIONS

The legal framework within which pricing decisions are made is also an important external factor in pricing. The various statutes pertaining to price setting that have been enacted by the several levels of government are discussed in Chapter 4. Suffice it to say, at this point, that such legal considerations are apparently becoming more important, and it is crucial that price makers, especially those in large business firms, take account of these factors.

Selected References

The concept of price elasticity of demand is discussed in detail in books on price theory and managerial economics and, usually, in general marketing books.

Demand analysis is dealt with in books on managerial economics such as Milton H. Spencer and Louis Siegelman, *Managerial Economics,* rev. ed. (Homewood, Ill.: Irwin, 1964), Chapters 5, 6, and 7. Many books on marketing research also cover demand analysis. Experimental and other research methods that can be used in studying the relationship between price and quantity demanded are discussed by Alfred R. Oxenfeldt in *Pricing for Marketing Executives* (San Francisco: Wadsworth, 1961), pp. 64–70. A technical discussion of the use of experimentation in marketing is found in Seymour Banks, *Experimentation in Marketing* (New York: McGraw-Hill, 1965). A good article on experimentation and research design in marketing is Ronald E. Frank, "Research Design in

Marketing Analysis," in Ronald E. Frank, Alfred A. Kuehn, and William F. Massy, *Quantitative Techniques in Marketing Analysis* (Homewood, Ill.: Irwin, 1962). Laboratory experimentation in marketing is dealt with in detail in Edgar A. Pessemier, *Experimental Methods for Analyzing Demand for Branded Consumer Goods with Applications to Problems of Marketing Strategy* (Pullman, Wash.: Washington State University Press, 1962). Field experimentation for the purpose of increasing productivity in marketing is discussed in Charles H. Sevin, *Marketing Productivity Analysis* (New York: McGraw-Hill, 1965), Chapters 6, 7, and 8.

Price leadership is discussed in Jules Backman, *Pricing: Policies and Practices* (New York: National Industrial Conference Board, 1961), pp. 50–54. Appendix D of this publication contains some excellent examples of price leadership.

For a discussion of pricing in a declining market, see Oxenfeldt, *Pricing for Marketing Executives,* pp. 82–87.

4

LEGAL AND ETHICAL CONSIDERATIONS

IN PRICING

All business executives must operate in an environment consisting of various technological, economic, social, and institutional factors or influences over which they have virtually no control. One of the most important factors in this uncontrollable environment is the legal framework. As we indicated in Chapter 3, the legal framework is one of the important external factors that must be considered in pricing. It is essential that all who take part in a firm's price-making activities be familiar with the legal boundaries within which they must make their decisions. In this chapter we will discuss the nature of the legal environment and its implications for pricing decisions. We will also consider various ethical aspects of pricing decisions.

LEGAL CONSIDERATIONS IN PRICING—
INTRODUCTION

In the early days of our nation's history, the various levels of government followed a laissez faire, or "hands-off," policy concerning the activities of business firms; they did not attempt to interfere by statute. Whatever control or regulation there was over business activities was based on the common law, which could be enforced through the state courts only by means of an action instituted by the injured party.

In the latter half of the nineteenth century, as business firms became larger, it became apparent that the state courts and the common law were unable to deal effectively with the abuses that had begun to occur. Many individuals and firms took unfair advantage of the situation and various excesses began to appear in the economy. As a consequence, the laissez-faire attitude began to weaken. Soon legislation was passed that was designed to control or prevent certain malpractices on the part of railroad companies in the 1870's and later to deal with monopoly in the industrial field. Since then a long series of steps taken by the states and the federal government have considerably modified the attitude toward business and have created a complex legal environment within which business firms operate. This environment is complex not only because of the nature of the laws themselves but also because of the interpretations that are given to these laws by regulatory agencies and the courts.

At the federal level, the initial step was the enactment of the Interstate Commerce Act [1] in 1887, which was designed to regulate the railroad industry. Since that time, many additional regulatory laws have been enacted by Congress. Those with important implications for the price maker, other than resale price maintenance legislation (discussed in Chapter 7), are the Sherman Antitrust Act, the Clayton Antitrust Act, the Robinson-Patman Amendment to the Clayton Act, and the Federal Trade Commission Act.

The Sherman Antitrust Act of 1890 attempts to outlaw all contracts, combinations, conspiracies, monopolies, and efforts to monopolize that restrain trade in interstate commerce. The Clayton Act of 1914 is designed primarily to strengthen the Sherman Act by prohibiting certain specific monopolistic practices, including unjust price discrimination. The Robinson-Patman Amendment to the Clayton Act, enacted in 1936, is intended to strengthen the law on price discrimination. These three laws have important implications for pricing. They are discussed in detail in later sections of this chapter.

Another law that affects price making is the Federal Trade Commission Act of 1914, which set up the five-member Federal Trade Commission. The other provisions of the Act itself added little to the Sherman and Clayton Acts, save for section 5, which provides

---

[1] Originally called the Act to Regulate Commerce.

that "unfair methods of competition" are unlawful. The Commission was assigned the task of determining what constitutes an unfair method of competition. On the strength of this provision, the Commission has attempted to put an end to a number of competitive practices such as deceptive advertising, misbranding, spying on competitors, and wrongfully appropriating trademarks. With regard to pricing, the Commission has ruled that such practices as deceptive pricing, selling below cost with the intent to injure competition, cutting prices arbitrarily to discipline a competitor, and conspiring to fix prices are "unfair." Section 5 of the Federal Trade Commission Act has also been applied successfully in cases involving basing-point pricing, on the grounds that such pricing involved conspiracies to fix prices.[2]

EXEMPTIONS FROM ANTITRUST LAWS

Certain exemptions from the antitrust laws have been provided. For example, the Clayton Act provides that labor unions cannot be held to be conspiracies in restraint of trade. The Shipping Act of 1916 exempts rate agreements between certain common carriers by water if approved by the Federal Maritime Commission. The Webb-Pomerene Act of 1918 exempts associations involved in export trade provided that no restraint of domestic trade results. The Transportation Act of 1920 exempts from prosecution under the anti-trust laws consolidations involving surface transportation companies that are approved by the Interstate Commerce Commission. Agricultural producers are permitted to form cooperative associations to process and market their products by the Capper-Volstead Act of 1922. The Agricultural Marketing Agreement Act of 1937 exempts agreements entered into by the Secretary of Agriculture and processors, producers, and others who handle agricultural commodities. The Civil Aeronautics Act of 1938 (now the Federal Aviation Act of 1958) exempts parties to agreements that have been approved by the Civil Aeronautics Board. In 1943 Congress provided that mergers of telegraph companies are exempt if approved by the Federal Communications Commission. Insurance companies subject to state control were

---

[2] The Federal Trade Commission Act is not discussed further in this chapter. Basing-point pricing, including the application of the Federal Trade Commission Act to this pricing practice, is discussed in Chapter 6.

exempted by the McCarran Act of 1945. The Reed-Bulwinkle Act of 1948 provides that price fixing among surface transportation companies is exempt from the antitrust laws as long as it receives the approval of the Interstate Commerce Commission. Finally, there is an exemption for resale price maintenance agreements. This will be discussed in Chapter 7.

ENFORCEMENT OF THE ANTITRUST LAWS

Enforcement of the antitrust laws is primarily the responsibility of the Department of Justice. This Department, which acts through its Antitrust Division, has sole responsibility for the enforcement of the Sherman Act and shares responsibility with the Federal Trade Commission for the enforcement of the Clayton Act. The Commission has sole responsibility for the enforcement of the Federal Trade Commission Act. Under both the Sherman Act and the Clayton Act provision is made for fines and prison sentences for violators; treble damages may be sought by those who are injured by a violation of the laws.

STATE LAWS

In addition to the federal laws, the states have enacted a number of similar laws, some of which apply to pricing. However, since such laws apply only to intrastate commerce and because they generally are not effectively enforced, they are relatively unimportant in comparison with federal legislation and are not treated further here.

PRICE FIXING AND THE SHERMAN ACT

PROVISIONS OF THE SHERMAN ACT

The Sherman Act of 1890 prohibits restraint of trade in interstate commerce by providing in section 1 that every contract, combination in the form of trust or otherwise, or conspiracy in restraint of trade or commerce among the several states or with foreign nations is illegal.

Section 2 provides that every person who shall monopolize or attempt to monopolize, combine, or conspire with any other person or persons to monopolize any part of the trade or commerce among the several states, or with foreign nations, shall also be deemed guilty of a misdemeanor. For pricing purposes the Sherman Act is relevant in those situations in which competing business firms are accused of agreeing on, or "fixing," the prices of the products or services they sell. The Act can also be applied to agreements between buyers and sellers to fix resale prices.

It is frequently said that the Sherman Act made contracts and conspiracies in restraint of trade or commerce explicitly illegal, when prior to the passage of the Act they had merely been void or unenforceable under the common law. According to Vernon L. Mund, however, this view is correct only with respect to contracts in general or unreasonable restraint of trade. Contracts or conspiracies to fix prices of "necessaries" were held from earliest times to be criminal offenses at common law, punishable by fines and imprisonment. For Mund the really important feature of the Sherman Act is that it committed the federal government to a policy of actively supporting the principles of market price and fair competition in interstate commerce.[3]

In any event, under the Sherman Act the government may bring criminal or civil action, or both, against a defendant. Maximum criminal penalties are a fine of $50,000 or a prison term of one year, or both, for each violation. When the government institutes criminal proceedings under the Sherman Act, a defendant may plead guilty, not guilty, or *nolo contendere* (no contest). The latter does not mean that the defendant admits guilt but simply that he does not choose to fight the case. By entering such a plea the defendant becomes subject to the penalties under the Act.

In civil cases instituted under the Sherman Act, injunctions can be issued to forbid certain practices, and dissolution, divestiture, and divorcement proceedings may result from the Sherman Act cases. A firm that is charged with violating the Sherman Act in a civil proceeding may arrange with the court and the Department of Justice to sign a consent decree without presenting its case to the court. By so doing, the defendant consents to accept a court order without having actually been found guilty.

[3] *Government and Business,* 3rd ed. (New York: Harper & Bros., 1960), p. 156.

ECONOMIC CONDITIONS THAT LEAD
TO PRICE FIXING AMONG COMPETITORS

Although agreements between competitors to fix prices have the effect of removing price as a competitive element, such agreements do not eliminate all competition between the firms involved. The non-price forms of competition may still be used. Nevertheless, the elimination of price competition is usually an important restriction on the competition in any given industry; it is considered extremely unfair to buyers since they are not allowed to choose among sellers on the basis of price but must do so on other bases. It may also mean that prices are unjustifiably high.

The most frequent cause of price-fixing attempts has been the desire to avoid destructive or ruinous competition. This is a particularly important motive when there has been considerable price cutting and the firms begin to fear that the general level of prices will eventually be so low that many or all firms in the industry will be ruined.

Such instability often characterizes an industry in which the product involved is relatively standardized or homogeneous and price is a very important factor in the purchase decision. This, in itself, does not necessarily bring on price cutting and instability, but when there are some sellers in the industry who are unwilling to avoid price cutting, then price cutting occurs, and other firms are forced to meet such lower prices because of the homogeneity of the product. One factor that often leads to such price warfare in industries with nearly homogeneous products is the existence of excess productive capacity.

A related factor that can cause sellers of homogeneous products to engage in price fixing is the difficulty of some producers in selling in distant markets because of the lower delivered costs (price of product plus transportation costs) offered by sellers who are located nearer to a given buyer. In such cases, in order to expand the geographic market for the firms in the industry, as well as to eliminate the possibility of severe price cutting, the firms within the industry sometimes attempt to eliminate price as a competitive factor by developing geographic pricing systems under which competing firms sell at the same delivered prices. Pricing arrangements of this sort are discussed in Chapter 6.

Aside from the instability factor, the desire to avoid destructive price cutting, and the geographic problems just referred to, price fixing can also result simply from an attempt to keep prices at a relatively high level for the purpose of increasing the profits of the firms involved. As such, price fixing is an efficient and relatively inexpensive method of eliminating competition. It avoids the complications and expenses of mergers, or acquisitions, while at the same time effectively eliminating a very important aspect of competition.

THE INTERPRETATION OF THE SHERMAN ACT IN PRICE-FIXING CASES

The Sherman Act uses the term "restraint of trade" without qualifying it in any way. Therefore, it is up to the federal courts to interpret the meaning of this term as best they can. Prior to 1911 the United States Supreme Court held the view that the Sherman Act forbade *every* agreement, combination, or conspiracy in restraint of trade. However, in 1911 the "rule of reason" was adopted by the Court in the case of *Standard Oil Company* v. *United States*.[4] As the court pointed out at the time, the language of the law did not intend to outlaw every contract that might have a restraining effect upon trade but only those contracts which, in terms of a "standard of reason," *unduly* restrained trade.[5] Such was the language of the common law, and the same interpretation was given in the American Tobacco case.[6] The "rule of reason" introduces an element of uncertainty as to what constitutes reasonable or unreasonable restraints. As a consequence, the unlawfulness of a contract or combination under the Sherman Act must be determined by the courts in each case.

However, although firms and individuals accused of price fixing may offer what appear to be sound reasons for engaging in the practice, the federal courts have consistently rejected such excuses and have held that price fixing is illegal *per se* regardless of the reasons or excuses that may be offered. In short, the rule of reason does not extend to price fixing.

J. F. Barron lists three justifications for price fixing that firms accused of the practice have offered. The first of these is that the in-

---

[4] 221 U.S. 1.
[5] 221 U.S. 1, 59–60.
[6] *United States* v. *American Tobacco Company*, 221 U.S. 106 (1911).

dustry is basically unstable and that, if the instability is not corrected by pricing agreements among producers, the result will be disad-- vantageous to the buyers of the product and to society in general in that the resultant uncontrolled price competition will eliminate a number of firms, thereby putting the survivors in a monopolistic posi- tion.[7] Furthermore, these firms argue that, if the product is important to national defense, the reduction in production capacity that results from this cutthroat competition may endanger the nation's security. The second justification offered for price fixing is that it sets prices that are only fair for the industry and for its customers, and that it does so without malice or evil intent. The third factor, according to de- fendants, is that price fixing is similar to agreements practiced by other economic entities, particularly labor organizations.[8]

In terms of the interpretation given to the Sherman Act by the courts, however, these three justifications are all irrelevant. It matters not what caused the price fixing or what the results of the price fixing are; whether the prices agreed upon are "reasonable" or not, the ac- tion of price fixing is itself illegal.[9]

It should be noted that the prices agreed upon by the producers in

[7] Causes of price wars are discussed by Ralph Cassady, Jr. in *Price Warfare in Business Competition,* Occasional Paper No. 11 (East Lansing, Mich.: Bureau of Business and Economic Research, Michigan State University, 1963).

[8] "Normal Business Behavior and the Justice Department," *Journal of Market- ing,* January, 1963, pp. 46–47.

[9] Cases that illustrate this interpretation of the Sherman Act are *United States* v. *Trans-Missouri Freight Association,* 166 U.S. 290 (1897); *United States* v. *Joint Traffic Association,* 171 U.S. 505 (1898); *Addyston Pipe and Steel Company* v. *United States,* 175 U.S. 211 (1899); *American Column and Lumber Company* v. *United States,* 257 U.S. 377 (1921); *United States* v. *Trenton Potteries Company,* 273 U.S. 392 (1927); *United States* v. *Socony Vacuum Oil Company,* 319 U.S. 150 (1940) (Madison Oil Case); and *Kieffer Stewart Company* v. *Seagram and Sons,* 340 U.S. 211 (1951). The only major ex- ception was *Appalachian Coals, Inc.* v. *United States,* 288 U.S. 344 (1933), which involved price fixing by a minority group of producers. The United States Supreme Court noted the distress and overcapacity of the coal mining industry during the Great Depression and ruled that sufficient competition from other producers existed despite the collusion. This, however, was only a tem- porary departure from the rule.

Price fixing has also been condemned by the United States Supreme Court under section 5 of the Federal Trade Commission Act. Thus, a multiple basing- point system was ruled to be illegal partly on this ground in *Federal Trade Commission* v. *Cement Institute et al.,* 333 U.S. 683 (1948). See Chapter 6 for a discussion of this case. Other cases in which section 5 has been applied to price-fixing agreements include *Federal Trade Commission* v. *Pacific States Paper Trade Association,* 273 U.S. 52 (1927) and *Fashion Originators Guild of Amer- ica, Inc.* v. *Federal Trade Commission,* 312 U.S. 457 (1941).

the industry do not have to be identical to be considered illegal. Agreements that establish minimum prices below which competitors will not go or fixed differentials in prices to be maintained between sellers are also illegal under the Sherman Act.

From an administrative standpoint, the Sherman Act is clearly easier to administer when *all* price fixing is treated as being unlawful *per se* than when certain kinds of pricing agreements are exempted. The problem of defining this distinction would be great. Furthermore, to accept the instability–cutthroat competition argument as a justification for price fixing would have the effect of preserving excess capacity in those industries where overcapacity is a cause of instability and the desire to fix prices. This would result in a misallocation of resources. Second, the argument that the prices agreed upon are "fair" or "reasonable" prices, is contrary to the basic intention of the Act, which is to promote competition. Even though the fixed prices may be reasonable, they are still illegal in that they result in the elimination of competition. Also, and perhaps more to the point, who is to be the judge of what is a "fair" price? According to Barron:

> Just as the seller is incapable of judging what is fair for the buyer, the antitrust authorities and the courts are in no position to judge when the seller is making the "proper" decision for both himself and the consumer and to excuse him from the antitrust laws when he does behave "properly." The only realistic alternative is to allow propriety to be determined as a result of the free interplay of market forces and to promote this freedom by punishing the emergence of market power which results from private coalitions.[10]

For these reasons it is difficult to argue with the attitude taken by the federal courts with respect to price-fixing agreements. Proving that price fixing has occurred is quite another matter, however. For this reason, the Antitrust Division of the Department of Justice has experienced serious difficulty in prosecuting price-fixing cases. Statistical comparisons of price movements over time in which changes in prices of different firms are compared do not necessarily prove that price collusion has taken place, for it can be shown that in some industries it is a natural result of the characteristics of the industry that prices of different sellers move together and, on occasion, are identical. Nonetheless, the federal courts have indicated in some cases that they tend to view as illegal similar behavior or practices among com-

---

[10] Barron, *op. cit.,* p. 49.

peting firms in oligopolistic industries if they result in undue restraint of trade, even though no proof of conspiracy is shown. Similar behavior among competitors is referred to as "conscious parallelism of action." [11] Such an interpretation of the antitrust laws creates an additional area of uncertainty. However, this situation has been clarified to a great degree by a decision of the United States Supreme Court that provides that proof of parallel action *alone* is not enough to violate the law. Such circumstantial evidence must also be sufficient to warrant the finding or the inference of *agreement* between the parties involved.[12]

It is interesting to note that the Sherman Act has not been used successfully against price leadership [13] or in situations where a few dominant firms in an industry follow the same prices, although in both cases there appears to be similar price behavior among competitors. Conceivably, these might be attacked on the ground that there exists the *power* to fix or control prices in the case of price leadership, and in the case of oligopolistic situations, on the principle of implied conspiracy.[14]

AN EXAMPLE OF PRICE FIXING—
THE ELECTRICAL EQUIPMENT CASES

The recent electrical equipment cases, which were decided in February, 1961, in the federal district court at Philadelphia, deal with many of the issues found in most price-fixing situations.[15] These cases are of particular interest not only because they illustrate some of the economic forces that lead to price fixing, but also because of the sheer size of the conspiracy, the amount of sales volume involved, the fact that several defendants were sentenced to prison, the large

---

[11] See *Bigelow* v. *RKO Radio Pictures, Inc.,* 150 F. (2d) 877 (1945) and 327 U.S. 251 (1946); *American Tobacco Company* v. *United States,* 328 U.S. 781 (1946); and *Milgram* v. *Loewe's, Inc.,* 192 F. (2d) 579 (1951), certiorari denied, 343 U.S. 929 (1952). Conscious parallelism of action was involved in cases concerning basing-point pricing, which are discussed in Chapter 6.

[12] This point of view was expressed in *Theater Enterprises, Inc.* v. *Paramount Film Distributing Corporation,* 346 U.S. 537 (1954).

[13] Price leadership is discussed in Chapter 3.

[14] Mund, *op. cit.,* p. 205.

[15] The cases have been well covered in the literature. For example, see Richard Austin Smith, "The Incredible Electrical Conspiracy," *Fortune,* Part I, April, 1961; Part II, May, 1961.

number of civil suits that have resulted from the cases, and the notoriety of these cases in particular and of price fixing in general since the 1961 decisions.

In the electrical equipment cases, twenty-nine producers of electrical equipment and forty-four of their employees were charged under the Sherman Act in eighteen indictments of conspiring to fix prices on such industrial products as condensers, generators, circuit breakers, insulators, switch gear, and transformers. Specifically, the firms were accused of violating section 1 of the Sherman Act by conspiring to

1. Fix and maintain prices, terms, and conditions for the sale of specified products.
2. Allocate among themselves the demand for specified heavy equipment used to generate, convert, transmit, and distribute electric energy.
3. Submit noncompetitive, collusive, and rigged bids for supplying specified equipment items to electric-utility companies, federal, state, and local governmental agencies, private industrial corporations, and contractors.
4. Refrain from selling certain types of equipment items to other manufacturers of electrical equipment.

The eighteen indictments covered actions that took place between 1956 and 1960 and involved sales of about $7 billion. In this instance, the basic motive for price fixing proved to be the existence of considerable overcapacity in the industry as a result of the entry of a number of new firms, and the fact that the products involved were often made to specification and sold under a bidding system. Since, for all practical purposes, the products were homogeneous, price was the critical factor in the purchase decisions. As a result of overcapacity and the homogeneity of the products, price cutting broke out. The subsequent price conspiracy was therefore an attempt to prevent destructive competition in the industry. According to our previous discussion, any arguments that attempted to justify these actions might be expected to be found unacceptable to the courts.

In eleven of the eighteen indictments the defendants were permitted to plead *nolo contendere.* In seven of the indictments, however, the defendants were required to plead either guilty or not guilty, and guilty pleas were entered. The advantages of a *nolo contendere* plea are that it avoids a costly trial that is damaging to good will, and that, since it is not an admission of guilt, when injured parties sue for treble damages, they must prove that the Act was violated. In contrast, when a defendant pleads, or is found, guilty, the violation is considered proven and injured parties need not prove it. As a consequence, subsequent suits for damages become merely a matter of establishing injury, and determining how much the injured parties are to receive in damages.

The net result of these proceedings was that the twenty-nine firms were fined a total of $11,787,000, that seven executives were sent to prison for thirty days each, and that they and thirty-seven other executives were fined a total of $137,500. Twenty-three executives received suspended thirty-day prison sentences and were placed on probation for five years. Jail sentences are not unheard-of in antitrust cases, but they are somewhat unusual.

Since seven of the indictments resulted in guilty pleas and, therefore, in the establishment of proof of guilt, a large number of treble damage suits have been filed against the firms by customers of the electrical equipment producers, including electric power companies and various governments. According to press reports, about 1,800 such damage suits have been filed and to date several hundred have been settled out of court, including one in the amount of $7,740,000 which was paid by the General Electric Company to the federal government. This amount represented 10 percent of the sales by General Electric to the Tennessee Valley Authority and various other federal agencies from 1956 to 1960.[16] According to one source, the General Electric Company alone had paid $173 million in out-of-court settlements as of August, 1964.[17] It is anticipated that most of the suits will be settled out of court, although there have been exceptions, such as a 1964 case in which six manufacturers of high-voltage transformers were ordered to pay $28,972,217 by a federal court on the basis of guilt established by the 1961 decisions.[18]

---

[16] "Will GE's Damage Formula Hold?" *Business Week,* August 4, 1962, p. 34.

[17] "Climbing Toll for the Price Fixers," *Business Week,* August 29, 1964, pp. 97–98.

[18] "Electrical Equipment Makers to Appeal $28,972,217 Price-Fix Damage Verdict," *Business Week,* June 6, 1964, p. 38. The problems involved in estimating damages that result from price fixing are discussed by Walter Jensen, Jr. and Harold A. Wolf in "A Legal and Economic Note on Price Fixing," *Michigan State University Business Topics,* Spring, 1962.

OTHER RECENT CASES

There have been a number of other price-fixing cases undertaken by the Antitrust Division in recent years. Among the industries involved are those that produce salt, drugs, electrical parts used in television sets and computers, copper and brass tube and pipe, temperature control systems, railroad wheels and pipe flanges and steel rings, bank services, flour, bleachers, carbon sheet steel, and structural steel. Considerable attention was given to "bid rigging" in some of these cases. This was due in part to the prominent role of bid rigging in the previous electrical equipment cases. Bid rigging occurs where sealed bids are required by a potential customer (private business or government) and are fixed by all or some of the bidders. In some bid-rigging agreements one firm offers a bid that is lower than the bids of the other conspiring firms; in other cases identical bids are submitted by all competitors. In 1962 the Justice Department made a study of identical bidding which showed that identical bidding was less frequent than had been suspected.[19]

THE PRICE MAKER AND THE SHERMAN ACT

Because the interpretation of the Sherman Act is quite clear on the topic of price fixing, the price maker is not faced with problems of uncertainty as serious as those he encounters when dealing with matters covered by the Robinson-Patman Act, which is discussed later in this chapter. Price-fixing agreements among competitors, regardless of their form, the reasons for them, or their various results are illegal. The current interpretation of the Sherman Act clearly makes illegal any attempt on the part of a seller to meet with his competition and agree on prices at which their offerings are to be sold.[20]

[19] "Identical Bid Fuss Cools Off," *Business Week,* August 25, 1962, p. 34. Identical bids are not necessarily the result of collusion, and government antitrust policy recognizes this. That identical bidding should be taken as a presumption of illegal conduct lessening competition and restraining trade is set forth by Mund in "Identical Bid Prices," *Journal of Political Economy,* April, 1960, pp. 168–69.

[20] For a discussion of the legality of exchanging price information among competitors, see John J. Galgay, "Antitrust Considerations in the Exchange of

Leaving aside for the moment the moral and ethical aspects of the problem of conforming with the Sherman Act and other antitrust laws, which are discussed in a later section of this chapter, the economic lesson of the Sherman Act is clear: businessmen should compete on a price basis. Although some persons concerned about problems of monopoly feel that the penalties provided under the Sherman Act are not severe enough and that the enforcement of the Act is not strong enough, the existence of the law is a constant reminder that price-fixing agreements are to be avoided. The recent electrical equipment cases have also demonstrated the willingness of the courts to levy rather severe penalties against price fixers compared to previous penalties. In short, the existence of the Sherman Act has probably reduced the frequency of price fixing.

Price fixing is also a shortsighted policy in an economic sense since it usually results in artificially high prices that keep inefficient firms in business and attract new entries into the industry. In the long run it only complicates the competitive picture. Another difficulty with price-fixing agreements is that other firms in the agreement may secretly depart from the prices that have been agreed upon and grant concessions to buyers at the expense of their partners. Indeed, as a rule, price-fixing agreements seldom last very long; the temptation to deviate from the prices agreed upon is too great.[21]

If business firms as a group were to try to ignore the Sherman Act, eventually the control exercised by the federal government over pricing would be expanded, conceivably resulting in the reorganization of entire industries by government decree. In other words, abuse of the freedom and responsibility to set prices may merely result in less freedom in the long run. As one author remarked when the court reached a decision in the electrical equipment cases, "In sum, no one has been served by this affair. The people directly involved will be punished, if guilty. The companies have been hurt, the stockholders have been victimized. The only beneficiaries are the enemies of the free enterprise system and the forces of Bigger Government." [22]

Price Information Among Competitors," in *Current Business Studies,* No. 45 (New York: Society of Business Advisory Professions, 1963).

[21] See Richard H. Buskirk, *Principles of Marketing* (New York: Holt, Rinehart and Winston, 1961), pp. 442–44.

[22] Ward Gates, "Anti-Trust Suits Expose Price Fixing Scandals," *Magazine of Wall Street,* February 11, 1961, p. 577.

PRICE DISCRIMINATION AND THE
ROBINSON-PATMAN ACT

FORMS OF PRICE DISCRIMINATION

Price discrimination, or differential pricing, occurs whenever two or more buyers pay different prices to the same seller for an identical product or service. Differences in prices charged different buyers may be based on the time of the purchase, as when a highly seasonal product is offered to the market at less than normal prices during the "off" season. Differences in prices may also be based on the quantities purchased; buyers of large quantities are often charged lower prices per unit than buyers of small quantities. The trade status of the buyers can also be used as a basis for price discrimination, as when wholesalers are charged lower prices than retailers. The use to which a product or service is put by buyers is used as a basis for price discrimination, too. For example, prices paid to farmers for fluid milk are determined by the uses to which the milk is to be put. Price differences may be based on the bargaining power of the buyers, wherein the more powerful buyers, or the buyers more skilled in negotiating, pay lower prices than other buyers. Price discrimination can also be based on whether the buyers are new or old customers, whether payment is made in cash or otherwise, and the ability to pay of the buyers. Discrimination can even consist of providing different services with the same product to different buyers at the same price. For example, a retailer may charge the same price for a given product with or without delivery of the merchandise sold. Similarly it is customary in many industries for a manufacturer to charge a uniform delivered price to all buyers wherever they may be and regardless of the cost of transporting the product.

In short, price discrimination takes many forms and is sometimes justified, economically and otherwise. Price discrimination is not wrong *per se,* although the term "discrimination" carries with it a pejorative connotation. For example, price discrimination that is based on the trade status of distributors who buy a product from a manufacturer can be justified on the grounds that certain distributors perform more services for the manufacturer than others. On the other hand, price discrimination that is based on bargaining power and negotiating skill is generally considered unjustifiable. However, the opinion one has of the propriety of any particular form of price discrimination depends in large part upon his point of view. Thus, price discrimination based on trade status may appear unjustified from the standpoint of the buyers who do not receive the lower prices, but justified from the standpoint of the seller and the buyers who do receive the lower prices. By the same token, price discrimination that is based on bargaining power or negotiating skill may be undesirable from the viewpoint of the buyers who do not receive the lower prices but highly desirable from the point of view of the favored buyer and also the seller, who feels that the sale to the favored firm, although at a relatively low price, is distinctly beneficial to him. Such a sale, for example, may enable the seller to stay in operation and to keep a labor force intact during a very depressed economic period.[23]

THE CLAYTON ANTITRUST ACT

The Clayton Antitrust Act of 1914 is designed primarily to strengthen the Sherman Act by prohibiting certain specific monopolistic practices. Thus, the Clayton Act contains provisions concerning exclusive dealing and tying contracts,[24] intercorporate stock acquisitions, interlocking directorates, and unjust price discrimination.

Section 2 of the Clayton Act attempted to outlaw unjust price discrimination in interstate commerce.[25] It forbade price discrimination practiced by sellers in interstate commerce when such differences in price were not based upon variations in grade, quality, quantity, selling or transportation costs, or the necessity of meeting bona fide com-

[23] For a discussion of the difference in the meaning of the term "price discrimination" in legal terminology and economic terminology, see Lucile Sheppard Keyes, "Price Discrimination in Law and Economics," *Southern Economic Journal*, April, 1961.

[24] Exclusive dealerships involve the sale of goods on the condition that the customer (dealer) will not buy the goods of a competitor. Tying arrangements make the lease or sale of a particular product conditional on the lessee's or purchaser's lease or purchase of associated products supplied by the same seller.

[25] Price discrimination can also be a violation of the Sherman Act if the result is to restrain trade, and a violation of section 5 of the Federal Trade Commission Act, which prohibits unfair methods of competition. The Clayton Act as amended is the principal price-discrimination law, however.

petition; and where the effect of such discrimination was substantially to lessen competition or to tend to create a monopoly in any line of commerce.

In addition to the reasons for price differentials allowable under the law, until 1929 the courts held that discrimination, to be unlawful, must injure competition between *sellers* rather than *buyers*.[26] Since most of the objections to price discrimination dealt with inequalities among, or effects on, buyers, the price-discrimination section of the Clayton Act was rendered quite ineffective by this interpretation. In 1929, however, the Clayton Act was successfully applied in a case decided by the United States Supreme Court [27] involving the lessening of competition among buyers.

This case did increase to some extent the effectiveness of the Federal Trade Commission in dealing with unjust price discrimination, but there still appeared to be important gaps in the law. At the same time, retail chain-store companies had been enjoying a tremendous rate of growth, and many people believed that one reason for the substantial growth was the price concessions—unavailable to "independent" retailers—that chain-store companies had received from manufacturers, wholesalers, and other suppliers.

In 1928 the Federal Trade Commission was directed by Congress to make a study of the growth of chain stores. Its final report was made public in 1934.[28] In general, the report bore out the contentions of the critics of chain-store companies. Many instances were cited in which price concessions had helped chain-store companies to undersell their independent competitors who had not been offered such concessions. Apparently the concessions were granted because of the greater size and importance of the chain-store companies. Among the examples of unfair price discrimination cited were certain volume allowances that were not related to costs, promotional allowances for which no promotional services were rendered in return, allowances for brokerage even though chains purchase directly and hence do not

---

[26] *Mennen Company* v. *Federal Trade Commission*, 288 Fed. 774 (1923), certiorari denied, 262 U.S. 759 (1923); and *National Biscuit Company* v. *Federal Trade Commission*, 299 Fed. 733 (1924), certiorari denied, 266 U.S. 613 (1924).

[27] *George Van Camp and Sons Company* v. *American Can Company*, 278 U.S. 245 (1929).

[28] Federal Trade Commission, *Final Report on the Chain Store Investigation*, 74th Cong., 1st sess., Senate Document 4 (Washington, D.C.: Federal Trade Commission, 1934).

make use of a broker, free goods in one form or another, freight allowances, and guarantees against price declines. Because it was generally believed that the Clayton Act could not cope effectively with many of these types of price concessions in its existing form, even after the stronger interpretation of the Act given in 1929, the Commission asked for new legislation.

THE ROBINSON-PATMAN ACT

Congress responded to the report of the Commission and to pressure to do something about price discrimination, by enacting in 1936 the Robinson-Patman amendment to the Clayton Act. The purpose of the Robinson-Patman Act was to fill in the gaps in the Clayton Act with respect to price discrimination, so as to curb the excessive growth of chain stores and other large buyers when such growth was based on price concessions granted because of sheer size and bargaining power. The Act was openly recognized as an anti-chain-store bill.[29]

The Robinson-Patman Act amended section 2 of the Clayton Act, which is now divided into six parts. Section 2a is a revision of the original section 2 and sections 2b through 2f are new. In addition, the Act added a new enforcement section (section 3). Under section 2a of the Act, it is unlawful for an individual or a firm engaged in interstate commerce to discriminate in price between different buyers of goods of like grade and quality, if such discrimination tends to lessen competition substantially or to create a monopoly in any line of commerce. Furthermore, such discrimination is illegal if it tends to injure, destroy, or prevent competition with any person who either grants or knowingly receives the benefit of the discrimination, or with customers of either of them, although prices may reflect differences in the

[29] Frederick M. Rowe, in his recent book on the Robinson-Patman Act, says: "It is now history that the Robinson-Patman law was a product of the economic crisis of the thirties, with its pessimistic outlook for competitive enterprise. The Act originated in the distress of the independent merchants in the grocery trades, fearful for their survival in competition with the chains whose success was blamed on discriminatory purchasing advantages. When confiscatory chain-store taxes fizzled and the restrictions of the NRA Codes of Fair Competition failed, the embattled wholesalers and brokers turned to the antitrust laws for relief. As Representative Patman reminisced: '. . . one certain big concern had really caused the passage of this act, the A. and P. Tea Co.' " See *Price Discrimination Under the Robinson-Patman Act* (Boston: Little, Brown, 1962), p. 534.

cost of manufacture, sale, or delivery resulting from differences in quantities sold, or in methods of sale or delivery. In addition, the Federal Trade Commission was given the power to fix and establish quantity limits for particular commodities or classes of commodities if it finds that available purchasers of large quantities of such commodities are so few as to result in price differences that are unjustly discriminatory or that promote monopoly in any line of commerce.

Under section 2b, upon proof that there has been discrimination in price or services or facilities furnished, the burden of rebutting the government's case by showing justification is upon the person charged with the violation. A seller may rebut a case by showing that his lower price or the furnishing of services or facilities to any purchasers was made in good faith for the purpose of meeting a competitor's equally low price or of matching his services or facilities.

Section 2c prohibits a seller from granting allowances for brokerage where such payments are not made to the person actually performing the brokerage service and where the broker is not independent of the purchaser. According to the law, such commissions may be paid only for services rendered. Section 2d provides that payments for services must be available on proportionally equal terms to all competing buyers, and under section 2e services or facilities must be made available on proportionally equal terms to all buyers, if they are furnished at all. Finally, under section 2f it is unlawful for any person knowingly to induce or receive a discrimination in price that is prohibited by the Act.

Section 3 provides that it is unlawful for one to be a party to, or to assist, a sale that he knows will discriminate between competitors who purchase the same quantity and quality of goods by giving one buyer a discount, rebate, allowance, or advertising service that is not at the time available to his competitors. Under this section it is also unlawful to sell goods at a lower price in one part of the United States than in another or to sell at unreasonably low prices in order to destroy competition or eliminate a competitor.

With the exception of the provisions in section 3, the Robinson-Patman Act is enforced by the Federal Trade Commission. When the Commission finds a violation, it issues a "cease and desist" order, which may be appealed to a circuit court of appeals and, if necessary, to the United States Supreme Court for annulment or enforcement. Any person injured by a violation of the Act—with the exception of violations of section 3—may sue and recover treble damages.

Under section 3, certain kinds of price discrimination are considered criminal offenses and as such are subject to maximum penalties of a $5,000 fine, or one year in prison, or both. The enforcement of this section is left to the Department of Justice.

In essence, the Robinson-Patman Act recognizes as valid two defenses or justifications for price discrimination: the cost defense, discussed in section 2a, and the "good-faith" defense, found in section 2b. According to section 2a, differences in costs that may be used as a defense are variations in costs of manufacture, sale, or delivery resulting from differences in the quantities sold or in the methods of sale or delivery. The good-faith defense can be used, according to section 2b, when a low price is offered or when services or facilities are furnished to a buyer for the sole purpose of meeting a competitor's equally low price or of matching his services or facilities.

Other kinds of price discrimination that result in injury to competition cannot be justified under the Act. Thus, a sale made to a large buyer at a low price that enables a seller to meet current expenses cannot be justified under sections 2a or 2b if cost savings, or the meeting of competition in good faith, cannot be shown to have been the prime motives.

In attempting to draft legislation that would bar unjust price discrimination, Congress was faced with the necessity of allowing some differential pricing and of using only those justifications that could be readily measured or quantified. Consequently, it established costs and competitors' prices as the permissible justifications, thereby ruling out more intangible factors, such as the practice of price discrimination in order to keep employees working or to meet a payment deadline on a bank loan.

In addition to the two justifications permitted under sections 2a and 2b, there are a number of other circumstances in which discrimination in pricing can be lawful, including the following situations:

1. The products involved are not identical.
2. A product is sold for different uses.
3. Other separate markets are involved (since there is then no possible injury to competition).
4. Sales take place at different times.

5. Discounts are given in accordance with the trade status of buyers.
6. Sales are made in intrastate commerce.
7. Sales are made to government agencies.[30]

INTERPRETATION OF THE ROBINSON-PATMAN ACT

There have been a great number of cases involving the Robinson-Patman Act since it was enacted in 1936, and no attempt is made here to cover the history of the application of the Act in depth. The following discussion is simply intended to point out several of the more significant decisions made by the Commission and the courts and to indicate the general trend in the interpretation and enforcement of the Act. We will then consider the implications of the Act for price makers.

Commodities of like grade and quality   The price discrimination outlawed by the Robinson-Patman Act is that practiced between different purchasers of commodities of "like grade and quality" (section 2a). However, neither the Commission nor the courts have given a uniformly consistent interpretation of the phrase "like grade and quality." Existing interpretations are conflicting and confusing.[31] For example, in some instances the Commission and the courts have ruled that the mere fact that identical products are branded differently is not sufficient to create a difference between goods of "like grade and quality." [32] In another case, however, the Commission has said that differentiated products must be presumed to be of like grade and quality if sold under the same brand name.[33] Recently a federal court of appeals overturned a decision of the Commission and ruled

[30] See Frederick D. Buggie, "Lawful Discrimination in Marketing," *Journal of Marketing,* April, 1962.

[31] See Ralph Cassady, Jr. and Ewald T. Grether, "Proper Interpretation of 'Like Grade and Quality' Within the Meaning of Section 2(a) of the Robinson-Patman Act," *Southern California Law Review,* April, 1957, and Jacky Knopp, Jr., "What are Commodities of Like Grade and Quality?" *Journal of Marketing,* July, 1963.

[32] For example, *Goodyear Tire and Rubber Company* v. *Federal Trade Commission,* 101 F. (2d) 620 (1939).

[33] *Federal Trade Commission* v. *General Foods Corporation,* 52 FTC 798 (1956).

that consumer preference for an advertised manufacturer's brand may make such advertised brand distinguishable in "grade" from a chemically identical private brand. The Commission had ruled that price differences could exist between two brands only to the extent that they reflected differences in the manufacturer's sales, manufacturing, and other costs. The court of appeals, on the other hand, said that commercial value in the market place must also be considered in determining "grade." The United States Supreme Court agreed with the Commission and reversed the decision of the court of appeals.[34]

Injury to competition The Robinson-Patman Act further provides that price discrimination is unlawful if such discrimination tends to lessen competition substantially or to create a monopoly unless the cost or good-faith defense can be used to justify such discrimination. Actually, there are three different levels of competition that price discrimination can substantially lessen or injure under the Act: competition between two or more sellers (the primary level of competition), competition between the customers of one seller (the secondary level of competition), and finally competition between customers of his customers.

In a landmark decision in 1948 the United States Supreme Court set forth an important principle regarding injury to competition that still applies. In *Federal Trade Commission* v. *Morton Salt Company*,[35] a case involving a quantity discount system, the Court ruled that it was not necessary that the Commission show that the discounts in question did, in fact, cause injury to competition, but only that there was a "reasonable possibility" that they "may" have had such an effect. By relieving the Commission of the necessity of showing actual injury to competition, the decision in the Morton Salt case greatly increased the possibility of effective enforcement of the Act. From the point of view of the business firm, on the other hand, the ruling presents a serious problem, even though the Commission and the lower courts, since 1948, have not always adhered strictly to the Morton Salt case doctrine relative to injury to competition. The Morton Salt decision suggests that almost any form of price differential, such as is found in any of the several kinds of discount systems that are widely used, may be subject to prosecution under the Act, since,

---

[34] *Federal Trade Commission* v. *The Borden Company,* 34 U.S.L. Week 4288 (U.S. March 23, 1966) (No. 106).
[35] 334 U.S. 37.

conceivably, it could be concluded that there is a reasonable possibility that almost any price differential may injure competition.

Quantity discounts and the cost defense   Many of the cases involving the Robinson-Patman Act have involved discounts based on quantities purchased, either in a single purchase (noncumulative) or over a period of time such as a year (cumulative, deferred, patronage).[36] The chief defense against a charge of price discrimination that is available to those who offer quantity discounts to their customers is that of cost differences. As we mentioned earlier, the Act provides (in section 2a) that prices may differ to the extent that there are differences in the cost of manufacture, sale, or delivery resulting from differences in quantities sold, or in methods of sale or delivery. In practice, however, it is interesting to note that, the cost differences that have been accepted by the Commission have been primarily costs of selling and physical distribution, not manufacturing. Cumulative quantity discounts are usually more difficult to justify on a cost basis than are noncumulative discounts since there may be no measurable cost savings involved. Regardless of the kind of quantity discount, however, the cost defense has been used successfully in only a handful of cases since the Act was passed.[37]

The Commission places the entire burden of proof on the seller and requires specific proof of any claimed cost savings. In trying to use the cost defense in cases of price discrimination, firms accused of the practice frequently encounter an apparent unwillingness on the part of the Commission to accept the kind of cost information the firm presents. Cost accounting is not an exact science, and accountants can disagree on accounting methods. The Commission has endorsed no particular cost-accounting principles, and in the past has often refused to accept cost estimates furnished in defense of dis-

[36] Quantity discounts are discussed along with other types of discounts in Chapter 8.

[37] W. David Robbins reports that up until 1949 there were only five formal cases in which cost justifications succeeded entirely as a defense. In three other cases cost studies were accepted as justifying in part some portion of a price differential. See "A Marketing Appraisal of the Robinson-Patman Act," *Journal of Marketing*, July, 1959, p. 17. Frederick M. Rowe reports that there were ten cases prior to 1962 (among the two dozen or so reported cases in which the cost defense had played an important part) in which the respondent firms had made a successful use of the defense. See Rowe, *op. cit.*, p. 296. The degree of success in using the cost defense is also discussed in Herbert F. Taggart, *Cost Justification*, Michigan Business Studies, Vol. 14, No. 3 (Ann Arbor, Mich.: Bureau of Business Research, University of Michigan, 1959).

counts. One exception was a 1948 ruling in which the Commission accepted the principle that a seller can classify customers into reasonable groups, based on the costs of serving each group, and that different prices that reflect these cost differentials can be charged to each group.[38] The United States Supreme Court also considers this a lawful type of price discrimination. However, the difficulty in applying this defense in practice is illustrated by the fact that the cost defense has been successful in so few cases. Perhaps one major element in the failure of most recent attempts to use the cost defense has been the use of excessively broad groups of customers, groups with too much internal variation.[39]

Another reason the cost defense has been so often unsuccessful is the fact that frequently businessmen have not attempted to collect cost information until *after* they were charged with unlawful price discrimination and it is then often too late to take such a step. The high cost of a thorough cost defense is also a factor in the failure of some business firms to respond adequately to a charge of unlawful price discrimination. The burden of computing costs adequate to show the savings required by the Act is too great to be continuously borne even by a large firm.[40]

Another feature of the Robinson-Patman Act that deals with quantity discounts is also found in section 2a. This section provides that the Commission, after finding that the number of purchasers who can qualify for the largest discounts offered by a seller is unduly small and hence that the discount is unjustly discriminatory or promotive of monopoly, may itself establish maximum discounts or quantity limits

---

[38] *Federal Trade Commission* v. *Minneapolis-Honeywell Regulator Company*, 44 FTC 351. See also *Minneapolis-Honeywell Regulator Company* v. *Federal Trade Commission*, 344 U.S. 206 (1952).

[39] Robert A. Lynn, "Is the Cost Defense Workable?" *Journal of Marketing*, January, 1965, p. 40. This article contains a good account of recent developments concerning the cost defense. For specific examples of recent cases involving customer groupings, see *United States* v. *The Borden Company* et al., 370 U.S. 460 (1962); *Federal Trade Commission* v. *Foremost Dairies, Inc.*, Docket 7475, May 23, 1963; and *Federal Trade Commission* v. *The Borden Company*, Docket 7129, November 28, 1962. Proposals for improving the determination of cost and price differences are found in Donald J. Fennelly, "On the Judging of Mince Pies," *Harvard Business Review*, November–December, 1964.

[40] Corwin D. Edwards, *The Price Discrimination Law* (Washington, D.C.: Brookings Institution, 1959), p. 612. Edwards cites the example of a cost study made by Sylvania Electric Products, Inc. that is reported to have taken 3,000 man-hours under supervision of the firm's executives and independent accountants.

for such a seller. The Commission has been very reluctant to use this power. Its only attempt to exercise this power was in a case concerning the rubber tire industry, which had been using a cumulative quantity-discount system for replacement tires and tubes based on annual purchases. Only 63 out of 48,198 dealers purchased $600,-000 worth of tires and tubes per year, yet $600,000 and over was the top discount bracket offered. The fact that a separate discount was granted to such a small percentage of buyers was deemed by the Commission unjustly discriminatory and promotive of monopoly. Accordingly, in 1952 the Commission ordered the industry to use 20,000-pound carloads as the maximum discount amount for a single order. However, this order was appealed by the industry and eventually nullified by a court of appeals on the grounds that, although the Commission had the right to regulate quantity discounts, there was a basic discrepancy between the Commission's order and the evidence upon which it was based. The court of appeals maintained that there was no relationship between the fact that there were few buyers who could qualify for the largest discount category, which was based on purchases of $600,000 per year, and the Commission's ruling fixing the maximum discount unit at a 20,000-pound carload on single orders.[41] The Commission then dropped further action in the case and has not shown further interest in making use of the provision.

The good-faith defense   In addition to the cost defense, the other defense against a charge of unlawful price discrimination that is recognized in the Robinson-Patman Act is the good-faith defense. As we have noted, section 2b of the Act provides that a seller may rebut a charge of price discrimination by showing that his lower price or the furnishing of services or facilities to any purchaser or purchasers was made in good faith to meet an equally low price of a competitor, or the services or facilities furnished by a competitor.

Here again, the attitude of the Commission has been generally negative throughout the history of the Act. Prior to 1951 the good-faith defense was not accepted at all as a legitimate defense by the Commission if the facts of the case involved indicated that injury to competition may have taken place. The Commission felt that the good-faith defense was null and void where injury to competition was involved. In *Standard Oil Company* v. *Federal Trade Commission* [42]

[41] *Federal Trade Commission* v. *B. F. Goodrich Company* et al., 242 F. (2d) 31 (1957).
[42] 340 U.S. 231.

in 1951, however, the United States Supreme Court ruled, in a case involving price differentials given by the Standard Oil Company of Indiana to gasoline jobbers in the Detroit area, that the good-faith defense is a legitimate defense whether or not there appears to have been actual or potential injury to competition. Theoretically, this shift in the position of the Court on the good-faith defense permits more freedom and flexibility in pricing than would have been the case had the Commission's interpretation of section 2b been allowed to stand. Nonetheless, as we shall discuss in later sections of this chapter, the good-faith defense has seldom been used effectively by those accused of unlawful price discrimination.[43]

Another aspect of the interpretation of the good-faith clause in the Standard Oil case had to do with a distinction between sporadic price adjustments and formalized pricing "systems." In 1951, the Supreme Court returned the Standard Oil case to the Commission with instructions to make a specific finding on whether the company had acted in "good faith." In reply, the Commission argued that there was an absence of good faith on the part of the company in meeting the lower prices of a competitor in that Standard's prices were part of an illegal price *system* and as such were not merely departures from a legal price scale. In 1958, however, the Supreme Court finally exonerated Standard, holding that the record showed that it had priced its gasoline in the Detroit market, not according to any illegal system, but in direct response to a competitive situation. Indeed, the evidence showed that Standard had lost three of its seven jobbers by not granting concessions, and that there had been a long history of haggling preceding price concessions.[44]

In other cases, the courts have upheld the Commission's view that the good-faith clause cannot be used in defense of a price system, but only for occasional or sporadic departures from normal pricing that were designed to meet the lower prices of a competitor. Several of the basing-point cases that we will examine in Chapter 6 involve this question. The distinction between sporadic pricing departures and systematic meeting of prices is not clear, however, and this is another important area of uncertainty for the price maker.

[43] Since 1951 a number of bills have been introduced in Congress with the general purpose of limiting the use of the good-faith defense in situations where the effect of the seller's discrimination may be to lessen competition substantially or tend to promote a monopoly. None of these has been passed.

[44] *Federal Trade Commission* v. *Standard Oil Company,* 355 U.S. 396.

It is equally unclear as to whether the good-faith defense may be used only in pricing actions designed to retain existing customers, or whether it may also be used in pricing actions designed to acquire new customers. The Standard Oil case involved actions taken to retain existing customers. The Commission recently interpreted this decision to mean that the good-faith defense can be used to justify price discrimination designed to retain customers but not differential pricing intended to acquire new customers, since new customers are technically not "purchasers" and the good-faith clause refers specifically to the lowering of prices to a "purchaser" or "purchasers." The Commission attempted, under this reasoning, to distinguish between "defensive" price cutting (to keep a customer) and "aggressive" price cutting (to obtain a new customer) that meets the competition.[45] Such an interpretation of the good-faith clause would result in significantly reducing its potential effectiveness as a defense. Furthermore, such a standard would be quite impractical because of the difficulty in distinguishing between old and new customers in a practical situation. It would also have the effect of reducing competition among sellers rather than of promoting it. Because of these considerations, a circuit court of appeals rejected the Commission's reasoning in a case decided in 1962, and directed that a complaint lodged by the Commission against Sunshine Biscuits, Inc. be dismissed.[46] The Commission did not appeal.

Other difficulties and uncertainties surrounding the use of the good-faith clause as a defense are illustrated in several cases involving the oil industry. For example, the American Oil Company claimed that it had granted a low price to certain retail dealers in good faith in order to meet the low price of a competitor. This defense was rejected by the Commission because the firm had attempted to meet a price that, in itself, was illegal since the competitor's price had not maintained the $0.02 differential in prices that traditionally existed between "major" and "private" gasoline brands. This ruling was made despite the fact that there is nothing in the Robinson-Patman Act requiring that the prices matched must be lawful or legal prices, although by implication the Supreme Court apparently added the word "lawful"

---

[45] The problem of trying to distinguish between "promotional" and "predatory" discriminatory price cutting is discussed in Robert C. Brooks, Jr., "Price Cutting and Monopoly Power," *Journal of Marketing*, July, 1961.

[46] *Sunshine Biscuits, Inc.* v. *Federal Trade Commission*, 306 F. (2d) 48.

to section 2b in the Standard Oil case discussed earlier.[47] In other cases subsequent to the Standard Oil decision the courts have upheld the idea that a competing price that is met in good faith under section 2b must be a "lawful price," although the definition of a "lawful price" is unclear. Obviously, the requirement that a matched price must be a lawful price poses a severe problem for the price maker because it is extremely difficult to determine the legality of a competitor's prices.

The American Oil case was appealed to a court of appeals, which did not rule on the Commission's interpretation relative to the meeting of lawful prices since the court could not find a reasonable possibility that the discrimination would substantially lessen competition. The court found that the actual economic loss to competing American Oil dealers who did not receive the price reduction had been both minor and temporary.[48]

In the same American Oil case, and in another case involving the Sun Oil Company, the Commission ruled that a reduction in price given by an oil company to its independent dealers so that such dealers might cut prices to meet competitors' prices in a local price war could not be classified as a price reduction made in good faith to meet an equally low price of a competitor since the "equally low price" being met was the price of its *customers'* competitors (retail dealers) and not the prices of its *own* competitors (other oil companies). Although the American Oil case was appealed to a court of appeals, the court did not rule on the questions raised by the Commission relative to the definition of a "competitor" since, as noted above, the court failed to find reasonable possibility that competition would be lessened substantially.

In the parallel Sun Oil case, on the other hand, the Supreme Court upheld the order of the Commission, ruling that the good-faith defense could be used only among competitors at the same level of competition.[49] The decision in this case adds to the uncertainty as to what is legal and what is not legal under the Robinson-Patman Act.

[47] It should also be noted that there is no statute that requires oil companies to maintain a certain differential in price between "major" and "private" brands.

[48] *American Oil Company* v. *Federal Trade Commission*, 325 F. (2d) 101 (1963).

[49] *Federal Trade Commission* v. *Sun Oil Company*, 371 U.S. 505 (1963). See also M. R. Lefkoe, "The Strange Case of Sun Oil, Which Is Damned If It Does and Damned If It Doesn't," *Fortune*, August, 1963.

The Commission has also attempted to disallow the use of the good-faith defense in situations in which firms have reduced the price of a heavily advertised "premium" product to the same level as the price of a product that is only sold and advertised locally. Such a price reduction might be interpreted as "beating" rather than "meeting" competition in that the usual differential in price between the premium and nonpremium brand is eliminated. For example, the Commission issued an order against Anheuser-Busch, Inc. for selling its Budweiser beer (a premium brand) in the St. Louis market at the same price as local brands of beer while holding the price of Budweiser at normal levels in other markets. This order was eventually set aside by a court of appeals, however, on the grounds that the price reduction, made in aid of the firm's declining overall position, was the result of robust competition, that the motives of the price cut were not vindictive nor were the effects punitive, and that the company did not misuse its economic power or size. In short, the price reduction in St. Louis was made in "good faith" [50] since no predatory abuse of power was involved.

Liability of buyers   Section 2f of the Act makes it illegal for buyers knowingly to induce or receive discriminatory prices. This part of the Act was not applied until 1953 when, in the case of *Automatic Canteen Company* v. *Federal Trade Commission*,[51] the Commission claimed that a buyer who had induced price concessions knew that the prices received were below list prices and were induced without inquiry of, or assurance from, the seller as to the cost differentials that might justify the price differentials. The issue before the United States Supreme Court was the burden of proof under section 2f; the Court held against the Federal Trade Commission by concluding that a buyer is not liable if the lower prices he induces are within one of the seller's defenses, such as the cost justification, or if the buyer is unaware that they are not within one of these defenses. In other words, mere knowledge on the part of the buyer that he is receiving a lower price does not violate the law; the burden of proof lies on the Commission to show that the buyer also knows that the lower price is unjustified. The difficulty of proving such knowledge in the Automatic

[50] *Anheuser-Busch, Inc.* v. *Federal Trade Commission,* 289 F. (2d) 835 (1961). A discussion of problems under the good-faith clause and a recommendation that the clause be revised are found in George R. Hall and Charles F. Phillips, "Good Faith, Discrimination, and Market Organization," *Southern Economic Journal,* October, 1963.

[51] 346 U.S. 61.

Canteen case led the Commission to drop all pending cases involving the question of buyer liability.[52] It is generally believed that the ruling of the Court in this case places an impossible burden of proof on the Commission.

Selling at unreasonably low prices   Section 3 of the Robinson-Patman Act contains the statement that it is unlawful to sell goods at unreasonably low prices for the purpose of destroying competition or eliminating a competitor. Although this section is to be enforced by the Department of Justice, the Department has generally ignored the provision. However, in 1961 the Department charged the National Dairy Products Corporation with making sales below costs in violation of the Act. In this case the United States Supreme Court upheld the constitutionality of section 3, reversing a lower court decision and holding that the proscription of business practices provided in section 3 was sufficiently precise. The Supreme Court found that "unreasonably low prices" simply meant selling below cost, unless mitigated by some acceptable business exigency. The Court did not define exactly what constitutes "selling below cost," however. It said that whether "below cost" refers to "direct" or "fully distributed" cost, or some other level of cost computation, could not be decided in the abstract. The Court cautioned that its opinion in the case was not to be construed as holding that every below-cost sale constitutes a violation of section 3. Below-cost sales are not illegal when made in furtherance of a legitimate commercial objective, such as the liquidation of excess, obsolete, or perishable merchandise, or the need to meet a lawful, equally low price of a competitor. In instances such as these, below-cost sales, according to the Court, neither would involve "unreasonably low" prices nor would they have been made with predatory intent. On the other hand, sales made below cost without legitimate commercial objectives and with specific intent to destroy competition would clearly fall within the prohibition of section 3.[53]

Under this very unclear interpretation of section 3, it is extremely difficult for a price maker to determine in advance whether a particular price would be considered unreasonably low. The Court has set no specific cost floor, and has not stipulated exactly what business condi-

---

[52] Merle Fainsod, Lincoln Gordon, and Joseph C. Palamountain, Jr., *Government and the American Economy*, 3rd ed. (New York: W. W. Norton, 1959), p. 558.
[53] *United States* v. *National Dairy Products Corporation* et al., 372 U.S. 29 (1963).

tions would warrant low prices. In the words of one writer: "It would take a miraculous business necromancer to ascertain, *ex ante,* when a business exigency would support a specific below-cost sale, particularly when the relevant 'cost' is not indicated by the Court." [54]

Furthermore, if the provision dealing with unreasonably low prices were to be generally enforced against price reductions, the difficulties of the price maker would be increased and the zone of price competition reduced. The federal government would be attempting to keep prices from being too high by enforcing competition while at the same time discouraging price competition by putting a floor below prices. Thus, in addition to the problem of uncertainty, the price maker would have to operate within a relatively narrow range of permissible prices.

Promotional allowances   Section 2d of the Robinson-Patman Act makes it unlawful for a seller to pay for any services or facilities furnished by a customer in connection with the processing, handling, sale, or offering for sale of any products or commodities manufactured, sold, or offered for sale, unless such payment or consideration is available on proportionally equal terms to all other customers competing in the distribution of such products or commodities. Section 2e contains a similar provision regarding the furnishing of services or facilities by sellers to buyers. No injury to competition is required to establish a violation under section 2d or 2e.

These provisions are of particular importance to manufacturers who wish to engage in some form of cooperative promotion or advertising with distributors (wholesalers and retailers). Notice, however, that to violate the requirements of these sections, there must actually be competition between the distributor to whom a payment is made, or a service or facility is furnished, and another distributor to whom such payment is not made or such service or facility is not furnished. This means, for example, that it is legal to grant advertising allowances to retailers in one market area without granting them to retailers in another market area because the two groups of retailers are not in competition with one another.[55]

In an attempt to remove any confusion that may exist in this area,

---

[54] Ray O. Werner, "Legal Developments in Marketing" section in *Journal of Marketing,* July, 1963, pp. 85–86. This is an excellent summary of the case.
[55] The Commission's interpretation of section 2d relative to cooperative advertising is discussed in Lawrence X. Tarpey, Sr., "The *Woman's Day* Case and Cooperative Advertising," *Journal of Marketing,* July, 1965.

the Commission publishes guides for advertising allowances and other merchandising payments and services.[56] For example, sellers have paid buyers to furnish the following services or facilities:

1. Advertising.
2. Handbills.
3. Window and floor displays.
4. Special sales or promotional efforts for which "push money" is paid to clerks, salesmen, and other employees of the customer.
5. Demonstrators and demonstrations.
6. Collecting of orders from individual stores.
7. Furnishing complete distribution of seller's line.

According to the Commission, when paying for or furnishing such services and facilities subject to the Robinson-Patman Act the seller must meet several requirements. First, a promotion or advertising plan must be made available to all competing customers on "proportionally equal terms." The Commission has interpreted this to mean that the plan must actually and openly be made known and available to all competing buyers in such a manner that they can avail themselves of the program if they so desire. The seller is obliged to advise all competing distributors of the plan even though it may be obvious that certain distributors are not likely to take advantage of the offer.

At one time the Commission interpreted the phrase "proportionally equal terms" to mean that the seller had to offer the very same promotion or advertising program to all competing distributors. If he offered a newspaper advertising plan to a retailer, the same plan had to be offered to all competing retailers. However, in more recent years the Commission has said that a seller may make alternate plans available to competing retailers. For example, he can pay for newspaper advertising for some, television advertising for others, and radio advertising for still others. However, every competing distributor should be able to participate in the plan on some basis and should be able to take advantage of at least one of the alternatives.

The Commission has further stipulated that all payments made to a distributor should have a reasonable relation to the value of the services performed by the distributor and that they must not be in excess of the amount spent by the distributor in the program. In addition,

---

[56] Federal Trade Commission, *Guides for Advertising Allowances and Other Merchandising Payments and Services* (Washington, D.C.: U.S. Government Printing Office, 1960).

the seller is expected to see to it that a distributor actually does what he is supposed to do before he is paid for his cooperation.

THE PRICE MAKER AND
THE ROBINSON-PATMAN ACT

It is probably true that many businessmen know very little about the provisions of the Robinson-Patman Act and consequently ignore them. Others have gone ahead with policies that they know may be considered illegal under the Act. On the other hand, many business executives have consciously attempted to price in such a way as to conform to the Act. In addition to a desire to obey the law, some are clearly motivated by a desire to avoid giving concessions to large buyers. All things considered, the net effect of the Act has probably been to simplify discount systems, reduce the use of discounts, encourage improved cost-accounting analysis, and discourage the practice of granting concessions to large buyers.

The general attitude of the Federal Trade Commission since 1936 has been toward a strict interpretation of the Act, as we have indicated, and the courts have often supported the Commission in this interpretation. Furthermore, the Commission has been reluctant to recognize justification for price discrimination. This is quite evident from the utter failure of business firms to use successfully either the cost defense provided in section 2a, or the good-faith defense provided in section 2b, except in a very few cases. The fact that business firms accused of price discrimination have typically been ill-prepared to defend themselves under section 2a or 2b of the Act is partially responsible for this lack of success, however. The fact remains that the average firm, once charged with price discrimination, has found it extremely difficult to present a successful defense.

We have said that the other principal problem confronting the price maker who wishes to conform with the provisions of the Act is his uncertainty as to what the Commission may consider to be unlawful price discrimination. In fact, even a judge has stated: "I doubt if any judge would assert that he knows exactly what does or does not amount to a violation of the Robinson-Patman Act in any and all instances." [57] These uncertainties include the matter of what are com-

[57] *United States* v. *New York Great Atlantic and Pacific Tea Company, Inc.* et al., 67 F. Supp. 626, 677 (1946).

modities or products of "like grade and quality," what constitutes injury to competition, what costs and costing systems are acceptable for use under the cost defense, when can the good-faith defense be used to justify the meeting of a competitor's price (price systems versus sporadic price adjustments, what constitutes defensive as distinct from aggressive price cutting, how one is to determine the "lawfulness" of a competitor's prices, how one is to define the term "competitor"), and at what point prices become "unreasonably low" under section 3, and how such low prices can be justified.

These two factors—the strictness of the Commission interpretation and the uncertainties surrounding the Act—have probably caused price makers who wish to comply with the Act to be reluctant to use price as an aggressive competitive weapon. In such situations price decisions are made on the basis of legal considerations and doubts rather than on the basis of marketing objectives.[58] This, in turn, means that prices are less flexible than they would be otherwise, that sometimes cost savings are not passed on to buyers where they might be, and finally that the benefits of greater efficiency are not reflected in lower prices. As a consequence, sellers have stressed nonprice aspects of competition to a greater extent than would otherwise have been the case. Thus, it is sometimes said that the Robinson-Patman Act has encouraged "soft" (nonprice) competition in lieu of "hard" (price) competition.[59]

It can also be said that the Robinson-Patman Act is discriminating in its effect upon different business firms. Indeed, a former member of the Federal Trade Commission once remarked: "While practically every company in interstate commerce could be found guilty of violating this Act, the Commission cannot indict the nation. So it selects a few to punish." [60]

---

[58] As Frederick M. Rowe states: "Confronted by restrictive FTC interpretations, and averse to costly 'test-casing' in the courts, cautious firms may forgo bold and aggressive maneuvers in favor of the safe and the conservative pricing routine." See Rowe, *op. cit.,* p. 550.

[59] Brian Dixon states that although price discrimination can be very advantageous to a seller, a firm should comply when a given pricing policy is in clear and direct conflict with the law. If any doubt exists, however, a firm should go ahead with the pricing policy in question making due allowance for possible litigation and damage expenses. See *Price Discrimination and Marketing Management,* Michigan Business Studies, Vol. 15, No. 1 (Ann Arbor, Mich.: Bureau of Business Research, University of Michigan, 1960), pp. 113–14.

[60] "Robinson-Patman Act: It Demands a Closer Look Now," *Printers' Ink,* October 20, 1961, p. 23.

In a monumental work on the Robinson-Patman Act, Corwin D. Edwards concluded that, although there is strong evidence that the Act has afforded effective protection against the price-cutting activities of predatory, would-be monopolists and that it has substantially reduced the discriminatory advantages in prices enjoyed by large buyers,[61] the law has gone further than it needed to go, and many of the cases have involved small firms and have been directed against injuries to competition that have had no relation to the big buyer or the predatory seller. According to Edwards this has resulted in an unnecessary harassing of business conduct, diminished efficiency, and less vigorous competition.[62]

Notice that there is a paradox between the Robinson-Patman Act and the Sherman Act. The Sherman Act attempts to force business firms into price competition by outlawing conspiracies and combinations. In contrast, although the Robinson-Patman Act attempts to promote competition by preventing large buyers from obtaining an unwarranted advantage over their small competitors, it has the effect actually of discouraging price competition and protecting competitors, not competition itself. Malcolm P. McNair calls the Robinson-Patman Act an attack on the Sherman Act since it is designed to prevent any kind of vigorous price competition.[63]

Obviously the Robinson-Patman Act and its interpretation have proven defective in practice. One cannot quarrel with the purpose of the Act—to prevent price discrimination that favors certain buyers because of their size and economic power. But, as our previous discussion indicates, the Act as it now stands and is interpreted, creates at least as many problems as it solves.[64]

Because of the tremendous uncertainty surrounding the interpretation of the Robinson-Patman Act, it is extremely important that the price maker study the Act and the various relevant Federal Trade Commission and court rulings. In addition, it is often wise to consult the Commission itself as to what is and is not lawful under the Act.

[61] Edwards, *op. cit.*, p. 622.

[62] *Ibid.*, pp. 627–30.

[63] "Competition and the Law," *Michigan Business Review*, March, 1951, reprinted in William Lazer and Eugene J. Kelley, *Managerial Marketing: Perspectives and Viewpoints*, rev. ed. (Homewood, Ill.: Irwin, 1962). See especially p. 61.

[64] It is beyond the scope of this book to make recommendations for amendment or replacement of the Robinson-Patman Act. Several writers have made suggestions in this direction, however. See, for example, Edwards, *op. cit.*, pp. 646–57.

ETHICAL CONSIDERATIONS IN PRICING

IMPORTANCE OF PRICING IN BUSINESS ETHICS

The problem of ethical conduct in business affairs has always been present; there have always been some people who have chosen to make business decisions that are contrary to accepted ethical or moral standards. Indeed, the fact that the federal government and the state governments have developed rather elaborate legal rules and regulations to govern business conduct testifies to the prevalence of unethical acts.

Of the many kinds of decisions that businessmen must make, those involving pricing receive considerable attention in terms of ethical and moral standards. This is perhaps because pricing is such a conspicuous facet of business activity, and one that is easily identified and measured, at least when compared with other business activities such as personal selling practices, the truth or falsity of an advertisement, or the reasons for the awarding of contracts to certain suppliers and not to others. The price-fixing cases involving the electrical equipment manufacturers have stimulated further interest in the general area of business ethics.

WHAT IS LEGAL AND WHAT IS RIGHT

In the electrical equipment cases, it was apparent that some, if not all, of the individuals who were accused of fixing prices believed that there was a distinction between what was illegal and what was dishonest, unethical, or wrong. In other words, they believed that, although price fixing was unlawful under the Sherman Act, it was not really wrong since it was required by the conditions that existed in the industry and therefore was part of everyday business practice in the electrical equipment industry and in other industries as well.

A person who is charged with pricing responsibility under circumstances like those of the electrical equipment cases is clearly in an extremely difficult position. Top management was pressing for more sales volume and profit at a time when the entire industry was suffering from overcapacity and a resultant tendency to slash prices. Furthermore, price fixing seemed to be an accepted thing among the companies involved, or at least this was the opinion of Judge J. Cullen Ganey, who heard the cases. Nonetheless, top executives denied that this was true and that they themselves had any knowledge of price fixing.[65] If price fixing was indeed expected of employees, there was considerable pressure and reason to fix prices; a well-paying job seemed to depend on it. However, since the law says that price fixing is illegal, such price fixing was also wrong, regardless of the reasons. Furthermore, it would seem that, unless laws are complied with, our free enterprise system of law and order could not survive and would be replaced by either anarchy or more rigid government control. Ideally, if one believes that a law is unjust or otherwise in error, he should work to have it repealed or amended, but in the meantime he should also attempt to comply with it.

In sum, although we must recognize that a price maker can sometimes find himself in a very difficult position relative to the law and even feel compelled to engage in price fixing or other illegal pricing practices, it is no excuse to claim that there is a difference between what is illegal and what is wrong. When imposing sentences in the electrical equipment cases, Judge Ganey commented on the serious implications of the failure to comply with the antitrust laws:

> This is a shocking indictment of a vast section of our economy, for what is really at stake here is the survival of the kind of economy under which America has grown to greatness, the free enterprise system. The conduct of the corporate and individual defendants alike . . . flagrantly mocked the image of that economic system of free enterprise which we profess to the country and destroyed the model which we offer today as a free world alternative to state control and eventual dictatorship.[66]

The obligation to comply with the law in pricing matters is part of every business firm's responsibility, and admittedly it can be a very difficult obligation to carry out in practice. Therefore, it is crucial that top management make a determined effort to comply with the laws as best it can, given the uncertainties that are sometimes involved, and to ensure that employees with price-making responsibility are aware

[65] For an interesting discussion of this issue, see Bernard D. Nossiter, "The Troubled Conscience of American Business," *Harper's,* September 1, 1963, p. 37.

[66] New York *Times,* February 7, 1961, p. 26.

of the laws and that they are expected to act in accordance with those laws. Training courses in the purpose and interpretation of the Sherman Act, Robinson-Patman Act, and other relevant legislation may be worthwhile in this regard. Such programs have been instituted by many firms subsequent to the decision in the electrical equipment cases.

OTHER ASPECTS OF ETHICS IN PRICING

In addition to price fixing, unjust price discrimination, and other unlawful pricing practices, pricing involves ethical questions with which the law does not deal effectively or at all. How ethical, for example, is the practice of "bait" pricing, whereby some retailers advertise a very low price on a product with the intention of enticing customers to buy higher-priced merchandise when they enter the store; or odd pricing—pricing at odd amounts such as $1.98 instead of $2.00, to give the impression of a lower price; or fictitious pricing —announcing a price "reduction" from the usual or customary price which is not, in fact, a reduction at all or which is a lesser reduction than claimed; or loss-leader pricing—pricing below some concept of costs.[67] Other ethical matters with which the law does not deal effectively or at all have to do with what prices are morally correct for products that have a great social importance, such as certain drugs; what is a "fair" amount of profit; whether a business firm is entitled to charge "the most profitable prices"; and whether a price maker is entitled to use unethical pricing methods because his competitors do. Indeed, the list of ethical and moral questions that are related to pricing decisions is very nearly endless.

The answers to some of the questions raised above would seem obvious to many persons; to others the answers are not as clear. Often such questions have no single correct answer that would be acceptable to all, or even most, persons; instead, the answer any individual would give would depend on his own set of values. For example, to engage in loss-leader pricing is considered by some businessmen a respectable practice, but others disagree. In any event, it is vital that those who are involved in price making recognize that there are

[67] Bait pricing, fictitious pricing, and loss-leader pricing are discussed in Chapter 7. Odd pricing is discussed in Chapter 8.

ethical and moral implications to their pricing decisions and that they give serious thought to the ethical nature of their actions.

NONSTATUTORY GOVERNMENT INFLUENCES ON PRICING DECISIONS

In addition to passing laws that affect price making, governments have also exerted an influence on pricing by nonstatutory means, particularly in recent years. Such nonstatutory methods include investigations made by legislative committees, and declarations, threats, and requests made by important government officials. At the federal level, these methods have taken the form of Congressional investigations, particularly those of the Senate Subcommittee on Antitrust and Monopoly, as well as pressure from the President of the United States. The investigations of the subcommittee have dealt largely with conspiracy, monopolistic pricing, and the effect of administered prices on inflation. Actions of the Chief Executive have been concerned primarily with the relationship between price increases and the general price level, or inflation. The intervention of President John F. Kennedy in the decision of steel companies to raise prices in the spring of 1962, the pressure applied by the Administration on the aluminum, copper, and steel-producing industries to encourage them to rescind price increases in late 1965 and early 1966, and the prescription of wage and price "guideposts" by both President Kennedy and President Lyndon B. Johnson are examples of how the Chief Executive can influence pricing.[68]

Government exhortation on the topic of prices is by no means a recent development. Arthur F. Burns points out that in its early days of secular authority the Church often spoke firmly on the need for just pricing. Later, governments frequently blamed profiteers for increases in the price of food or other key commodities. In the post-

---

[68] The guideposts suggest that wage increases be limited to the annual trend increase in national productivity. As to prices, if an industry's productivity rises less than the national trend of productivity, its prices can rise enough to accommodate the rise in labor costs per unit that is indicated by the wage guideline. When an industry's productivity rises more rapidly than the national average, its prices should be lowered in keeping with the decline in unit labor costs. For criticisms of the wage and price guideposts, see Charles A. Bliss, "Flaw in the Wage-Price Guideposts," *Harvard Business Review,* May–June, 1966.

World War II years it has become customary for governments to lay particular stress on the importance of stability in the general level of prices rather than on the rightness of individual prices. In the past few years, however, governmental attempts to influence pricing have become more frequent and more urgent, to the point where, according to Burns, "Trade unions and business firms . . . are no longer merely asked or admonished to moderate their private power in the public interest; they are advised with a show of specificity *how this can best be done.*" [69]

Generally speaking, of course, nonstatutory government pressure is a problem faced primarily by larger firms, particularly those in certain heavily concentrated, "basic" industries, such as automobile and steel manufacturing. Most business firms are not directly affected by the problem and do not regard their pricing decisions as being that important to the economy as a whole. For an executive in one of the more important basic industries, however, pressure from government can be a very real problem.

What is the responsibility of the price maker when the government attempts to influence his pricing decisions through investigations, threats, declarations, or requests? As with other questions of a primarily ethical nature, there is no single correct answer. One's personal value system must be considered. On the one hand, it could be said that businessmen do not have the responsibility to control economic conditions or to carry out the economic policy of the federal government, and that, as a consequence, under the free enterprise system they have the right and the responsibility to charge the prices that they think are the most profitable. If these prices are out of line in some way, the market will eventually reject them. In other words, according to this view it is the market, rather than the government, that should be the judge of price making. On the other hand, it cannot be denied that the executives who are responsible for carrying out the pricing function in giant firms in heavily concentrated industries must at least consider the broad social and economic implications of their pricing decisions because of the sheer importance of those decisions. Furthermore, pressure by government and public opinion force pricing executives in such firms to consider the economic and social consequences of their decisions, even though these decisions may not be altered by such consideration.

[69] "Wages and Prices by Formula," *Harvard Business Review*, March–April, 1965, p. 57.

Selected References

Detailed treatment of the general subject of government regulation of business is found in the several books on this broad topic, such as Vernon L. Mund, *Government and Business,* 3rd ed. (Harper & Bros., 1960).

A recent book on the legal aspects of marketing, including those related to pricing, is Marshall C. Howard, *Legal Aspects of Marketing* (New York: McGraw-Hill, 1965). See especially Chapters 2 and 3. General marketing texts usually contain some discussion of government regulation of pricing. See, for example, Theodore N. Beckman and William R. Davidson, *Marketing,* 7th ed. (New York: Ronald, 1962), Chapter 34. The "Legal Developments in Marketing" section of the *Journal of Marketing* contains brief discussions of current cases involving the Sherman Act and the Robinson-Patman Act.

The approach the businessman might follow in dealing with the antitrust problem is discussed by Jerrold G. Van Cise, "How to Live With Antitrust," *Harvard Business Review,* November–December, 1962. Reasons for price fixing and the rationale of the government in price-fixing cases are dealt with by J. F. Barron in "Normal Business Behavior and the Justice Department," *Journal of Marketing,* January, 1963. A tongue-in-cheek discussion of methods that should be used in price fixing is found in John Q. Lawyer, "How to Conspire to Fix Prices," *Harvard Business Review,* March–April, 1963.

Reasons for the existence of identical bids are discussed in Paul W. Cook, Jr., "Fact and Fancy on Identical Bids," *Harvard Business Review,* January–February, 1963. Criticisms of identical bidding are set forth in Mund, "Identical Bid Prices," *Journal of Political Economy,* April, 1960. The details of what went on in the electrical equipment cases are spelled out by Richard Austin Smith in "The Incredible Electrical Conspiracy," *Fortune,* Part I, April, 1961; Part II, May, 1961. See also Clarence C. Walton and Frederick W. Cleveland, *Corporations on Trial: The Electric Cases* (Belmont, Calif.: Wadsworth, 1964).

The outstanding general sources on the Robinson-Patman Act are Corwin D. Edwards, *The Price Discrimination Law* (Washington, D.C.: Brookings Institution, 1959), which examines the economic impact of the law, and Frederick M. Rowe, *Price Discrimination Under the Robinson-Patman Act* (Boston: Little, Brown, 1962) which is written in terms of legal principles. There is also a supplement to this book published by Little, Brown in 1964. See also Edwards, "Twenty Years Under the Robinson-Patman Act," *Journal of Business,* July, 1956, and W. David Robbins, "A Marketing Appraisal of the Robinson-Patman Act," *Journal of Marketing*, July, 1959.

The problem of determining what are commodities of "like grade and quality" under the Robinson-Patman Act is discussed in Ralph Cassady, Jr. and Ewald T. Grether, "Proper Interpretation of 'Like Grade and Quality' Within the Meaning of Section 2(a) of the Robinson-Patman Act," *Southern California Law Review*, April, 1957, and Jacky Knopp, Jr., "What Are Commodities of Like Grade and Quality?" *Journal of Marketing*, July, 1963.

The question of competitive injury under the Robinson-Patman Act is examined in Robert C. Brooks, Jr., "Injury to Competition Under the Robinson-Patman Act," *University of Pennsylvania Law Review*, July, 1961; "Competitive Injury Under the Robinson-Patman Act," *Harvard Law Review*, July, 1961; and Brooks, "Businessmen's Concepts of 'Injury to Competition,'" *California Management Review*, Summer, 1961.

The cost defense under the Robinson-Patman Act and how it has been interpreted are discussed in Herbert F. Taggart, *Cost Justification*, Michigan Business Studies, Vol. 14, No. 3 (Ann Arbor, Mich.: Bureau of Business Research, University of Michigan, 1959); Donald F. Fennelly, "On the Judging of Mince Pies," *Harvard Business Review*, November–December, 1964; and Robert A. Lynn, "Is the Cost Defense Workable?" *Journal of Marketing*, January, 1965.

Problems under the good-faith clause of the Robinson-Patman Act are treated by George R. Hall and Charles F. Phillips in "Good Faith, Discrimination, and Marketing Organization," *Southern Economic Journal*, October, 1963.

Ethics in business has been the subject of several articles in recent years. See, for example, Raymond C. Baumhart, S.J., "How Ethical Are Businessmen?" *Harvard Business Review*, July–August, 1961. Ethical problems in marketing are discussed in William N. Borton, "Respectability for Marketing?" *Journal of Marketing*, October, 1959; D. Beryl Manischewitz, "Marketing Under Attack," *Journal of Marketing*, July, 1962; and Eugene J. Kelley, "Ethics and Science in Marketing," in George Schwartz, (ed.), *Science in Marketing* (New York: John Wiley and Sons, 1965). Specific discussions of pricing and ethics are found in Alfred R. Oxenfeldt, *Pricing for Marketing Executives* (San Francisco: Wadsworth, 1961), pp. 13–16, and Bernard D. Nossiter, "The Troubled Conscience of American Business," *Harper's*, September, 1963.

5

NORMATIVE PRICING MODELS

In recent years, many writers in the marketing field have become increasingly interested in various methods for making the decision process more scientific, including operations research and the use of scientific models as decision aids. In this chapter we will examine some of the recent developments that pertain to pricing decisions. The discussion begins with a brief description of decision theory. This is followed by an account of the nature of operations research and scientific models and how these techniques can be used in making marketing decisions. With this background we will then devote the bulk of the chapter to a consideration of some normative models that have been developed for use in making pricing decisions.

ELEMENTS OF DECISION THEORY [1]

The growth in interest in the decision-making process in business has resulted in the building up of a good deal of theory concerning decision making. No attempt is made here to discuss this theory in detail. The intention is only to point out its essential elements.

Decisions made by business executives may be broken down into several basic elements for purposes of theoretical analysis. Let us consider each element separately.

---

[1] Our discussion of decision theory is based in large part on that of David W. Miller and Martin K. Starr, in *Executive Decisions and Operations Research* (Englewood Cliffs, N.J.: Prentice-Hall, 1960), Chapters 3, 4, and 5.

OBJECTIVES

We mentioned in Chapter 2 that business firms and executives pursue a variety of objectives. Clearly, an executive's approach to a decision problem depends on his objectives. Only on the basis of these objectives can he choose the appropriate strategy from the alternatives available to him. Therefore, the first step in the decision process is to formulate, or recognize, the relevant objectives.

DEVELOPMENT OF THE PAYOFF MEASURE

After the executive has recognized his objectives, he needs a *payoff measure*—some indication of the degree of utility to be achieved by his decision in terms of given objectives. In other words, he needs a measure of the degree of success of the decision. Ideally, this measure of payoff should be a numerical unit that indicates the extent to which goals are realized. For some business decisions there is a "natural" payoff measure of the degree of achievement in the various economic indices that are relevant to many business objectives. Dollars can be a natural measure of payoff for objectives concerning profits and costs, for example. Other natural payoff measures are market share, volume of sales, order size, number of customers, and repeat-order rate.

Some objectives, however, do not have a natural measure of payoff. The payoff cannot always be expressed in quantitative terms, and, in cases where it cannot, decision theory is less useful. In such cases the decision maker may employ devices such as the ranking of possible outcomes.

STRATEGIES AVAILABLE

A decision maker who has alternative ways in which he can use the resources under his control must select among these alternative strategies. The selection of a strategy is his decision regarding what he will do with these resources (including his own time and effort). Although there may be a large number of strategies that could be used in any decision situation to achieve the desired payoff, various factors limit the number of strategies that will be considered as practical alternatives. For example, some possible strategies are illegal or unethical and can therefore be ruled out immediately. Other possible strategies may be rejected because they do not conform to usual practices in the industry or because the decision maker is reluctant to introduce any substantial change in his customary approach. In short, the executive's next step is to determine which strategies represent real alternatives for the situation in question.

OUTSIDE FACTORS

In decision theory, factors that are beyond the control of the decision maker, such as weather conditions, economic conditions, labor strife, and technological developments, are termed "states of nature." The reactions of buyers and competitors to decisions made by the decision maker are also important forms of states of nature. These outside factors create the environment in which the decision is made. The decision maker, wishing to achieve a particular objective, selects a strategy from those available to him, and the interaction of this strategy with the existing states of nature determines the degree to which his objective is attained. It is important that the decision maker identify as many states of nature as possible and that he try to understand their relative importance; some will be relevant in a given decision situation and some will not.

SELECTION FROM ALTERNATIVE STRATEGIES

In an attempt to set forth the different approaches that could be taken in the selection of the ideal strategy, decision theory classifies decision problems according to the degree of certainty, uncertainty, or risk that is involved. Various criteria that may be used in the selection of strategies have been isolated by decision theory, including the criteria of optimism, pessimism, regret, and rationality, and the minimax, maximax, maximin, Laplace, and Wald criteria. If, for example, a businessman chooses to be guided by the maximin criterion in a given situation, he would select the strategy with the largest minimum payoff. Using such a strategy the decision maker could be sure that he would be in as favorable a position as possible if the worst

possible payoff occurred. Thus, in the selection process, he determines the worst that could possibly happen for each possible strategy
and then picks the strategy that is "least worst."

In contrast to the cautious maximin approach, the decision maker
might select the strategy that permits the largest maximum payoff. He
would then be using the maximum maximum or maximax criterion.
Here the businessman is choosing "that gamble whose first prize is
highest, no matter what the dangers in the relative values of the other
prizes and penalties." [2] Still another strategy would be chosen if the
decision maker used the Laplace criterion, which calls for the maximum *average* payoff.[3]

OPERATIONS RESEARCH

THE NATURE OF OPERATIONS RESEARCH

What is now called "operations research" (OR) was first developed during World War II in England and later in the United States
as a method of solving military problems. After the war it was picked
up by private industry and government, and since about 1950, it has
rapidly become an extremely powerful and flexible tool.

The term "operations research" seems to mean different things to
different people and enjoys no generally accepted definition. One
common definition is that OR is the application of scientific method
to the solution of business problems and the use of quantitative methods in business decisions. But this does not tell us very much; cost
accounting and quality control are two well-known techniques that
also meet this definition.[4]

Some definitions of operations research have stressed the role of
mathematical models; other definitions stress the "systems" approach
to problem solving. The systems approach is basically a recognition of

---

[2] William J. Baumol, *Economic Theory and Operations Analysis* (Englewood
Cliffs, N.J.: Prentice-Hall, 1961), p. 371.

[3] The *average payoff* is the expected value of the payoff over all possible states
of nature.

[4] Alfred Oxenfeldt, David Miller, Abraham Shuchman, and Charles Winick,
Insights into Pricing (Belmont, Calif.: Wadsworth, 1961), pp. 8–9.

the fact that many business problems, such as inventory management, involve more than one of the organizational divisions, or departments, in a firm and should therefore be analyzed from the point of view of the "total system." [5] The "team approach"—the combined efforts of people with diverse backgrounds—has also been stressed as a unique feature of OR.

Probably the most acceptable definition of operations research is that suggested by David W. Miller and Martin K. Starr, who maintain that operations research is applied decision theory, which makes use of any available scientific, mathematical, or logical means for coping with the problems that confront the executive when he tries to achieve a thoroughgoing rationality in his approach to decision problems.[6] Several techniques and tools are used frequently in OR, including algebra, calculus, queueing theory, Markov chains, linear programming, dynamic programming, regression analysis, game theory, probability theory, and simulation.[7]

If we accept the tenet of decision theory that the principal task of the executive is to choose between alternative courses of action in the face of an uncertain future, then we may say that an objective of OR is to provide executives with a scientific basis for making these decisions. Proponents of operations research claim that it can help the executive's decision-making task by contributing the following:

1. A better and more logical description of his objectives and of the assumptions on which they are based.
2. A more precise and illuminating definition of his problems and of the critical factors involved, the relative importance of each, and the relationships among them.
3. A clear indication of the information required in order to determine the "best" solution.
4. The ability to take into account, in determining the "best" solution, a larger number of relevant factors.
5. A precise description of many more of the possible solutions of the problem, the assumptions underlying each, and the costs, benefits, and risks involved in each.

[5] See, for example, C. West Churchman, Russell L. Ackoff, and E. Leonard Arnoff, *Introduction to Operations Research* (New York: John Wiley and Sons, 1957), pp. 6–9.

[6] Miller and Starr, *op. cit.,* p. 104.

[7] The reader should consult the literature on operations research which is referred to at the end of this chapter for explanations of any of these techniques or tools.

6. The ability to compare many more possible solutions and to locate the "best" among them, rapidly, efficiently, and with considerable confidence.
7. A basis for predicting the consequences of change in his firm's procedures or in the environment.[8]

THE NATURE OF SCIENTIFIC MODELS

Paralleling recent work in decision theory, operations research, and scientific decision making has been an increase in interest in model building as one of the tools in business management. Models have long been used in accounting, econometrics, and marketing research,[9] and they are an intrinsic part of the scientific method in all fields of human endeavor.

OR . . . applies the scientific method to the study of business problems. It applies, in particular, the method of research which has been used with such great success in the natural sciences. An important ingredient in this method is the formulation of an hypothesis or theory regarding the nature of the mechanism underlying a phenomenon. This theory is then tested against observed facts and modified in the light of test results. The modified theory is then tested and itself modified and this process is continued until the scientist is satisfied that his theory accounts for the observed facts with sufficient accuracy for his purposes.

Scientists can rarely obtain interesting and useful results by studying a phenomenon directly as it takes place in nature. More commonly, in order to test a theory, they must reproduce the mechanism that they believe to be responsible for the phenomenon under controlled conditions in a laboratory. They must construct a replica of the cause and effect relationships which, as they see it, are producing the phenomenon and must study and analyze this replica, rather than the natural phenomenon in its natural setting. The replica is, therefore, an embodiment in physical, graphical, or mathematical form of the scientist's theory of the origin or nature of a phenomenon. It is a representation of the underlying causal mechanism. It is not, however, a perfect and complete representation but contains only those elements which the scientist considers important.

[8] Abraham Shuchman, *Scientific Decision Making in Business* (New York: Holt, Rinehart and Winston, 1963), pp. 8–9.
[9] See Robert D. Buzzell, *Mathematical Models and Marketing Management* (Boston: Graduate School of Business Administration, Harvard University, 1964), pp. 31–33.

In the language of science, such replicas are known as *models*. And in the methodology of science, models occupy a key position. It follows that models are of central importance in the methodology of OR.[10]

In other words, a model is a representation of reality that attempts to explain the behavior of some aspect of the object or situation in question.[11] Thus, a road map is a model that represents a given geographic area; a corporate profit-and-loss statement is a model that represents the performance of a business firm; and a model airplane in a wind tunnel represents the behavior of the "real thing" under certain conditions.

Some models are very concrete; others are highly abstract. Churchman, Ackoff, and Arnoff distinguish between *iconic, analogue,* and *symbolic* models. An *iconic model* is designed to look like reality. Examples are sculptures, photographs, and model ships. In an *analogue model* a property in the model is substituted for a property in the object or situation. A graph of the demand curve for a given commodity in which distance on the graph is substituted for quantities demanded is an analogue model, for example. So are the different colored lines on a map that are used to indicate different classes of highways. Finally, there are *symbolic models* in which objects, events, and processes are represented by symbols of some kind, such as mathematical symbols. A formula in which physical distribution cost is represented by a certain number of dollars or by a symbol such as A' is a symbolic model. The iconic model is usually the easiest to conceive and is also the most concrete and specific. Its function is primarily descriptive rather than explanatory, in that it can seldom reveal causal relationships. In contrast, the symbolic model is usually the most difficult to conceive, perhaps because it is also the most general and abstract. The function of a symbolic model, however, is primarily explanatory rather than descriptive. Analogue models fall between iconic and symbolic models in both respects.[12]

The kind of model with which we will be concerned in this chapter is the symbolic or mathematical model. It is usually impossible as a practical matter to include in a model all the major and minor elements of which a particular business problem is composed because the analysis would become hopelessly complicated or even impossi-

---

[10] Shuchman, *op. cit.,* pp. 61–62.
[11] Miller and Starr, *op. cit.,* p. 115.
[12] Churchman, Ackoff, and Arnoff, *op. cit.,* pp. 158–62.

ble. Therefore, the model builder often finds it necessary to ignore or omit certain elements, or changes in certain elements, of the object or situation he is describing. The difficulties of statistical fact-finding and mathematical computation mount rapidly with the degree of complication of the model. Therefore, the decision to omit an element from a model must be a matter of balancing off the loss in realism against the gain in reduced difficulty of computation.[13]

Mathematical models are developed for various purposes. Robert D. Buzzell, for example, distinguishes between *descriptive, predictive,* and *control* models. The *descriptive model* is intended only to describe some object or process in the real world. A model describing the physical distribution system of a firm would fall into this category. *Predictive models* are designed to facilitate the prediction of future events, as well as to describe objectives and events. A sales-forecasting model would be predictive if it were designed to predict the overall result of a group of purchase decisions made by customers of a firm. A *control model* is the most comprehensive. It not only describes and predicts events, but it also provides a basis for choosing among alternative courses of action. This, of course, is the kind of model that is most closely associated with decision theory, since it is best suited to the task of helping decision makers choose among alternative strategies. As Buzzell points out, a purely predictive sales-forecasting model might include only factors such as population and consumer income, which are essentially uncontrollable from the viewpoint of the firm. If, however, a sales-forecasting model includes the prices charged by a firm, it may help the executive make an intelligent choice among various possible prices. To this extent it is functioning as a control model. There can be some overlapping between these different kinds of models, and the dividing line between them is not always clear.[14]

In this chapter we will concentrate on mathematical control models that are designed to provide a basis for choice among alternative strategies. These are termed *maximizing* or *optimizing* or *normative* models because they help the executive make decisions that will be consistent with certain predetermined objectives. Mathematical models have two important advantages over other decision aids. They make possible a faster, less expensive, or more accurate determination of results, and they can be used when it is impossible for one

---

[13] Baumol, *op. cit.,* p. 413.
[14] Buzzell, *op. cit.,* pp. 16–17.

reason or another to use the events or the physical objects themselves for this purpose.[15]

APPLICABILITY OF OPERATIONS RESEARCH AND MODEL BUILDING TO MARKETING

Operations research is not intended to be a substitute for marketing research, distribution-cost analysis, sales forecasting, or any other tool used by marketing management. It is rather an *additional* tool, or approach.

> Operations research draws on information from these subjects [marketing research, distribution-cost analysis, sales forecasting, etc.], calls on the services of varied company specialists, and cuts across the lines of functional authority in sublimating the objectives of subgroups to the overall objective of the company. It is not designed to reduce the responsibilities of marketing management but rather to add new scope and dimensions to the marketing tasks and to help marketing managers deal more effectively with the crucial decisions they must make.[16]

Although theoretically OR can provide a great deal of help to marketing executives, it has been used to only a limited extent to date in solving marketing problems. Marketing men have been much slower in learning about OR and in attempting to apply it than have the managers of other functional areas of the firm, particularly production.

The principal reason there has been relatively little progress in applying the techniques of operations research to marketing problems is that marketing problems are very complex and many of the important variables involved in these problems are not quantifiable. Part of the reason marketing problems appear to be more complicated and less precise than production problems is that marketing problems involve to much greater extent the human element, such as consumer attitudes and motives, the reaction of middlemen to decisions of manufacturers, and the effectiveness of personal salesmanship or advertising in dealing with customers. This means that the operations researcher must deal with a much greater number of uncertainties in

---

[15] *Ibid.*, p. 13.
[16] William Lazer, "Operations Research and Marketing Science," in George Schwartz, ed., *Science in Marketing* (New York: John Wiley and Sons, 1965), p. 436.

attempting to apply the OR approach to marketing problems than to production problems.

In further support of this argument Miller and Starr point out that OR solutions must be based on some set of costs and that, although such cost estimates are readily available in production and the clerical side of administration, good estimates of the relevant costs are not generally available in marketing. Therefore, the solution to the decision problem is one step further removed. Furthermore, Miller and Starr argue that whereas most of the elements of a given problem are under the decision maker's control in the area of production, many of the crucial elements of a problem are outside his control in marketing. Even when the factors are under control in marketing it can be an extremely difficult task to disentangle the interrelationships between them. Thus, in the marketing area a solution will often depend on laborious attempts to disentangle the interactions of the various factors and will, even then, require some rather unrealistic assumptions.[17] Because of these differences between the types of problems encountered in production and marketing, operations-research solutions are less likely to be forthcoming and less reliable in the marketing area than in the production area. "Since the probability of a return from a search for a solution in the marketing area is smaller, it follows that fewer companies can afford to undertake the search. Thus, experience accumulates more slowly in the development of suitable marketing models." [18] Thus it is not surprising that the most frequent use of OR in marketing has been in dealing with problems of physical distribution and inventory where there is a greater opportunity to quantify and the least problem with the human element.

William Lazer adds that marketing executives are usually unskilled in mathematical and statistical methods. They tend to be "people oriented" rather than "analytically oriented." "They have tended to follow the lore of the trade, to use rules of thumb, and often to apply various generalizations. Moreover, many of them have been extremely successful." [19]

Model building To construct a mathematical model one must first identify the controllable and uncontrollable variables in the situation in question and the relationships that exist among these variables. Then one must figure out ways of measuring events in terms of

[17] Miller and Starr, *op. cit.*, pp. 410–11.
[18] *Ibid.*, p. 411.
[19] Lazer, *op. cit.*, p. 438.

objectives.[20] As we have just indicated, however, in the marketing field it is difficult to untangle the variables and their relationships, and it is often impossible to quantify them. As a consequence, only a few marketing managers have made use of mathematical models to date. As Buzzell observes:

> . . . one of the major obstacles to progress in the use of mathematical models in marketing is that well defined, generally acceptable procedures for measuring many of the factors involved do not as yet exist. Such factors are often designated as "qualitative," but this does not mean they are inherently different from "quantitative" factors. It *does* mean that they are not readily measurable.[21]

Because of the difficulty in quantifying marketing factors and in specifying the relationships among these factors, some model builders have assumed away such critical marketing factors as demand, consumer behavior, competitive strategies, and size of market share. When what may be the most important variables are assumed away, the solutions reached are somewhat meaningless. "What is often obtained by operations research procedures are neat mathematical formulations that need not pertain to marketing reality, that are ineffective as decision tools, but that furnish impressive looking manuscripts for esoteric journals." [22]

As of 1963, according to Buzzell, the use of mathematical models for purposes of decision making in marketing could be described as "practically none," or "slight." Most of the firms who said they were using mathematical models in marketing were actually still in the exploratory stages with this approach. In very few cases were firms using mathematical models in a manner even approaching "complete reliance." Futhermore, Buzzell discovered that the most common application of mathematical models in marketing was "diagnostic" in that the models were being used to clarify objectives, to determine what alternatives were available, and to determine what facts were relevant in the marketing decision.[23] According to Lazer:

> Some of the more sophisticated mathematical models have received widespread acclaim for their accomplishments. Yet, when evaluated

---

[20] Discussions of the technicalities of model construction may be found in the literature on operations research. See, for example, Buzzell, *op. cit.*, Chapter 3; Churchman, Ackoff, and Arnoff, *op. cit.*, Chapter 7; and Shuchman, *op. cit.*, Part 2.

[21] Buzzell, *op. cit.*, p. 27.

[22] Lazer, *op. cit.*, p. 441.

[23] Buzzell, *op. cit.*, pp. 66–69.

against the spectrum of significant marketing problems, the accomplishments of models, and particularly mathematical models, have been sparse indeed. The value of mathematical models in solving marketing problems, perhaps with the exception of linear programming, is quite limited. In fact, it is the promise of *potential applications* in marketing, rather than *actual application*, to which operations researchers refer fondly.[24]

Despite the difficulties and limitations inherent in the use of mathematical models in marketing, such models may be of considerable help to marketing management in the future. Specifically, models can help identify and sort out the various factors involved in a decision problem and organize data systematically for analysis. They can lead to better understanding of problems even if the factors and payoffs involved cannot be quantified. In sum, the application of mathematical models to marketing problems promises to advance the development of marketing science in the following ways:

1. The models are useful in theory construction. When quantitative models are formulated and data from the real world is mapped into them, a theory is generated about the data.
2. Simulation, or experimentation, on the models can generate further theories and hypotheses about marketing and provide valuable insights for marketing science.
3. Models have provided the most successful predicting system developed so far, namely, the predicting system used in science.
4. Quantitative models help portray marketing situations in simplified forms for the purpose of analysis. They help explain critical relationships and reactions.
5. Quantitative models tend to be objective rather than intuitive, and they often permit analyses that are not feasible with other techniques.[25]

Thus, OR, and mathematical models in particular, promises to become an important tool of marketing management in the future. Like other decision makers, marketing executives are faced with the problem of choosing among alternative strategies. The operations researcher can sometimes assist in such situations, as he can in other areas of business decision making, although, admittedly, it is more

[24] Lazer, *op. cit.*, p. 440.
[25] *Ibid.*, pp. 430–31.

difficult to apply the OR approach to marketing than it is to some other phases of business management.

PRICING MODELS

Normative pricing models have long existed in economic theory. Such models attempt to explain the pricing mechanism, or how prices that will maximize profits are determined under certain kinds of market-structure situations. In Chapter 1, we discussed the normative models of pure competition, pure monopoly, monopolistic competition, and oligopoly. The weakness of such models, as we mentioned, is that, to a great extent, they do not describe the "real" world because of the unreal assumptions upon which they rest. Furthermore, these price theory models have been developed primarily as a tool for the analysis of broad economic changes and the evaluation of social controls, rather than as an aid in business decision making.

OR has pricing models of its own. These differ from the pricing models of the economist in purpose and in the viewpoint of the model builder. Since OR is applied decision theory, it follows that the pricing models developed through OR methods are designed primarily as aids for business decision making, not for analyzing economic changes or evaluating social controls. The viewpoint is that of the individual firm and the individual decision maker, in contrast to that of the economist's model in which an "outsider" attempts to evaluate pricing from the point of view of society as a whole. Thus, operations research provides a new way of looking at pricing problems. Furthermore, OR pricing models can offer a method for handling the problem of uncertainty, which economic theory does not do. The economist assumes perfect knowledge on the part of the price maker, which is rarely the case in the real world. "The whole of decision theory . . . can be considered a careful analysis of what constitutes rational behavior in the face of uncertainty. Consequently, familiarity with these approaches will be useful to those who make price decisions as well as to others faced with uncertainty." [26]

Despite the fact that the concept of model building has proved

---

[26] Oxenfeldt, Miller, Shuchman, and Winick, *op. cit.,* p. 119.

difficult to apply to marketing, some models have been developed for the purpose of helping executives make pricing decisions. In the remainder of this chapter, we will examine briefly several of the mathematical normative pricing models, including two models designed to guide decisions to reduce prices, a model intended to aid in pricing a new product, and a competitive bidding model.

DECISION TO REDUCE A PRICE— A BEVERAGE MANUFACTURER

When a firm is losing sales to less expensive, competing brands it must face the question of whether or not to reduce the price of its product. Critical issues in such a decision are the degree to which price is to be reduced and the effect that such a reduction might have on sales volume. Will volume increase sufficiently to make up for the decrease in price? In other words, what amount of increased volume is needed to break even?

William J. Baumol has suggested a pricing model for such a situation.[27] He describes a beverage manufacturer who found that he was losing sales to less expensive, competing brands. Prices in the industry had not changed in recent years so there was no available data on which to base an estimate of the nature of the demand function. There was, however, a rough estimate of marginal cost per unit, and there was reason to believe that marginal costs would not vary substantially over the range of output under consideration. The problem thus became one of determining whether a reduction in price from the current P cents per unit, to some lower price, P* cents per unit, would be profitable. This meant that the problem could be structured around the following data:

Q = the current quantity of the product sold at the current price
P = the current price in cents per unit
P* = the proposed new price in cents per unit
C = the marginal cost per unit

The symbol Q* was used to designate the unknown new quantity of output that would be sold at the new lower price, P*. Then if current revenue was PQ, potential revenue became P*Q*. To produce

[27] Baumol, *op. cit.,* pp. 396–97 and 406–07.

the increased quantity, $Q^* - Q$, it would cost the firm $C (Q^* - Q)$ dollars. The net change in profits resulting from the price reduction would be equal to the increase in total revenue minus the change in costs, that is, it would be equal to $P^*Q^* - PQ - C (Q^* - Q)$. Clearly, this net change in profits could not be less than zero or the firm would lose out. In other words, the required condition may be expressed as

$$P^*Q^* - PQ - C (Q^* - Q) \geqq 0$$

which was solved to give

$$Q^* \geqq \frac{P - C}{P^* - C} Q$$

The solution to this last statement tells us the smallest increase in quantity sold that is necessary to ensure that the firm will not lose by the reduction in price.

In this example Baumol found that a 70-percent increase in sales was necessary before the firm would break even on the price reduction proposed. Although the firm did not have adequate information on the nature of demand, it appeared unlikely that this price reduction would result in a 70-percent increase in sales. Furthermore, the firm did not have the productive capacity to handle a 70-percent increase in sales, even if it were to occur. In short, the analysis indicated that the proposed price reduction definitely should not be made.

This rather simple model illustrates how much can be done with very little information. In this case, the decision maker had no information about how customers or competitors would react to a price change, so he made use of the information he did have concerning price, cost, and quantity sold. Although the model does not help the executive determine whether or not a specific price will produce an increase in sales volume, it does help him decide whether or not a specific price reduction would be *practical* assuming that it is successful in producing larger sales volume. The particular illustration used by Baumol yields very clear-cut results—a 70-percent increase in sales volume was required to break even at the proposed lower price. This was out of the question. A smaller break-even level of increased volume such as 5, 10, or 15 percent might be less conclusive since such an increase in sales might be quite possible and the firm might easily be able to produce the additional output required.

PRICING A NEW PRODUCT

The pricing of new products is one of the most interesting as well as one of the most difficult aspects of pricing. The uncertainties surrounding the reactions of the market and of competitors are usually greater when the decision maker faces the task of pricing a new product than when he is considering a change in the price of a product that has already been thoroughly exposed. Robert S. Weinberg has suggested a mathematical model for use in pricing a new product.[28]

Weinberg takes as his example a firm that planned to introduce a new product and wanted to set a price on this product that would maximize its profits. The firm's market research department had estimated the demand for the product at various selling prices, and the firm's financial department had gathered various estimates of the costs associated with producing and marketing the product.

Specifically, four market forecasts were projected for four possible prices. The estimates showed that demand would vary along with prices, and that a linear relationship existed between price (the independent variable) and quantity demanded (the dependent variable). These forecasts yielded the results listed in Table 1.

Table 1   Market Forecasts

Price	Estimated demand (units)
$ 50	7,500
100	5,000
150	2,500
200	0

Source Association of National Advertisers, *An Analytical Approach to Advertising Expenditure Strategy,* 1960, p. 98, by permission.

[28] See Association of National Advertisers, *An Analytical Approach to Advertising Expenditure Strategy,* 1960, pp. 89–116. This has been reprinted under the title, "The Uses and Limitations of Mathematical Models for Market Planning," in Frank M. Bass, *et al., Mathematical Models and Methods in Marketing* (Homewood, Ill.: Irwin, 1961) and in Shuchman, *op. cit.*

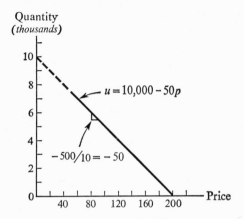

Figure 10   New-Product Price—Demand Relation

Source   Association of National Advertisers, *An Analytical Approach to Advertising Expenditure Strategy*, 1960, p. 99, by permission.

The interrelationship between price and demand could be represented by the generalized equation for a straight line, $Y = a + bX$, where Y is the dependent variable (in this case, quantity demanded) and X is the independent variable (in this case, price). The exact interrelation between Y and X is determined by the two parameters, a and b. The parameter a represents the intercept (i.e., the value of Y when $X = 0$) of the line, and the parameter b represents the slope of the line. The intercept could be determined from the diagram in Figure 10, in which the estimates given in Table 1 are plotted, by extending the u curve as shown by the broken line segment. This tells us that at a zero selling price, the firm could expect to "sell," or give away, 10,000 units of the product. The broken segment of the line only existed for mathematical purposes, however, to establish a value for a.

The parameter b measures the slope of the line, or the price sensitivity of demand for the new product. To determine the value for the b parameter, or the net change in demand associated with a unit change in price, all one had to do was consult the data given earlier in Table 1 showing the estimated volume of demand associated with given prices. There we saw that each $50 increase in price was expected to result in a reduction in demand of 2,500 units, or, in other words, a reduction in demand of 50 units for each $1 increase in price ($-2,500/50 = -50$). On the other hand, each $1 reduction in price was expected to result in an increase in demand of 50 units.

This inverse relationship between demand and price is represented by the negative value for b. Substituting the values for a and b into the generalized equation, $Y = a + bX$, we have

$$u = 10,000 - 50p \qquad \text{(Eq. 1)}$$

where

$$u = \text{expected unit sales}$$
$$p = \text{price}$$

On the basis of cost estimates prepared by the firm, it was estimated that it would cost \$50,000 (a fixed cost) to "tool up" for production of the new product and that each unit produced would cost \$45 in materials and labor (a variable cost). It was also estimated that physical distribution and other marketing costs would amount to \$25 per unit (a variable cost). The new product's share of the firm's "overhead" was estimated at \$35,000 (a fixed cost). These cost factors are summarized in Table 2.

Table 2   Cost Elements

Fixed costs		*Variable costs*	
Tooling	\$50,000	Production (materials and labor)	\$45 per unit
Overhead	35,000	Physical distribution, etc.	25 per unit
Total	\$85,000	Total	\$70 per unit

Source   Association of National Advertisers, *An Analytical Approach to Advertising Expenditure Strategy*, 1960, p. 101, by permission.

When these cost elements were combined, they yielded the relationship

$$C = \$85,000 + \$70u \qquad \text{(Eq. 2)}$$

where

$$C = \text{total costs}$$

and

$$u = \text{expected unit sales}$$

Profits could be then determined by means of the simple equation

$$P = S - C \qquad \text{(Eq. 3)}$$

where

P = profits (in dollars)
S = sales (in dollars)
C = total costs (in dollars)

Total costs could be determined from the cost equation (Eq. 2) above. Equation 1 provided an estimate of the firm's unit sales, but not its dollar sales. Accordingly, a fourth equation was needed to define dollar sales. This equation can be expressed as

$$S = up \qquad \text{(Eq. 4)}$$

where

S = dollar sales
u = expected unit sales
p = price

Combining Equations 1 and 4 the following relationship between dollar sales and selling price was derived:

$S = up$		(Eq. 4)
$u = 10,000 - 50p$		(Eq. 1)
$S = (10,000 - 50p)p$	(substituting Eq. 1 into Eq. 4)	
$S = 10,000p - 50p^2$		(Eq. 5)

Equations 1 through 4 represent the complete pricing strategy model that allows the decision maker to compute quickly the level of ultimate profits associated with any given new-product selling price. The required computational sequence is as follows (given price $[p]$, determine profits $[P]$):

1. Substitute p into Equation 1 to derive u
2. Substitute u into Equation 2 to derive C
3. Substitute u and p into Equation 4 to derive S
4. Substitute S and C into Equation 3 to derive P.

In this example of a new-product pricing problem the only variable over which the firm had control was the sales price; the demand and cost relationships were given and assumed to be fixed. Given the demand and cost situations, the decision maker's choice of action (assuming that it had already been decided that the product would be introduced) was to select the sales price that would maximize profits from the product.

The model we have just discussed provides the decision maker with a method of determining the ultimate level of profits associated with *any given* possible price. Weinberg offers two mathematical methods of quickly determining *which* of the specific prices would maximize profits on the new product. He calls these the "marginal cost = marginal revenue" solution and the "profit maximization" solution. The first method is based on the economic principle that profits are at a maximum when marginal revenue equals marginal cost and employs calculus to develop equations that represent the firm's marginal revenue and marginal cost. From these equations, the decision maker can determine the optimal price that will maximize profits. Weinberg's second approach consists of maximizing the new-product total profit relation itself by combining Equations 1, 2, 3, and 4 and by using calculus to determine the optimal price. These two methods amount to the same thing and are really applications of price theory as it is discussed in Chapter 1.

Weinberg also offers a generalized solution to the new-product pricing problem that we have just discussed. According to Weinberg, the basic relationships developed above may be used to derive a generalized pricing formula that is applicable to any situation in which there is a linear demand relationship and a linear cost relationship. This equation is as follows:

$$p_o = \frac{v}{2} - \frac{b}{2e} \qquad \text{(Eq. 6)}$$

where

$p_o =$ optimal selling price (optimal value for p)
$v =$ total variable costs (in dollars per unit)
$b =$ the intercept of the demand relation (i.e., unit sales when price $= 0$)
$e =$ the slope of the demand relation (i.e., price sensitivity of demand)

In essence, Equation 6 states that the optimal price for a new product is a function of three variables: the total variable costs, the intercept of the demand relation, and the slope of the demand relation.[29]

---

[29] The same basic techniques may be used to develop similar pricing models for nonlinear cases.

When Equation 6 was applied to the example above, it was found that the optimal price was $135 when the following values were assumed,

$$v = 70$$
$$b = 10,000$$
$$e = -50$$

then

$$p_o = \frac{v}{2} - \frac{b}{2e}$$
$$p_o = \frac{70}{2} - \frac{10,000}{2(-50)}$$
$$p_o = \frac{70}{2} - \frac{10,000}{-100}$$
$$p_o = 35 - (-100)$$
$$p_o = 35 + 100$$
$$p_o = 135$$

It is apparent, however, that this new-product pricing model can be criticized because of the assumptions upon which it rests. For example, it is assumed that maximization of profits from the product is the objective—a "quantifiable" objective. In practice, however, other objectives may be paramount in a pricing decision problem. Another assumption is that the firm is able to estimate accurately the demand for the new product at various prices and that it can estimate its costs accurately as well. Assumptions such as these tend to oversimplify the problem of demand and cost estimation. Furthermore, linear relationships are assumed between price and demand and between costs and volume, and this, too, may be highly unrealistic. However, the model does serve to illustrate the techniques that can be used, possibly with more involved mathematics, to handle the difficult problem of selecting a price for a new product.

DECISION TO REDUCE A PRICE—
A PLASTICS MANUFACTURER

Buzzell [30] and Paul E. Green [31] have provided an example of the application of decision theory to the pricing problem of whether a company should reduce price, and, if so, to what level.

[30] Buzzell, *op. cit.*, Chapter 6.
[31] "Bayesian Decision Theory in Pricing Strategy," *Journal of Marketing,* January, 1963.

The Everclear Plastics Company manufactured a plastic called Kromel which sold for $1 per pound. Anticipating that in the next year or two there would be an oversupply of the product because of a somewhat stagnant demand accompanied by an expected increase in the production capacity of the entire industry, management in 1960 began to consider the possibility of reducing the price of Kromel for the purpose of enlarging demand.

Kromel was basically a modification of an older plastic named Verlon. Because Kromel was superior to Verlon in several respects, its price was about 10 percent higher than that of Verlon. Both products were sold to textile manufacturers for use in upholstery materials sold to four market segments labeled A, B, C, and D. Kromel was very successful in replacing Verlon in all segments except segment A; Everclear executives were sure that if segment A could be penetrated, then, for various reasons, demand in the other three segments would increase substantially.[32]

Everclear was the largest seller of Kromel with a market share of about 40 percent. The other three competing sellers were all large firms. The product was highly standardized. Therefore, it appeared certain that any price reduction introduced by Everclear would be met immediately by the other three sellers, but that lower Kromel prices might *not* lead to retaliation by sellers of Verlon since margins on Verlon were already very low.

If a price reduction did result in increased sales of Kromel, a substantially higher level of output would be required. It was felt, however, that this increase in production could be handled by existing facilities without any additional investment in production facilities. Hence the Everclear management decided that the proper criterion for comparing alternative prices was total dollar profit.[33]

At the same time it was expected that a price reduction would lead to *lower* profits for at least a year or two since some time had to elapse before the market would expand. Because profits would start accruing to the company at different times under alternative prices, management needed to compound the profits from all different approaches in some way in order to put them on an equivalent basis at some future time. Only in this way could a meaningful comparison be

---

[32] In this context, penetration is defined as any significant amount of sales in the market segment.

[33] It should be noted that Everclear's basic objective for all divisions and products was to maintain a rate of return on investment of at least 20 percent before income taxes.

made of varying streams of profit that extended over different time periods. In this particular study rates of interest of 6 percent and 10 percent were used to represent two possible opportunity costs on potential use of funds over a given time period.

It was decided that only a limited number of significantly different (well-spaced) alternative prices (strategies) would be considered since it would be difficult to estimate the impact of different prices if the differences between them were small. The lower limit selected for alternative prices was somewhat above variable cost—$0.80 per pound. The other two alternative prices selected for comparison were $0.85 and $0.93 per pound, in addition to the then current price of $1.00 per pound. For various reasons it was decided that the analysis should cover a five-year period. Thus, the problem could be stated briefly as follows:

> Which of the four alternative prices—$0.80, $0.85, $0.93, or $1.00
> —will yield the greatest total net profits after taxes (valued at the
> *end* of the five-year period, using either a 6-percent or a 10-percent
> discount rate) over the next five years?

Predictions of the combined sales of Kromel and Verlon for the next five years had been made. These were subject to considerable error. There were three separate forecasts—optimistic, pessimistic, and most probable. It was decided that all three predictions would be incorporated into the analysis. The total cost of the Kromel sold could be estimated within a small margin of error, which also meant that the net profit could be derived fairly readily for any given level of sales.

Clearly, this was a decision that involved some risk. Essentially, a choice had to be made among several pricing alternatives, the payoffs of which depended on which of several possible states of nature (i.e., customer response and reaction of competitors) would prevail. The actual states of nature that would prevail could not be predicted with certainty, but it was possible to estimate the *probability* that a particular state of nature would exist if a given price alternative were chosen.

What the management of Everclear needed was a prediction of what *might* happen if a given price change were made, as well as estimates of the *likelihood* of each possible series of events. Estimates of these possible states of nature and probabilities of their occurrence were built up from the combined judgment of Everclear's own sales personnel.

A "tree diagram" of possible chains of events was drawn up. A simplified version of this diagram is shown in Figure 11. Each "branch" of the "tree" represents one specific series of possible events. At stage 1, for example, Everclear had four price alternatives. If one of these were followed, then competing sellers might reduce their prices (stage 2) to any of the same levels. (It was assumed that if any Kromel producer lowered his price, the others would follow.) For any of these possible levels of Kromel prices, Verlon producers might retaliate by meeting the reduction fully, by meeting it half way, or by standing pat (stage 3). Under each of the four price strategies, present or potential producers might add to or initiate industry capacity (stage 4). For a given combination of Kromel and Verlon prices, penetration of segment A might be achieved by 1961, by 1962, and so on (stage 5). Assuming that segment A was penetrated, the Kromel share of it might be as low as 25 percent or as high as 100 percent (stage 6). Finally, for any given market share in segment A, Kromel market shares in the other three segments might follow a basic (predicted) pattern of growth or might be speeded up a year (stage 7).

For any of the possible series of events depicted in Figure 11, the sales and profit consequences for Everclear were then traced out. Included in the tree diagram (but not shown in Figure 11) were the three alternative forecasts (optimistic, pessimistic, and most probable) of combined Kromel-Verlon sales that had been made for the next five years. Thus, by following any one of these forecasts and any one of the complete "chains" of Figure 11, it was possible to arrive at a five-year forecast of Everclear's Kromel sales for each of the three alternative combined Kromel-Verlon sales figures. Since costs could be estimated from sales volume, the profits on Kromel sales could then be derived from the sales forecasts.

The next step was to collate the estimates of the probabilities assigned by Everclear sales personnel to each possible chain of events. (*Probability* measures the relative frequency with which one can expect an event to occur in the long run, or on the average. Thus, if one tosses a coin 1,000 times, he can expect heads to fall about 500 times [1/2].)

Once the estimates of probabilities were gathered, the decision model was programmed on an electronic computer for simulation of the various alternatives. In the computer simulation the sequence of possible subsequent events was laid out for each price alternative,

Figure 11   Everclear Plastics Company
Simplified "Tree Diagram" of Possible Chains of Events for Alternative Kromel Prices

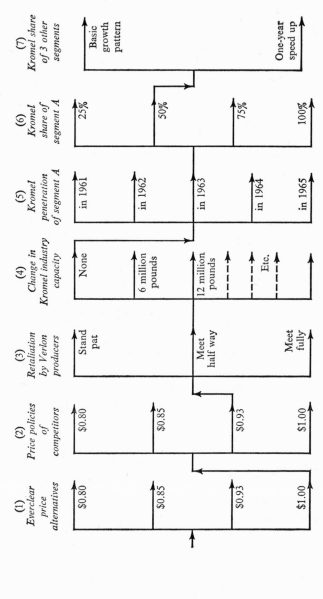

Source   Robert D. Buzzell, *Mathematical Models and Marketing Management* (Boston: Graduate School of Business Administration, Harvard University, 1964), p. 128, by permission.

and the appropriate probability estimates were assigned to each event on the basis of the estimates of the sales force. Then each price alternative was traced through to its possible results in terms of sales and profit. Next the cumulative, compounded profit at the end of five years associated with each outcome was computed from the equation

$$5\text{-year profit} = \sum_{i=1}^{5} (1 + r)^{5-i} (D_{ij} - Z_{ij}) (K_{ij}M_{ij})$$

in which

r = rate of interest on profits—either 6 percent or 10 percent per year

D_{ij} = Kromel price per pound in year i, under the jth outcome

Z_{ij} = total cost per pound of Kromel in year i, under the jth outcome

K_{ij} = Everclear's overall market share of Kromel sales in the ith year under the jth outcome

M_{ij} = total Kromel sales (in pounds) in year i under the jth outcome

Probabilities for each final result were computed by multiplying the probabilities of the events leading up to it. The computation procedure for one portion of the complete tree is illustrated in Figure 12, which shows some of the possible outcomes of the $1.00 price alternative. Here we see that if the price is kept at $1.00, the probability that Kromel would penetrate market segment A was estimated by the sales forces at 0.05, or five chances in 100.[34] Further along the left hand branch of the tree, the probabilities assigned to various market shares of segment A were multiplied by the 0.05 "probability of penetration" to derive the figures shown at the upper left of Figure 12. Thus, for example, if market segment A were penetrated, the probability of attaining a 25-percent share of the segment in 1961 was estimated by the sales force at 0.15. Since the probability of penetrating segment A at a price of $1.00 was 0.05, the *joint* probability of achieving penetration *and* attaining a 25-percent share was computed by multiplying the two probabilities, thus 0.05 (0.15) = 0.0075.

If Kromel did not penetrate market segment A during the first year at $1.00 per pound, a probability of 0.80 was attached to the likelihood that competitive producers of Kromel would reduce price to

[34] All the various probabilities estimated by the sales force are not given here.

$0.93 per pound. Multiplying this probability of 0.80 by 0.95 (probability of penetration) yielded a joint probability of 0.76 to the possibility of Kromel not penetrating A and Kromel price being reduced to $0.93 per pound.

However, if the price of Kromel were reduced to $0.93, Verlon retaliation had to be considered, which led to the joint probabilities assigned to the next set of tree branches. The joint probabilities of all possible sequences of events were determined in similar fashion by multiplying out the estimated probabilities at each stage. The probabilities for each possible final outcome were determined by following the procedure (shown in Figure 12) for all branches of the probability tree (sometimes referred to as a "decision tree").

For each price alternative, the expected values of compounded net profits over the five-year period were computed as follows:

$$\text{expected profit at a given price} = \sum_{j=1}^{n} P_j \left\{ \text{5-year profit of } j\text{th } outcome \right\}$$

in which P_j represented the probability of the jth final outcome for the given price.

These computations provided the estimates of expected cumulative net profits for the five-year planning period as shown in Table 3. These figures are based on a 6-percent interest rate and the "most probable" sales forecast for industry sales.

Table 3   Estimates of Expected Cumulative Net Profits

Price	Total net profit valued at end of period
$1.00	$6,625,000
.93	7,575,000
.85	8,475,000
.80	8,725,000

Source   Robert D. Buzzell, *Mathematical Models and Marketing Management* (Boston: Graduate School of Business Administration, Harvard University, 1964), p. 124, by permission.

Charts were prepared to depict the probabilities of penetrating segment A at the different alternative prices, the differences in estimated

Figure 12 Everclear Plastics Company: Simulated Experience—Kromel
(Portion of Probability Tree)

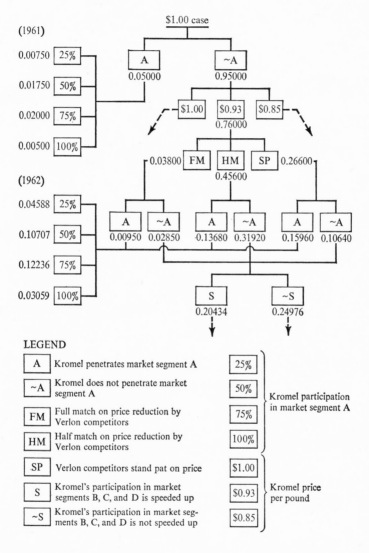

LEGEND

A	Kromel penetrates market segment A	25%	
~A	Kromel does not penetrate market segment A	50%	Kromel participation in market segment A
FM	Full match on price reduction by Verlon competitors	75%	
HM	Half match on price reduction by Verlon competitors	100%	
SP	Verlon competitors stand pat on price	$1.00	
S	Kromel's participation in market segments B, C, and D is speeded up	$0.93	Kromel price per pound
~S	Kromel's participation in market segments B, C, and D is not speeded up	$0.85	

Source Robert D. Buzzell, *Mathematical Models and Marketing Management* (Boston: Graduate School of Business Administration, Harvard University, 1964), p. 132, by permission.

Everclear sales of Kromel for each price reduction as compared with the price of $1.00, and the differences in compounded net profit at the different prices. When the results were compared for the two alternative interest rates (6 percent and 10 percent), and for the three industry sales forecasts (optimistic, pessimistic, and most probable), it was found that differences in these factors did not affect the profitability ranking of the four price strategies. In other words, the results clearly indicated that a price reduction was in order.

The calculations discussed above were based on the assumption that a price reduction would effectively discourage growth in total industry production capacity. A separate series of computations was then undertaken on the assumption that price reductions would *not* discourage the growth of productive capacity. These calculations yielded estimated total net profits for the firm as shown in Table 4.

Table 4   Estimates of Expected Cumulative Net Profits

Price	Total net profit valued at end of period
$1.00	$6,625,000
.93	6,725,000
.85	6,850,000
.80	6,300,000

Source   Robert D. Buzzell, *Mathematical Models and Marketing Management* (Boston: Graduate School of Business Administration, Harvard University, 1964), p. 125, by permission.

Comparing the two tables it became clear that the key factor underlying the differences in total net profits was Everclear's share of total Kromel sales. If it were assumed that a price reduction would discourage additions to industry capacity, then Everclear would probably win a higher share of the expanding market by reducing prices. If, however, the industry's capacity were increased despite Everclear's price cut, then it was possible that the increased volume of Everclear sales resulting from penetration of segment A would just about balance the lower revenue per unit, and the expected payoffs from alternative price strategies would be more nearly equal.

In short, the principal findings of the study were that any price reduction strategy would result in higher expected payoffs than that associated with maintaining a price of $1.00, that a price of $0.80 would lead to the highest expected profit among the alternatives considered (assuming that a price reduction would discourage growth of industry production capacity), and that the higher payoffs associated with the price reductions were largely dependent on the assumption that Everclear's future market share would be favorably influenced by reductions in the price of Kromel.

In sum, this model approached the problem of determining what price would be most profitable by attempting to predict the responses of customers and of present and prospective competitors. The task became essentially one of selecting appropriate ways of expressing possible changes in market behavior and then estimating the likelihood of each pattern of response.[35]

Among the weaknesses of this and other pricing models are the assumptions upon which they rest, particularly the assumption that a sales force can estimate accurately the probabilities that certain events will occur. However, it shows what can be done when information from the "field" is not available. The model also has the obvious advantage that it forces the executive to take a rigorous approach to decision making and makes possible the consideration of strategies under several different "states of nature." [36]

COMPETITIVE BIDDING

The term *competitive bidding* refers to situations in which a buyer asks two or more competing suppliers to submit bids on a proposed purchase or contract. The buyer then makes his purchase from the bidder who offers the best proposal. What is "best" to any given buyer depends on his particular interest, such as price, delivery time, reputation for quality of products, or past performance on contracts.

Competitive bidding is prevalent in the industrial-goods market. The majority of government agencies are required to request competitive bids on most of their purchases. It is of major importance in the growing defense industry, for example.[37]

[35] Buzzell, *op. cit.*, p. 205.
[36] Green, *op. cit.*, p. 14.
[37] Pricing in the defense industry is not discussed separately in this book. Two recent articles on the subject are Ralph C. Nash, Jr., "Pricing Policies in Government Contracts," *Law and Contemporary Problems,* Spring, 1964, and Walter F.

Where purchase orders or contracts are awarded largely on the basis of price (when all other factors, such as quality and service, are equal), the low bidder is normally the winner.[38] In such a situation the bidder has the problem of trying to submit a bid that will help his firm achieve its objectives, should the bid be accepted, while at the same time trying to beat competing bids if possible. To aid the seller in such situations, competitive bidding models—probably the most advanced normative models in the pricing field—have been developed. The problem to which they address themselves primarily is how a firm should determine the price that it submits as a competitive bid. The competitive bidding model that we will discuss briefly was originally developed by Lawrence Friedman.[39]

The course of action that a firm is best advised to follow in a competitive bidding situation depends to a great extent upon its objectives. There are, as we indicated in Chapter 2, many possible objectives that a firm could pursue. In the model we are examining it is assumed that the objective is the maximization of immediate profits. *Immediate profit* is defined as the difference between the bid made and the costs involved in fulfilling the contract if it is won.

The firm, of course, does not know if it will get the contract. If it gets the contract, its profit will indeed be the bid less the costs involved in fulfilling the contract. If it does not get the contract, however, its profit will be zero. Therefore, strictly speaking the profit to be derived from any particular bid is a matter of uncertainty. Clearly, probability theory is relevant in competitive bidding since as a rule the higher the bid, the less is the probability that the bidder will be awarded the contract in question.

Pettit, "The Defective Pricing Law and Implementing Regulations—A Year and a Half Later," *Law and Contemporary Problems,* Spring, 1964. See Arthur J. Katz, "The Dilemma of Selling to Uncle Sam," *Journal of Marketing,* April, 1965, for a discussion of the general problems involved in selling to the federal government.

[38] The term *contract* will be used here to indicate the business sought after in a competitive bidding situation.

[39] See Lawrence Friedman, "A Competitive Bidding Strategy," *Operations Research,* February, 1956. This model is also discussed in Miller and Starr, *op. cit.,* pp. 223–38; in Oxenfeldt, *Pricing for Marketing Executives* (San Francisco: Wadsworth, 1961), pp. 47–53; and in Oxenfeldt, Miller, Shuchman, and Winick, *op. cit.,* Chapter 3. The discussion presented here is derived from the latter publication. A recent version of a competitive bidding model may be found in Franz Edelman, "Art and Science of Competitive Bidding," *Harvard Business Review,* July–August, 1965.

Probability theory offers the concept of *expected profit,* a concept that was used in the Everclear Plastics Company model. Expected profit is the profit that can be expected from a given bid, given the probability that the bid will be accepted and a contract awarded. In essence, expected profit represents the average return per bid that the firm could expect if it repeated the same bid on a large number of contracts with precisely the same costs and if the probability of its being awarded the contract remained fixed. Suppose, for example, that on a particular contract the costs involved in fulfilling the contract would be $20,000 and that a bid of $40,000 has a probability of 0.30 of being accepted, while a bid of $30,000 has a probability of .70 of being accepted. Which of the two bids should the firm submit? If it is awarded the contract, the profit on the $40,000 bid would be $40,000 less $20,000, or $20,000. Its profit on the bid of $30,000 would be $30,000 less $20,000, or $10,000. If the bid is $40,000, there could be a return of $20,000 with a probability of 0.30, or a return of zero with a probability of 0.70 (i.e., $1 - 0.30$). Therefore, the expected profit on the bid of $40,000 is 0.30 ($20,000) + 0.70 ($0) = $6,000. For a bid of $30,000 there could be a return of $10,000 with a probability of 0.70, or a return of zero with a probability of 0.30 (i.e., $1 - 0.70$). Consequently, for the bid of $30,000 the expected profit is 0.70 ($10,000) + 0.30 ($0) = $7,000. Since the bid of $30,000 has the larger expected profit, it is the bid that should be submitted according to this approach.

To underscore the importance of the concept of expected profit in competitive bidding, the objective of the model is changed from "maximize immediate profit" to "maximize expected immediate profit." The equation for the firm's expected profit is

$$\text{expected profit} = p(X - C) + (1 - p)(0) = p(X - C)$$
since $(1 - p)(0) = 0$

where

p = probability of being awarded the contract, given the bid price
X = bid price
C = costs involved in fulfilling the contract

If the decision maker is able to calculate the probability that the firm will be awarded the contract for a given bid, he can calculate the expected profit. This probability is related to the size of the bid. In general, for a given contract, the higher the bid, the lower the probability that the firm will be awarded the contract.

Suppose that all the necessary information were available and that the relationship between the probability of award and the size of the bid were known. For example, assume that a firm is bidding on a contract that will cost $8,000 to fulfill. To simplify matters, let us further assume that all bids must be in units of $1,000. Then the relationship between the probability of award and the size of the bid might be presented as in Table 5.

Table 5 Size of Bid and Probability of Award

Bid X	Probability of award p
$ 7,000	1.00
8,000	0.95
9,000	0.85
10,000	0.60
11,000	0.30
12,000	0.10
13,000	0

Source From *Insights into Pricing* by Oxenfeldt, Miller, Shuchman, and Winick, p. 49. © 1961 by Wadsworth Publishing Company, Inc., Belmont, California. Reprinted by permission of the publisher.

It shows that for each bid there is a given probability of being awarded the contract if the bid is made. A bid of $7,000 would certainly win the contract, but a bid of $8,000 has a probability of only 0.95 of being awarded the contract. This is because there is a chance that one or more competitors will submit a bid of $7,000. The probability of obtaining the award decreases further as the bid price increases, and the chances that competitors will undercut the given price become greater and greater.

On the basis of the above information, one is able to calculate the expected profit for any bid. Ignoring for the moment the possibility of ties (equal bids), let us suppose that a bid of $9,000 is submitted and that the costs involved are $8,000. Table 5 tells us that the probability of the firm being awarded the contract is 0.85. Translating this data into the equation for expected profit we have

$$\text{expected profit} = p(X - C)$$
$$= 0.85(\$9,000 - \$8,000)$$
$$= \$850$$

By using the same approach, the expected profit for each bid can be calculated to yield the data listed in Table 6.

Here we see that the maximum expected profit of $1,200 accompanies a bid of $10,000. This then is the bid that the firm should make if its objective is to maximize its expected immediate profit because this bid, if it were to be repeated a large number of times under identical circumstances, would give the firm an average return of $1,200 per bid, greater than that for any other bid.

In the preceding example, it was assumed that the costs of fulfilling the contract were known to be $8,000. In reality, however, a firm is not likely to know exactly what its costs will be. What the decision

Table 6 Calculation of Expected Profit

Bid	Expected profit		
$ 7,000	1.00 ($ 7,000 — $8,000) =	—	$1,000
8,000	0.95 ($ 8,000 — $8,000) =		0
9,000	0.85 ($ 9,000 — $8,000) =		850
10,000	0.60 ($10,000 — $8,000) =		1,200
11,000	0.30 ($11,000 — $8,000) =		900
12,000	0.10 ($12,000 — $8,000) =		400
13,000	0 ($13,000 — $8,000) =		0

Source From *Insights into Pricing* by Oxenfeldt, Miller, Shuchman, and Winick, p. 51. © 1961 by Wadsworth Publishing Company, Inc., Belmont, California. Reprinted by permission of the publisher.

maker can do is to accumulate information on the relationship between the firm's estimates and the actual costs of the contracts that it has been awarded in the past. Ideally, the executive will be able to refer to records showing the ratio between the estimated costs on which the bids were based, and the actual final costs. A distribution of these ratios can be developed. However, it will have no effect on the bid as long as the errors in cost estimates are not related to the probabilities given in Table 5. As long as this is the case, then errors in estimating costs will have no effect on the bid, since they would average out in the calculations even if they were included. Suppose, for example, that the actual costs in the example discussed above turned out to be anywhere between $6,500 and $9,500, but that they were estimated at $8,000. In such a situation, the actual amount of profit on a contract awarded for any one bid could range from $1,500 below to $1,500 above the expected profit for that bid. The point to remember, however, is that the expected profits on all bids would be affected equally by this uncertainty; therefore, the $10,000 bid would still give the maximum expected profit. In other words, the uncertainty about costs increases the variability of actual profits without affecting the relative advantages of various bids.

The discussion thus far suggests that it is possible for a firm to determine the bid that will maximize its expected profit if it knows the distribution of probabilities of award as a function of the amount of the bid. The question is how to determine this distribution.

Since it is customary for buyers to announce the bids received on contracts after they have been awarded, it is usually possible to study the bidding behavior of competitors. Suppose firm A has one competitor, B, bidding for a particular contract. Firm A would like to know what this competitor has bid on every previous contract for which A has made a cost estimate. When this information is available it is possible to determine the ratio of B's bid to the cost estimate (not the bid) of A. The ratio we are interested in is B's bid divided by A's cost estimate. Thus, if on a particular contract A's cost were $8,500 and B's bid were $10,200, the ratio would be $10,200/$8,500, or 1.2. If similar information on all past contracts is available, it could be summarized in tabular form showing the total number of times that each ratio occurred, as in Table 7.

There are a total of fifty ratios in Table 7. Out of the fifty ratios, the ratio 1.2 occurred eleven times. Therefore, the probability of its occurrence is 11/50, or 0.22. If the probability of occurrence is computed for each ratio, we can show these probabilities as in the second column of Table 8.

This table indicates that, for example, 30 percent of the time (a probability of 0.30), competitor B submitted bids that were 1.3 times A's cost estimate for the contract. Table 8 is a probability mass function. The probability that the competitor's bid will be more than or equal to any particular ratio to A's cost estimate can be determined by summing the probabilities from the bottom of the table. The results are presented in the third column of Table 8, which is called a

Table 7   Relation of B's Bids to A's Cost Estimates

Ratio of B's bids to A's cost estimates	Number of occurrences
0.9	1
1.0	3
1.1	5
1.2	11
1.3	15
1.4	8
1.5	4
1.6	3
Total	50

Source From *Insights into Pricing* by Oxenfeldt, Miller, Shuchman, and Winick, p. 53. © 1961 by Wadsworth Publishing Company, Inc., Belmont, California. Reprinted by permission of the publisher.

Table 8   Probabilities of Given Ratios

Ratio of B's bids to A's cost estimates	Probability of ratio	Probability that B's bid $\geq$ ratio
0.9	0.02	1.00
1.0	0.06	0.98
1.1	0.10	0.92
1.2	0.22	0.82
1.3	0.30	0.60
1.4	0.16	0.30
1.5	0.08	0.14
1.6	0.06	0.06

Source Columns 1 and 2 from *Insights into Pricing* by Oxenfeldt, Miller, Shuchman, and Winick, p. 54. © 1961 by Wadsworth Publishing Company, Inc., Belmont, California. Reprinted by permission of the publisher. Column 3 prepared by author.

probability distribution function. Thus, for example, B will bid at a level more than or equal to 1.5 times A's cost estimate with probability $0.06 + 0.08 = 0.14$.

A can reconstruct its own table of probabilities for obtaining the award by underbidding B. To eliminate the possibility of tie bids it is simple to lower A's bid slightly. Thus, one can say that there is a probability of 1.00 that a bid of 0.89 times A's cost estimate will be lower than B's bid. By the same token, a bid of 0.99 times A's cost estimate will be lower than B's bid with the probability of $1 - 0.02 = 0.98$, and a bid of 1.09 times A's cost estimate will be lower than B's bid with the probability of $1 - 0.02 - 0.06 = 0.92$. Such computations yield the data listed in Table 9.

Table 9 gives the probability that any particular bid, expressed as a multiple of A's cost estimate, will be lower than B's bid. Furthermore, assuming that B is the only competitor of A, the table shows the probability that the contract will be awarded to A, as a function of the amount of the bid. It is similar in concept to Table 5. With this information firm A can now determine the bid that will give the maximum expected profit, still assuming that B is the only competitor. Suppose, for example, that a bid of 1.09C (where C = A's estimated costs of fulfilling the contract) is made. Table 9 indicates that the

Table 9   Probability That Certain Bids Will Be Lower Than B's Bids

Bid, as multiple of A's cost estimate	Probability that bid is lower than B's bid
0.89	1.00
0.99	0.98
1.09	0.92
1.19	0.82
1.29	0.60
1.39	0.30
1.49	0.14
1.59	0.06
1.69	0

Source   From *Insights into Pricing* by Oxenfeldt, Miller, Shuchman, and Winick, p. 55. © 1961 by Wadsworth Publishing Company, Inc., Belmont, California. Reprinted by permission of the publisher.

probability is 0.92 that the contract will be won. If the contract is won, the firm will make an actual profit (not expected profit) of $X - C$, where X = bid price and C = estimated costs of fulfilling the contract, or $1.09C - C = 0.09C$. The expected profit is determined by the equation for expected profit

$$\text{expected profit} = p(X - C)$$

Since $p = 0.92$ then

$$\text{expected profit} = 0.92(0.09C)$$
$$= 0.0828C$$

If the firm bid 1.19C, then

$$\text{expected profit} = 0.82(1.19C - C)$$
$$= 0.82(0.19C)$$
$$= 0.1558C$$

Proceeding in the same way with the other bids listed in Table 9, we obtain the data shown in Table 10.

Clearly, a bid of 1.29C will yield the maximum expected profit, which is 0.1740C. If C = \$8,000, the bid of 1.29C represents 1.29(\$8,000), or \$10,320, which will produce an expected profit of 0.1740(\$8,000), or \$1,392.

The approach discussed above enables the firm to select the profit-maximizing bid when there is only one competitor. If there is more than one known competitor involved, the same procedure is followed, except that now the price maker must derive a probability distribution showing the probability that a given bid will be lower than that

Table 10   Expected Profits from Certain Bids

Bid, as multiple of cost estimate	Expected profit where B is the only competitor		
0.89	1.00 (0.89C − C)	=	− 0.1100C
0.99	0.98 (0.99C − C)	=	− 0.0098C
1.09	0.92 (1.09C − C)	=	0.0828C
1.19	0.82 (1.19C − C)	=	0.1558C
1.29	0.60 (1.29C − C)	=	0.1740C
1.39	0.30 (1.39C − C)	=	0.1170C
1.49	0.14 (1.49C − C)	=	0.0786C
1.59	0.06 (1.59C − C)	=	0.0354C

Source   From *Insights into Pricing* by Oxenfeldt, Miller, Shuchman, and Winick, p. 56. © 1961 by Wadsworth Publishing Company, Inc., Belmont, California. Reprinted by permission of the publisher.

of *each* competitor. The final probability of award distribution is then determined by multiplying, for each bid, the entries of each competitor for that bid. This distribution provides the necessary information for calculating the expected profit for each bid, enabling the decision maker to choose the bid with the maximum expected profit.

When the price maker does not know his competitors and thus has no specific information about the bidding behavior of each of them, he is forced to rely upon less precise information in selecting his bid. Instead of using information based on specific competitors, the firm can use information about its "average" or "typical" competitor and project the overall behavior of all past competitors on those contracts for which the firm has made cost estimates. The procedure is the same as before except that all competitors are lumped together into one probability mass function.

Suppose that the decision maker does not know the identity of his competitors but does know how many of them there are on a particular contract. In such a situation he might use the average distribution function for the average or typical competitor as if it applied to each of the unknown competitors and then proceed as in the case where competitors were known. If the firm does not know the number of competitors on a particular contract, it must estimate the number in some way.

Like any models, competitive bidding models are as "realistic" as the assumptions upon which they rest. In the model we have just described one might question the assumption that maximization of profits is the firm's objective, or that information about past bidding by competitors is available. Also, what happens when an *industry* has had no experience in bidding and hence no past information to go on? Furthermore, what if a given *firm* has no bidding experience (although the industry does) and hence can provide no cost estimates to compare against the past bids of competitors? The difficulties in making accurate cost estimates are also overlooked by such models. For reasons such as these competitive bidding models rarely can be as precise as our example might suggest. Decision makers usually do not have accurate estimates of the probability of bids made by competitors or of the profits they would make on given contracts.

Despite the fact that all the information necessary for a competitive bidding model may not exist, such a model helps pinpoint for the price maker the basic elements in a competitive bidding situation and their relationships with one another. It also helps to reduce the uncertainty involved in selecting the best bid.

PREDICTIVE MODELS

The pricing models we have discussed so far are normative, or control, pricing models. In addition to such normative models, there are other pricing models designed primarily to permit prediction of future events, as well as to describe objectives and events. A few examples of such predictive models should be noted, although a detailed discussion of such models would be beyond the scope of this text.

William M. Morgenroth, for example, has developed a model intended to assist in identifying and understanding various determinants of prices under a situation of price leadership.[40] The model, which makes use of a "binary flow chart," [41] attempts to describe the pricing process, thereby enabling one to predict the behavior of a follower firm when a price leader makes a price adjustment.

A pricing model of decision making in one department of a large retail department store is offered by Richard M. Cyert and James G. March.[42] This model could easily be generalized to apply to other departments in that department store, as well as to other department stores. It consists of flow charts representing the decision-making process dealing with the department's sales and markup goals. Its objective is to enable one to predict the actions that management might take when certain conditions arise.

Finally, William F. Massy and Ronald E. Frank have developed a mathematical model, which they call a "distributed lag" model, that is designed to predict how a firm's changes in price and "dealing" activity (special price cuts at retail) will affect its market share over a period of weeks for frequently purchased food and household products.[43] It can also be used to determine whether or not the market for the products studied should be divided into segments because of different response patterns to variables such as price and dealing activity.

[40] "A Method for Understanding Price Determinants," *Journal of Marketing Research,* August, 1964.
[41] The "binary flow chart" used by Morgenroth is a form of a tree diagram in which at each successive step the possibilities are limited to two—yes and no.
[42] *A Behavioral Theory of the Firm* (Englewood Cliffs, N.J.: Prentice-Hall, 1963), Chapter 7.
[43] "Short Term Prices and Dealing Effects in Selected Market Segments," *Journal of Marketing Research,* May, 1965.

Selected References

Decision theory has been dealt with in a number of publications. Good examples are David W. Miller and Martin K. Starr, *Executive Decisions and Operations Research* (Englewood Cliffs, N.J.: Prentice-Hall, 1960), Chapters 3, 4, 5, and 14; William J. Baumol, *Economic Theory and Operations Analysis,* 2nd ed. (Englewood Cliffs, N.J.: Prentice-Hall, 1965), Chapter 24; and Alfred Oxenfeldt, David Miller, Abraham Shuchman, and Charles Winick, *Insights into Pricing* (Belmont, Calif.: Wadsworth, 1961), Chapter 1.

There is a voluminous literature available on the general subject of operations research and OR models. One standard book in the field is C. West Churchman, Russell L. Ackoff, and E. Leonard Arnoff, *Introduction to Operations Research* (New York: John Wiley and Sons, 1957). Other good texts are Maurice Sasieni, Arthur Yaspan, and Lawrence Friedman, *Operations Research: Methods and Problems* (New York: John Wiley and Sons, 1959); Miller and Starr, *Executive Decisions and Operations Research;* and Abraham Shuchman, *Scientific Decision Making in Business* (New York: Holt, Rinehart and Winston, 1963).

Discussions of operations research and scientific models as they might be applied to marketing decisions are found in Frank M. Bass, *et al., Mathematical Models and Methods in Marketing* (Homewood, Ill.: Irwin, 1961); Ronald E. Frank, Alfred E. Kuehn, and William F. Massy, *Quantitative Techniques in Marketing Analysis* (Homewood, Ill.: Irwin, 1962); Wroe Alderson and Stanley J. Shapiro, eds., *Marketing and the Computer* (Englewood Cliffs, N.J.: Prentice-Hall, 1962); Ralph L. Day, ed., *Marketing Models* (Scranton, Pa.: International Textbook, 1964); Robert D. Buzzell, *Mathematical Models and Marketing Management* (Boston: Graduate School of Business Administration, Harvard University, 1964); George Schwartz, ed., *Science in Marketing* (New York: John Wiley and Sons, 1965), Chapters 15 and 16; and Peter Langhoff, ed., *Models, Measurement, and Marketing* (Englewood Cliffs, N.J.: Prentice-Hall, 1965).

Complete descriptions of particular pricing models can be found in the publications cited in the footnotes in the section of this chapter where specific pricing models are discussed.

6

PRICING BY MANUFACTURERS

THE NATURE OF THE PRICING DECISION
OF MANUFACTURERS

As we mentioned in Chapter 2, manufacturers generally have more need for a price policy than do, say, producers of primary products or distributors because they generally have more discretion or latitude in pricing. The chief reason for this greater discretion is that there is generally more product differentiation in manufactured goods and that the firms involved are larger and fewer in number. For reasons such as these, price policy is generally of more importance in manufacturing than in other kinds of economic activity.

Generally speaking, pricing by manufacturers also receives more attention from government agencies, labor unions, consumer organizations, and other groups than pricing by firms in primary production or in distribution. Although all prices produce repercussions in the economy as a whole, the impact on the economy of the prices of manufacturers is crucial. This is particularly true of the prices established by the larger firms; pricing decisions made by large corporations such as automobile manufacturers, steel companies, and appliance makers have important effects on a vast number of people, including distributors, industrial buyers, consumers, and employees.

In contrast to other sectors of the economy, primary producers in particular, manufacturers have more latitude in the marketing approaches available to them. It is much easier for them to adjust production, make changes in marketing or selling programs, and

169

make use of the various nonprice modes of competition, such as quality and services, in addition to changing price itself to meet changing market conditions. Here again the reason is that there is greater product differentiation among manufacturers and a greater frequency of oligopoly-type competitive situations.

It is difficult to generalize about the topic of present pricing policies and procedures of manufacturers, or about what these policies and procedures should be. Manufacturers differ greatly in kinds of products produced, size of firm, and in their approaches to their pricing problems. By the same token, the pricing problems themselves vary considerably from industry to industry. It is possible, however, to isolate some basic characteristics of pricing by manufacturers, some basic pricing problems that they face, the kinds of decisions that must be made, and the manner in which such problems are, and should be, handled.

SOME BASIC PRICING DECISIONS THAT MANUFACTURERS MUST MAKE

DETERMINATION OF THE LEVEL OF PRICES

One important decision that any manufacturer must make is the price level at which the firm is to position itself in relation to other firms in the industry. A firm may choose to price "at the market," "below the market," or "above the market." Whichever approach is taken will directly affect other decisions that must be made about prices and other marketing tools. Sometimes the price level is dictated by the attributes selected for the product the firm is to manufacture. In other cases, the choice of price level is less clear-cut.

Pricing at the market   As a general rule, it is wise to set prices approximately equal to those of competitors if there is little product differentiation between the offerings of competing firms in an industry. As noted earlier, the ability to price above competitors is sharply limited in such a situation, and prices that are below those of competitors may lead to retaliation and even price warfare.

Other factors that may induce a manufacturer to price his product at the market are that the buyers of the product may expect the prices of different sellers to be the same or similar (in fact, firms sometimes deliberately design and produce a product that they will be able to sell at "established" prices); or that certain prices are traditional or customary in the industry (as in the case of soft drinks and chewing gum); or that the firm is anxious not to upset the status quo in the industry, thus avoiding "ruinous competition"; or that the firm is following a price leader(s) for one or more of the reasons stated in Chapter 3; or that the firm's management is uncertain about the nature of the demand for the product and chooses to match competitors' prices "to be on the safe side." [1]

In some of the situations cited above, sellers who price at the market are, in effect, assuming that they face a kinked demand curve such as the one used in Chapter 1 to describe an oligopoly situation. The firm assumes that a higher price than those of competitors would reduce sales substantially, whereas a lower price than that charged by competitors would not appreciably increase sales. In other words, they believe that the demand curve for their products is "kinked" at the current price.[2]

When a firm prices at the market, price plays a relatively more neutral role in the marketing mix than would otherwise be the case, and other elements in the mix become relatively more important in building sales volume.

Pricing below the market   Pricing below the prices of competitors is the most aggressive way in which price can be used to build sales volume. Factors that might induce a manufacturer to price his products below the market are a desire to expand market share, to give customers the best value for the money paid, or to discourage the entry or growth of competitors. A firm might also price below the market if it has lower costs than competitors have or if its product is of lower quality.

Before initiating such a policy, the decision maker should definitely

---

[1] In a study of small manufacturers (250 or fewer employees) it was found that such firms very often match prices of their principal competitor, or, in effect, they are price followers. The authors conclude that: "These small manufacturers are, for the most part, not sufficiently informed about their own costs and market conditions to make fully rational price decisions. Under these circumstances, a 'followership' policy, even if not forced upon them, is both logical and simpler from their point of view." See Robert F. Lanzillotti and Gordon O. Parrish, *Pricing, Production, and Marketing Policies of Small Manufacturers* (Pullman, Wash.: Washington State University Press, 1964), pp. 15–16.

[2] This fact is pointed out by Edward R. Hawkins in "Price Policies and Theory," *Journal of Marketing,* January, 1954, pp. 236–37.

consider the nature of the demand for his firm's product. Unless the price elasticity of demand for the product is such that the lower prices will result in a meaningful increase in sales, it is generally unwise to adopt such a price policy. When there is sufficient price elasticity of demand, however, pricing below the market may give the firm an advantage over its competitors. But there are at least two possible dangers in pricing below the market. The first is that competitors may retaliate by matching the low prices, thus leaving the initiating firm with no advantage but merely a lower total revenue. As we have seen, retaliation is most likely to occur in those industries in which there is little product differentiation. Only when a firm enjoys some product differentiation does it feel that it need not match the prices of its rivals. The second danger is that selling below the market may "cheapen" the image of the product in question in the eyes of customers. As pointed out in Chapter 2, customers, particularly the buyers of consumer goods, frequently equate price with quality. To the extent that buyers feel this way, the low prices may actually discourage sales rather than increase them.

Pricing above the market   Charging higher prices than those of competitors is generally not possible unless there is a high degree of product differentiation that causes customers to be willing to pay the higher price. Otherwise the price elasticity of demand for the product in question will cause sales volume to fall off.

There are several reasons that might cause a firm to adopt such an approach to pricing. For example, a firm may have higher costs than its competitors (although this is no guarantee that customers are willing to pay the higher prices), or perhaps the firm expects to build a "prestige" image for the product or the firm as a whole, or perhaps the product is genuinely superior and "worth" more than those of competitors, or perhaps the manufacturer is eager to obtain the aggressive cooperation of middlemen in selling the product by offering them above-average margins.

ONE-PRICE POLICY VERSUS VARYING PRICES

A firm is said to follow a "one-price" policy if it charges uniform prices so that all buyers who purchase a product under substantially similar circumstances pay the same price. However, a one-price policy should not be confused with what is sometimes referred to as a "single-price" policy, which means the seller charges all customers the same price for a product, regardless of quantities purchased or other factors that make the circumstances surrounding the sales dissimilar. Under a one-price policy those who buy different quantities of a product may be charged different prices. Nonetheless, the terms of sale are known and administered uniformly and all who buy the same quantity pay the same price.

A one-price policy does not mean that prices do not change or that they do not change very often. Prices may change quite frequently under a one-price policy, but, at any one time, all customers who buy the same quantities under similar circumstances pay the same price.

In contrast, when different prices are charged different buyers of the same quantity of goods depending on competitive factors or the bargaining ability of the buyer, they are called "varying prices." Thus, in the case of varying prices there is the added element of bargaining or negotiation.

A one-price policy is found most often at the retail level in the United States, although it is growing in importance in manufacturing and wholesaling because of its peculiar advantages. The question of whether or not a manufacturer should use a one-price policy or resort to varying prices is, of necessity, related to the legal limitations imposed by the Robinson-Patman Act, which was discussed in some detail in Chapter 4. Therefore, in the following discussion we will confine ourselves to those nonlegal considerations that affect the choice between a one-price policy and a varying-prices policy.[3]

Varying prices Under a policy of varying prices, adjustments in prices are made when competitive conditions seem to call for a change. In such a case different buyers ordering the same quantities of the product under virtually identical conditions may pay very different prices. Price may be lowered in order to make a sale or raised if conditions indicate that such a move is possible.

If a policy of varying prices is to be successful, different buyers must have different price elasticities of demand for the product. Otherwise a one-price policy should generally be adopted. Furthermore, buyers must be separated geographically or in some other way so that if the firm grants a low price to one, it does not have to grant a low price to other buyers as well.

The principal advantage in following a policy of varying prices is

[3] Varying prices by giving discounts to buyers will be discussed in depth in Chapter 8.

that prices can be adjusted to meet changing conditions in the market place, thereby enabling the firm to make sales that otherwise would not be made. In addition, varying prices are often a particularly effective method of attracting new customers. Thus, in general, by taking advantage of the different price elasticities of demand that buyers display for the product, total revenue may be more nearly maximized than under a one-price policy.

However, there are several possible disadvantages in using varying prices.

1. Varying prices often requires that pricing authority be delegated to sales managers or salesmen. This often necessitates a higher caliber and more expensive sales force than the firm needs when using a one-price policy.
2. Price bargaining is a time-consuming process, a factor that also increases the cost of selling.
3. Delegation of pricing authority means the loss of centralized control over prices, which may be vital in light of other circumstances.
4. Some customers may be expected to raise objections to the policy if it means that they must pay higher prices than other customers under the same circumstances.
5. Permitting sales personnel to manipulate prices may encourage them to cut prices whenever they are faced with a difficult sale and if this happens frequently the result will simply be a lower overall level of prices. Indeed, it is probably true that the less effective a salesman is, the more likely it is that he will resort to price cutting to obtain a sale.
6. The use of varying prices can lead to legal complications involving the Robinson-Patman Act for firms that engage in interstate commerce.

One-price policy A one-price policy has certain advantages of its own and, at the same time, permits the firm to avoid many of the disadvantages of varying prices. A principal advantage of following a one-price policy is that it is easier to administer. It also simplifies the selling process by eliminating any bargaining over price. This, in turn, means that the sales task delegated to sales people does not involve price making. In practice, this means that the attributes of the product in question tend to be emphasized to a greater extent in the sales approach.

Another advantage of the one-price approach is that it is considered to be fair to all buyers, regardless of their ability to bargain or of the competitive situation surrounding the transaction. Such an approach to pricing is less likely to endanger the good will of buyers than is the use of varying prices.

Because of these clear-cut advantages over varying prices, manufacturers seem to be adopting a one-price policy to a far greater extent in recent years than in the past, although considerable price negotiation between manufacturers and their customers still takes place.

MARKET SEGMENTATION

When manufacturers find that the total heterogeneous market they serve is composed of various homogeneous submarkets, or segments, and try to take advantage of this fact in their marketing program, they are said to practice "market segmentation." The segments may be based on geography or on some characteristic of the product's buyers, such as income, education, occupation, kind of industry, size of firm, or product preferences. Given this segmentation, the manufacturer may be able to design a marketing program in which each segment is appealed to in a way that will maximize sales to that segment.

If different market segments respond differently to price changes, they are dissimilar in price elasticity of demand. Prices can be established so that they appeal only to the most important segment(s) in the market, or so that they appeal to the largest number of segments in the market. But in order to use price effectively in this manner it is imperative that the firm have some knowledge of the price elasticity of demand for each of the different market segments.

Thus, assuming that a given manufacturer's total market is made up of several segments, each of which is willing to pay up to a given amount for a given quantity of the product, there are two kinds of decisions to be made. First the firm must decided to *which* segment(s) it should try to appeal, and second, it must decide *how* to make price appeals to the several segments.

Which segments to appeal to   The firm must decide which of the segments it has identified it should try to reach. This is a basic marketing decision that affects all aspects of the marketing program, not just price. It is based on factors such as the size of the potential market in each segment, the ability of the firm to produce and market the product to one or more segments, the location of the segments (if based on geographic factors), and the competitive situation within each segment.

How to appeal to multiple segments   Once it is decided which segments of the market are to become targets of the marketing program of the firm, management must determine the timing of the pricing designed to appeal to these segments. The various segments can be approached over a period of time or simultaneously. If the former approach is taken, then it is possible to have one product and one price at any particular time and yet change this price over time. Thus, a new product may be introduced at a fairly high price, which is designed to attract that portion of the market that is relatively insensitive to price. After a period of time the price may be lowered a step in order to reach another segment of the market. Thus the firm may lower its price by steps and, by "sliding down the demand curve," eventually tap each of the segments of the entire market. Notice, however, that it is highly unlikely that a firm would find the reverse of this procedure successful, that is, raising the price over time to reach additional market segments.

Experience indicates that "sliding down the demand curve" can be used successfully only if the firm is able to wait before it taps the entire market that it wants to reach eventually, if the life expectancy of the product is sufficiently long to permit such a pricing procedure, and if the product in question is a fairly well-differentiated new product for which there is an inelastic demand in the initial target segment.[4]

If, on the other hand, it is decided that a price appeal will be made to two or more segments of the total market simultaneously, there are several methods from which to choose. The first alternative is to offer different segments different prices for the same product depending upon their price elasticity of demand. One serious problem with this approach for firms in interstate commerce is that charging different prices for a product that is designed to appeal to different broad market segments is likely to constitute a violation of the Robinson-Patman Act. Such a policy may also cause much ill will in some segments of the market. Another difficulty with this approach is the

----

[4] Pricing of new products is discussed in detail on pp. 185–90 of this chapter.

problem of keeping proper separation of the various segments so that, if a low price is offered to one segment, the firm will not encounter demands for equally low prices in other segments.

The second alternative is to offer the market several different products, all in the same generic class of product. The different products in the line may differ in size or quality (based on both tangible and intangible attributes) but still carry the same brand name. Differences between the products in the line may be small or large. Alternatively, the products may carry different brand names and may either differ or not in size or quality. In any case, the several products in the line may be priced so that each appeals to a particular segment of the market.

The multiple-product approach avoids most of the legal problems involving the Robinson-Patman Act as long as the products in the line can be shown to be different. Problems of ill will are not as likely to arise, and it is easier to keep segments separated. Now let us consider the actual problem of pricing a multiple-product line.

PRODUCT-LINE DECISIONS

Although many manufacturers produce just one type of product, almost every manufacturer produces more than one version of such a product. Usually, the manufacturer produces the product in several different sizes, colors, structural strengths, flavors, or with different horsepower or accessories so that, in effect, he has a "line" of products to offer to the market, rather than a single product.[5] Many manufacturers also produce two or more generic products and several different versions of each product type. Thus, the products in the product line may be different versions of the same generic product, and hence substitutes for one another, such as different sizes of a detergent with the same brand name or different brands of the same generic product, or they may be different, but related, complementary products, such as cameras and film. On the other hand, the different products may be entirely unrelated in so far as the market is concerned (this may even be true of the costs of producing these products if entirely different manufacturing plants are involved), ex-

---

[5] In the following discussion different versions of the same generic product are referred to as "different products."

cept to the extent that the reputation of one helps or hinders the sale of the others. Clearly, the pricing approach should differ for each of these kinds of relationships.

The fact that the firm is selling more than one product makes the pricing function, and other marketing functions, much more difficult than would be the case if there were only one product. When establishing a price for a product in such a situation, one must take into account the impact of the price of one product on another product and the proper relationship that should exist between them.

SOME BASIC CONSIDERATIONS

Joel Dean has pointed out that several alternative policies might be followed in product-line pricing.[6] One possibility is to price the different products in the line in proportion to some concept of costs, such as full costs, incremental costs, or conversion costs.[7] Although this is a popular approach to product-line pricing, it has an important drawback in that it ignores entirely the demand side of the picture.

A better approach is to relate product-line pricing to price elasticity of demand for the different products to be priced and to the nature of competition surrounding each product, as well as to costs.[8] The price maker must evaluate each product individually in light of these three concepts. Consideration then also must be given to the effect of the price of one product on the sales of other products in the line.

PRICING SUBSTITUTES

When a firm produces different versions or models of the same generic product, the different products in the line are often, in effect, substitutes for one another. To this extent, the firm is actually competing against itself. Dean discusses in some detail the problems of pricing products that differ in size and products that differ in quality.[9]

---

[6] *Managerial Economics* (Englewood Cliffs, N.J.: Prentice-Hall, 1951), pp. 472–77. See also his "Problems of Product Line Pricing," *Journal of Marketing,* January, 1950.

[7] Conversion costs are the labor and overhead costs incurred in the conversion of raw materials into finished products.

[8] Dean, *Managerial Economics,* p. 477.

[9] *Ibid.,* pp. 485–90.

Pricing products that differ in size The first question to be answered when products of the same generic kind differ in size is whether prices should also differ. If the benefits to buyers do not vary with size (as is the case, for example, with some kinds of clothing), the manufacturer may only be able to charge a uniform price regardless of size since buyers would be unwilling to pay different prices. If benefits to buyers do vary with size, however, and if it is decided that prices should vary accordingly, the problem then becomes one of deciding how the differences in prices should be determined. Should differences in prices be based solely on differences in size? Such an approach would be relatively simple from an administrative point of view but would only by accident provide the prices that would enable the firm to reach its objectives. The same can be said of pricing according to differences in costs. The problem with both methods is that they ignore price elasticity of demand and competition or, in short, the market side of the problem. The ideal approach is to price each size in the line in terms of elasticity and competition, as well as in terms of size and costs.

Pricing according to differences in size or costs alone also fails to recognize the fact that a given price on one product can affect the sales of other products. The smallest size in the line, for example, may be priced very low in order to encourage "trial" purchases by buyers in the hope that they will later purchase larger sizes as regular buyers. On the other hand, the firm may want to encourage the purchase of the largest sizes in the line and price these sizes lower per pound, ounce, foot, etc., than the smaller sizes in order to attract customers to the larger sizes.[10] Pricing according to differences in size or costs also overlooks the reasons for having different sizes in the line. For example, the firm's primary purpose of having different sizes in the product line may be to appeal to several different market segments. In such a case the price elasticity of demand in each segment is probably more important to the price maker than differences in size or costs as a determinant of differences in prices.

Pricing products that differ in quality The approach to pricing products in a line that differ in quality is similar to that for products that differ in size. The first question, again, is whether the different

---

[10] Informal studies of package sizes, their contents, and their retail prices indicate, however, that for some consumer products, as one moves from the medium sizes up to the very largest sizes, prices sometimes increase rather than decrease per unit.

products should carry different prices. Although the answer to this question is obviously yes, unless buyers of the product recognize the quality differences and the benefits they derive from them, it will be difficult to charge different prices for products that differ in quality. On the other hand, if different prices are to be charged for products of different quality (or size), then the differences in prices must be great enough to be noticed and considered meaningful by the buyer.

Assuming that it is decided that prices should be different, a firm might attempt to price its products according to differences in quality (if they can be measured) or according to differences in costs. Here again, although such an approach is relatively easy to administer, it ignores the demand side of the problem by failing to consider price elasticity of demand and competition. Only by coincidence would the resultant prices help to reach the objectives of the firm. Thus, as before, each product in the line must be appraised according to price elasticity of demand and competitive situation.

The relationship between the prices charged for the products must also be considered. To assess this relationship accurately, the firm must study it in light of its own objectives in putting several different quality levels in the line. For example, as Dean points out, the purpose of the highest-quality product in the line may be to bring prestige to the entire line; such products should be priced so that they will help bring about the desired effect on buyers' attitudes toward the other products in the line.[11] In contrast, the chief objective of the lowest-quality products may be to counter or discourage price competition from other firms without lowering prices on the other products in the line. In such a situation the lower-quality products are in the line primarily to protect the prices of the other products. Consequently, the prices of competing products very nearly dictate the prices to be charged on products included in a line for such a purpose. Lower-quality, low-price products may also be added to a line in order to attract new buyers, who may later trade up to more expensive products in the line. In other situations products are added to a line largely for the purpose of making use of excess capacity. As indicated in Chapter 2, relatively low prices may be charged for such products, in contrast with the "normal" prices charged for other products in the line.

[11] *Managerial Economics,* pp. 487–88.

PRICING COMPLEMENTARY PRODUCTS

When a manufacturer produces two or more products that comple-
ment one another, meaning that they are used in combination by the
customer, he faces a slightly different pricing situation. Sometimes
complementary products are components of the same final product,
as, for example, are all the products from which a diesel locomotive
is made. In other cases, the products are used together but do not
comprise some other final product, as in the case of golf clubs and
golf balls.

For most complementary products, the price of one product has an
effect on the sales of the other and vice versa. As before, the firm
must also consider elasticity, competition, and costs. Thus, in the
cases where the products are used together, one of the products can
be priced to encourage purchase of the other. The classic example of
razors and razor blades illustrates this practice. An extremely low
price on a razor can encourage high volume purchases of the blades
that are designed for that particular razor.

Where one manufacturer's products are components (perhaps in
conjunction with products produced by others) of some other final
product, such as an automobile, house, or sewing machine, similar relationships exist. The price of one product may encourage or discourage the sales of another. However, pricing is complicated in such
situations by the fact that the firm now is dealing with derived rather
than direct demand.

PRICE LINING

Price lining is the term used to describe the practice of offering
products or services to the market at a limited number of prices.
These prices are called *price lines*. A manufacturer who follows such
a practice does not attempt to sell his product(s) at a large number
of different prices, but instead confines his efforts to products that sell
at a limited number of prices—say two or three—with nothing priced
at points in between. Thus, a manufacturer may produce a line of

men's hats which are priced at retail at $10, $15, and $20, while another hat manufacturer may produce a line of hats with retail prices of $20, $25, and $30. Price lining is most prevalent at the retail level, although it is also practiced by manufacturers of both consumer and industrial goods.

Price lines are usually fairly inflexible and are adhered to for some length of time. Once price lines have been established, the seller tends to feel that the only decision he has to make is what costs will be; no longer does he have to decide what price to charge. When costs or other conditions change, sellers using price lines often change the products or services rather than the prices at which they are sold in order to preserve their traditional price lines. Part of the reason for this reluctance to change lines is that sellers in such a situation often become identified with certain price lines in the mind of the buyer.

Sometimes price lines are used to indicate the "good," "better," and "best" products in the line, while in other cases a firm may concentrate on just two broad lines—one for the economy-minded market and one for the market that is more interested in such things as extra quality and fashion than in economy.

Although price lining does not necessarily make it any easier to arrive at a price, it does tend to enable a manufacturer to avoid frequent price changes. It simplifies inventory control for the manufacturer as well as the purchase decisions and inventory control problems of the buyers of the product, whether they be middlemen or final consumers, by reducing the number of prices and groups of products from which to choose. On the other hand, price lining has the basic disadvantage that it may be difficult to maintain given price lines during periods of rapidly rising costs without substantially reducing quality in the process.

Manufacturers of consumer goods often practice price lining because their products are typically sold at certain retail prices. To preserve price continuity, they design and manufacture products that can be sold profitably at those prices. For example, if a dress manufacturer wants to sell dresses in the $19.95, $29.95, and $39.95 retail-price brackets, he takes these prices as given and designs a product that can be sold at sufficient profit at those prices.

According to Martin Zober, the practice of price lining has three objectives, to appeal to the many different income brackets and tastes in the market place, to facilitate buyers' selection of goods that will satisfy their needs, and to keep the variety of products offered for sale within economical boundaries so that there may be savings in production and inventory.[12]

Sellers who elect to practice price lining should bear in mind that in order to have the desired effect of classifying products in the line and of simplifying the price aspects of the buying and selling functions there must be enough difference between price lines to be meaningful to the buyer. However, the price differences cannot be so large that they are out of proportion to the differences in the products offered or so far apart that the customer might prefer something "in between."

PRICING REPLACEMENT PARTS

Many manufacturers have the problem of pricing replacement parts to be used in their products. In some situations the manufacturer sells a set or partial set of replacement parts along with the original equipment. For example, commercial airlines generally purchase spare parts along with a new airplane. In other cases, the sale of the original equipment and the sale of the parts are separate transactions.

Another important distinction is that sometimes the sales of replacement parts are actually more important in dollar terms than are the sales of the original product, while in other cases the stocking and sale of replacement parts is a nuisance to the manufacturer since sales are very small and erratic. The sale of parts for older products or models generally falls into the latter category, for example. Some manufacturers solve this problem by refusing to stock parts for older products, but for others the public-image and customer-relations consequences of such action may make this policy inadvisable.

In any case, the competitive situation is the primary consideration in pricing replacement parts. The competitive situation surrounding the sale of replacement parts varies considerably from industry to industry and from firm to firm, of course. In some cases the manufacturer has, in a sense, a captive market in that he is the only available supplier of the parts. In other cases, replacement parts may be obtained from several sources, and in still other cases buyers may be

[12] Martin Zober, *Marketing Management* (New York: John Wiley and Sons, 1964), p. 94.

able to make the parts themselves. It follows, therefore, that parts that are widely available should be sold at relatively low prices, while parts that are sheltered from competition should be priced to reflect this profit opportunity.[13]

Cost and demand considerations cannot, of course, be ignored in the pricing of replacement parts. Like any other aspect of product-line pricing, the pricing of replacement parts cannot be performed in isolation. The price maker must take into consideration the relationship between the prices on the parts in question and the sales of other replacement parts and of the original product. It is not unusual for a manufacturer to establish relatively low prices for his replacement parts in order to promote good will among customers for the firm and its products.

Another factor to be considered is the cost of labor associated with making repairs, and the relationship between the labor costs and the prices of parts. If labor costs are very high relative to the prices of replacement parts, the prices of parts are not likely to be the critical item for the customer, and he will probably be less concerned about such prices as a consequence. A relatively high price may be charged for replacement parts under such circumstances.[14] The opposite may be true if labor costs are relatively low in comparison with the prices of parts.

However, many manufacturers, particularly manufacturers of consumer goods, have little control over the prices that the firms that do the actual servicing of the product charge customers for parts. The service industry has been troubled with unethical practices of many kinds, and the manufacturer may find that service firms are "gouging" customers in their pricing of replacement parts. This may cause the manufacturer to lose customer good will. To combat this situation the manufacturer can try to exercise better selection and control of independent servicing firms who handle the parts. Alternatively, the manufacturer may decide to handle the servicing himself.

Finally, the manufacturer is usually concerned about the quality of the service provided by independent servicing firms. Manufacturers usually are anxious that good service is provided on their products so that customers will be able to derive the greatest satisfaction from their use. The pricing of replacement parts may have a bearing on

---

[13] Dean, *Managerial Economics,* p. 496.

[14] This point is made by D. Maynard Phelps and J. Howard Westing in *Marketing Management,* rev. ed. (Homewood, Ill.: Irwin, 1960), p. 311.

the quality of service to the extent that it determines the adequacy of the margins permitted servicing firms.

AGE OF THE PRODUCT

PRICING NEW PRODUCTS

Perhaps the most challenging and interesting of all the problems associated with pricing by manufacturers is that of pricing a new product. Like other marketing decisions that involve new products, pricing decisions are usually made with very little information to go on concerning demand, costs, and other factors and with little certainty of success. Indeed, the fact that most new products introduced by American manufacturers fail in the market place may be attributed, at least in part, to the difficulty in arriving at a proper price for such products.

The difficulty in pricing new products varies depending upon whether the product is completely new or is similar to other products that are already on the market. In the former case the firm has few, if any, guides to pricing while in the latter case experience with other products can be of considerable help.

Although the general pricing factors discussed throughout this book, such as characteristics of the product, price elasticity of demand, nature of the buyers, and costs, should be taken into consideration in any attempt to price a new product, the special nature of new-product pricing has triggered attempts to formulate pricing approaches designed specifically for new products.[15]

Approaches to pricing new products Probably the best-known and most widely accepted approach to the pricing of new products is that first suggested by Dean. He distinguishes between two basic alternatives in pricing a new product, one which calls for a relatively

[15] In a study of 146 firms, respondents identified nearly forty factors that influence the determination of new-product prices. These were grouped into five general categories: (1) profit and cost considerations; (2) competitive considerations; (3) product characteristics; (4) market or sales expectations; and (5) other factors. See G. Clark Thompson and Morgan B. MacDonald, Jr., "Pricing New Products," *Conference Board Record*, January, 1964, pp. 7–9.

high price, called "skimming" pricing, and one which calls for a relatively low price, called "penetration" pricing.

A skimming price, according to Dean, is appropriate for products that represent a drastic departure from accepted ways of performing the service in question. A manufacturer might want to use a high skimming price under these circumstances for the following reasons:

1. Demand is likely to be somewhat inelastic since customers know little about the product and there are very few, if any, close rivals.
2. This method of pricing a new product is one of breaking the market up into segments that differ in price elasticity of demand —in a sense, the initial high price "skims the cream" of a market that is relatively insensitive to price, and subsequent price reductions tap successively more elastic sectors of the market.
3. A skimming policy is a safer approach when little is known about the nature of costs and the price elasticity of demand for the product since a high initial price may easily be lowered later, whereas a price that is too low is difficult to raise.
4. High prices produce a quick payback of product introduction costs, which may be important for the firm.

In contrast, a penetration price is a low price that is designed to penetrate mass markets as quickly as possible. According to Dean, the conditions that call for a penetration approach are:

1. High price elasticity of demand for the product.
2. The possibility of large savings in production costs as a result of high volume.
3. The absence of an adequate segment of the market that will accept a high price—no "elite" market.
4. A strong threat of potential competition. To meet this threat the penetration price may be used to raise entry barriers to prospective competitors, sometimes referred to as "keep-out" pricing.[16]

Alfred R. Oxenfeldt cautions that any decision involving the pricing of a new product must take into consideration the various parties

[16] Dean, "Pricing Policies for New Products," *Harvard Business Review,* November, 1950. See also his *Managerial Economics,* pp. 419–24; "Pricing a New Product," *The Controller,* April, 1955; and *How to Price a New Product,* Management Aids for Small Manufacturers, No. 62 (Washington, D.C.: Small Business Administration, April, 1955).

who are directly or indirectly involved in pricing decisions including other members of the firm, customers, potential rivals, resellers, suppliers, and the government. This will help at the outset to narrow the range of feasible prices to some degree. Once this has been done, Oxenfeldt suggests the "differential" method as a means of setting the price on a new product. The logic of this method is simply that in the world of existing products there will be one or more that can serve as a foundation on which to build a price for a new product. Such a product might be one that performs the same function as the new product; or it might be one that is similar in general appearance and apparent cost, even though it performs a different function; or it might be a product that potential customers consider comparable to the new item. Once such a product has been isolated, then, according to Oxenfeldt, it is up to the price maker to determine the differential (higher or lower than the price of the foundation product) that the customers the firm is trying to attract would be willing to pay. Any new product must be fitted into an established population of products, since most customers form their opinions of the value and price of the new product by comparing it with existing products.[17]

Another approach to the new product pricing is suggested by Stephen J. Welsh. His approach to the pricing of a new product involves a seven-step process:

1. Approximate the impact of price on the volume the firm expects to achieve.
2. Appraise marketing requirements and define the marketing plan in broad terms.
3. Plot projected growth curves at several selected price levels.
4. Approximate cost data.
5. Appraise the capabilities of competitors, including timing.
6. Estimate competitors' costs.
7. Select the price.

Some of the possible alternatives in pricing a new product include a choice between a skimming strategy and a penetration strategy, and a choice between trying to get as much profit as possible as soon as possible and trying to maximize profit with a somewhat lower price

---

[17] Oxenfeldt, *Pricing for Marketing Executives* (San Francisco: Wadsworth, 1961), pp. 77–82.

schedule at a slower pace. Welsh also discusses the possibility of establishing a price that will discourage competitors.[18]

The approaches suggested by these three authors are somewhat different from one another. It is clear, however, that, although Welsh's approach is more specific and "practical" than Dean's in that he sets forth actual steps to be taken while Dean stresses considerations of a more theoretical nature, the two approaches are very much alike in that they both approach the pricing task chiefly in terms of extremes of high and low. In contrast, Oxenfeldt's approach stresses the fact that, once the range of feasible prices has been narrowed as far as possible by consideration of the parties involved in pricing, the new product should be priced by analogy to the prices of existing products. In this respect and in the sense that it does not offer the extremes of high and low as the basic pricing alternatives, Oxenfeldt's approach differs significantly from the other two.

There is a great deal of merit in the Oxenfeldt differential method. It is a relatively simple approach to new-product pricing that, for the most part, forces the price maker to take into account all the factors that Dean and Welsh believe should be considered in the pricing of a new product. The weakness of this method lies in the assumptions upon which it rests:

1. The prices of products that are already in the market place are proper prices.
2. The price maker can identify the products that can serve as guides for the pricing of his new product.
3. The price maker can measure or predict the differential that customers will be willing to pay.

In some cases one or more of these assumptions will be invalid. For example, although it is likely that prices in the market place are close to being "proper" prices, there is no guarantee that they are. Furthermore, for an entirely new product that has not been on the market before, it may be difficult to identify existing product(s) that will serve as valid pricing guides. Finally, as we mentioned in Chapter 3, it is often quite difficult to find out what people will pay for a new product.

In short, it is clear from a consideration of these three suggested

[18] Welsh, "A Planned Approach to New Product Pricing," in American Management Association, *Pricing: The Critical Decision,* AMA Management Report No. 66 (New York: American Management Association, 1961).

approaches that there are special factors to be taken into account in pricing a new product. The high skimming price and the low penetration price are the two basic available alternatives, but it must be kept in mind that new-product pricing is not always an either-or proposition —either high or low. The two basic extreme alternatives, and the conditions under which each one is appropriate, are simply intended to be broad guidelines for pricing a new product. There are many situations in which the conditions will not call for either extreme alternative but rather for some compromise position.

Other considerations in pricing new products Another possible reason that a firm might adopt a skimming policy, at least temporarily, is that its production and marketing facilities may be inadequate to serve a large market. Still another possible reason is that the firm may want to provide extra large margins for middlemen in order to encourage their cooperation in the introductory phases of the product. The major disadvantage of a skimming policy is that it attracts competitors into the industry and, if entry is relatively easy, the results can be disastrous.

One of the key elements in the successful use of a high skimming price for a new product is whether or not there is product differentiation. This factor is reflected in the price elasticity of demand for the product. For example, products that have strong patent protection are usually very well insulated from competition and enjoy a relatively high degree of inelasticity of demand. Other forms of protection include situations in which unique managerial production know-how is required, the firm controls raw-material sources, or the necessary specialized labor force is in limited supply. In situations of this sort a firm enjoys near monopoly power and can capitalize on its position by setting a high price on a new product.[19] It is important to note, however, that all this product protection is of little consequence if customers fail to recognize and appreciate the product differentiation that results from these conditions.

Another factor to be considered in pricing new products is the probable effect on older products in the firm's line. For example, if the new product is to replace an older product of the firm, then timing considerations are all-important. Substantial inventory losses may be incurred by middlemen and the manufacturer himself if the new

---

[19] Kenneth R. Davis, *Marketing Management* (New York: Ronald Press, 1961), p. 682.

product is introduced prematurely on a wide scale through a low-price approach. There may also be losses involved with special production facilities and materials used in the old product. These losses are only qualifications on the basic timing decision for the introduction of the new product; if the new product is expected to have little or no relationship to the sales of the older products, then a more independent pricing approach is possible.

The specific reason for introducing the new product obviously affects the pricing decision. If the product is introduced in order to add prestige to the line of products sold by the firm, then a high price is called for. If, on the other hand, the product is introduced with the purpose of warding off or meeting competition at the low end of the product line, then a relatively low-penetration-type price is in order. Again, if the product is added to the line for the purpose of making use of excess production capacity, an underutilized sales force, or some other facility of the firm, then a relatively low price may be advisable. Or, if a new product is introduced in order to gain entry into an industry in which the firm has not been before, a low price might be best.

PRICING OLDER PRODUCTS

Every product has a life cycle that begins when it is introduced to the market and ends when it is withdrawn from the market. This cycle will take a long or a short time to run its course, depending upon product characteristics and other factors.

As a product moves through various stages in its life cycle, a firm must be ready to adjust its price accordingly. A price that is appropriate when the product is introduced may be entirely inappropriate two years later, and one that is suitable two years later may be entirely inappropriate in five years.

Eventually every product reaches a state of maturity when some or all of the following characteristics are present:

1. Competing products are very similar.
2. Brand preference on the part of buyers is weak.
3. A number of private labels are available.
4. The market is, to a great extent, saturated in the sense that most sales are replacement rather than new-equipment sales.

5. Production methods in the industry are fairly well standardized or stabilized.[20]

Although it is difficult to state with certainty that any given product is in a "mature" state, signs such as these indicate that it may be approaching such a condition. When this is the case, what is a proper pricing policy to follow? Under such conditions a manufacturer usually finds that he has little pricing discretion or independence because there is very little product differentiation. He cannot successfully price his product above the prices of competing products, and price reductions are likely to lead to retaliation and a generally lower level of prices throughout the industry. Although such low prices may help forestall the eventual death of the product at the hands of newer substitute products, the recommended approach is to avoid price reductions and try to maintain the existing price level as long as possible. In such a situation, a manufacturer will usually find that it is wiser to try to offer the customer a lower "real" price by giving him more for the established price. For example, such an approach might take the form of additional services, better credit terms, or product changes of one kind or another.

CONSIDERATIONS INVOLVING DISTRIBUTORS

Aside from the fact that distributors, such as wholesalers and retailers, represent one kind of market and, as we discussed in Chapter 3, influence pricing by manufacturers in the capacity of buyers (in terms of their size and number), distributors also influence pricing by manufacturers in the capacity of distributors.

In order to achieve the basic marketing objective—the exchange of

[20] Dean, "Pricing Policies for New Products," *Harvard Business Review,* November, 1950, p. 52, and *Managerial Economics,* pp. 424–26. See also R. S. Alexander, "The Death and Burial of 'Sick' Products," *Journal of Marketing,* April, 1964; Philip Kotler, "Phasing Out Weak Products," *Harvard Business Review,* March–April, 1965; Donald K. Clifford, Jr., "Leverage in Product Life Cycle," *Dun's Review and Modern Industry,* May, 1965; and Theodore Levitt, "Exploit the Product Life Cycle," *Harvard Business Review,* November–December, 1965. An interesting account of the history of some very successful old products is Velma A. Adams, "Why the Old Products Last," *Dun's Review and Modern Industry,* April, 1965.

goods or services—someone must perform the necessary marketing functions, including transportation, warehousing, personal selling, advertising, and financing. Most manufacturers, particularly those in the consumer-goods field, find that they must rely on distributors to perform some of these functions. To the extent that this is done, marketing becomes a cooperative effort between the manufacturer and the distributors.

Since most manufacturers are heavily dependent upon distributors of one kind or another for the effective marketing of their products, it follows that in making most marketing decisions manufacturers should take into account their relationship with the distributors, particularly in matters that affect pricing.

PRICING AND THE MANUFACTURER–DISTRIBUTOR RELATIONSHIP

In setting a price on their products, most manufacturers are anxious to find a price that will help accomplish the following objectives:

1. To attract the right kind of distributors to the product in order to project the proper image to consumers and to ensure adequate promotion of, and/or service for, the product.
2. To attract a sufficient number of distributors of the product in order to provide adequate market coverage.
3. To encourage distributors to provide the kind of cooperation the manufacturer desires.

The extent of a manufacturer's concern with each of these factors will vary depending upon the type of product involved—industrial or consumer good, raw material or finished product, convenience good or specialty good—but in every case the manufacturer should be concerned with all three factors to some degree.

The price that the ultimate consumer, or user, of the product pays and the margins earned by distributors will clearly affect the three objectives mentioned above. Thus, an extremely high or an extremely low retail price on a consumer good will automatically rule out a number of retailers who do not wish to handle a product that is priced at that level. It will also dictate to some extent what kinds of retailers are attracted to the product—exclusive retailers, discounters, or cut-rate retailers. This will help determine the quality of the retailers who are to handle the product.

The *margins* that distributors feel they will be able to earn also affects how many will be interested in handling a product and what kind of distributors they will be. Margins earned by distributors also greatly influence the amount of cooperation a manufacturer can expect from them. Naturally distributors tend to put more effort into selling products or brands that carry the highest margins.[21]

Manufacturers cannot expect distributors to handle a product that does not permit them to earn what they think is an adequate return. Some manufacturers run into difficulty in this respect, however, because they distribute their products through several kinds of middlemen—such as several different classes of retailers—each of which has different costs and performs different aspects of the distribution function for the manufacturer's product. It is difficult for all of these distributors to obtain the same margin from handling the same product. As a consequence, some will have higher margins than others, and these margins will be considered adequate by some and inadequate by others.[22] Indeed, this problem can exist among distributors of the same class, such as department stores, since they do not all have the same operating costs.

Assuming that the manufacturer has control over the situation, he should take the following factors into account in determining what margins a distributor should be allowed to earn:

1. The size of the margins customarily earned by distributors in the industry.
2. The operating costs of the distributors if they are known to the manufacturer.
3. The costs of selling to different kinds of distributors.
4. The margins offered to distributors by competing manufacturers.
5. Whether or not distributors handle competing brands in addition to the manufacturer's brand (including both brands of other manufacturers and private labels of the distributors).

[21] The influence of a manufacturer's pricing policies on the willingness and ability of distributors to promote a product is discussed by Martin R. Warshaw in "Pricing to Gain Wholesalers' Support," *Journal of Marketing*, July, 1962.

[22] The use of discounts that affect the margins earned by distributors is discussed in Chapter 8.

6. Whether or not distributors are given exclusive territorial rights to sell the manufacturer's product.
7. The amount of service, such as promotional assistance, the manufacturer may expect from distributors and the amount of service he expects to give to distributors.
8. The ease or difficulty that distributors have had in moving the product, a factor that is related to brand acceptability. (Sometimes a manufacturer of a very popular consumer brand can allow distributors very low margins because distributors feel that they must carry such brands.)
9. The size and importance of individual distributors or classes of distributors (chain stores, discount houses, department stores, etc.) to the manufacturer in terms of sales volume.
10. The implications of the Robinson-Patman Act regarding price discrimination.

As we indicated earlier, manufacturers sometimes start out with the price they want the ultimate customers to pay for their product and then work backward, trying to develop a product that can be sold at those prices. The fact that some manufacturers approach pricing in this way, and in so doing must provide for adequate distributor margins in order to have a successful marketing program, means that manufacturers often determine the gross amount they will receive from distributors by simply taking the difference between the margins distributors will earn and the price established for ultimate customers of the product.

CONTROL OF PRICES CHARGED BY DISTRIBUTORS

The size of the margins earned by wholesalers and retailers is, of course, directly affected not only by the prices they pay to the manufacturer or to other distributors but also by the prices charged by the distributors themselves. Although a manufacturer might like to control or influence the prices charged by distributors to ultimate customers, he is not always able to do so.

For example, the chief reason manufacturers have attempted to control resale prices is that they are anxious to satisfy the demands of those distributors who desire protection against price cutting by competing distributors. Another reason for the keen interest that manufacturers take in the prices charged by distributors is the fact that manufacturers sometimes feel that price is a very important element in sales volume, and as a consequence they would like to use price in advertising their product to potential customers with some assurance that the prices they quote are the prices the customer will be asked to pay. In still other cases manufacturers have felt that price cutting by distributors tends to cheapen the product in the eyes of the ultimate purchasers and that the reputation of the brand and of the firm is hurt by this.

Another possible reason that manufacturers try to control the prices charged by distributors is the fear that general price cutting by distributors may simply result in a significant reduction in distributor margins, and that they, in turn, might then pressure manufacturers for lower prices, which would reduce the profit earned by manufacturers.

In attempting to control the resale prices charged by distributors, however, the manufacturer faces several risks. By preventing price cutting among distributors, he may create a lot of dissatisfaction among those who would like to engage in the practice, and these distributors may refuse to handle the product, or they may fail to give it adequate sales support. Since these would-be price cutters may be large distributors, the manufacturer who attempts to control resale prices must consider the possible loss of significant sales volume. Furthermore, controlling resale prices may be a very costly procedure and not worth the extra time and expense necessitated by the substantial policing problems that it involves. This is particularly true if a large number of distributors are involved. Another factor that may discourage a manufacturer from attempting to control resale prices is that price cutting among distributors may actually be beneficial to the extent that it encourages the sale of his products. The argument that price cutting tends to damage the reputation of the brand and the firm is sometimes difficult to substantiate.

Although many manufacturers make no overt attempt to influence or control resale prices charged by distributors, some manufacturers feel that it is important to do so. But what can the manufacturer do, aside from trying to gain cooperation from distributors by ensuring that they receive good service and adequate margins and promotional assistance, in order to encourage them to set what he believes to be a suitable price on his product? Actually, he can approach this problem in five different ways.

1. For many years manufacturers of consumer goods who were interested in controlling resale prices could rely upon state resale price maintenance laws to support them in their attempt to fix minimum, or actual, prices charged by retailers.[23] In recent years, resale price maintenance laws have encountered considerable difficulty, and the number of states which have effective laws of this kind is declining. However, it is still possible in some states to rely on state resale price maintenance laws and to require retailers to charge no less than a specified minimum price or some particular price specified by the manufacturer. In any case, the manufacturer who does rely on resale price maintenance laws must be ready to undertake the expense of enforcement to make such a program work.

2. To control resale prices some manufacturers have turned to consignment selling, whereby the manufacturer retains title to the product in question and merely pays the distributor, as an agent, a commission that is based on the quantities sold. By retaining title the manufacturer keeps control over price, but he also incurs all the risks associated with keeping title.[24]

Until recently, manufacturers practicing consignment selling have had no serious legal problems. However, in 1964 the United States Supreme Court ruled that the combination of a lease and a consignment agreement between an oil refiner and its lessee-dealers that allowed the refiner to control the retail prices of gasoline was a violation of the antitrust laws. The Court held that the lease and consignment agreements had forced the dealers into an arrangement under which their supplier was able to impose noncompetitive prices on thousands of dealers whose prices otherwise might be competitive.[25] What effect this decision will have on the practice of consignment selling is

---

[23] Resale price maintenance or "fair trade" laws are discussed in greater depth in Chapter 7.

[24] Control of retail prices by a manufacturer by means of consignment selling is considered lawful only if the retailer involved is a true "agent." Certain criteria have been established as a test of agency: (1) accounting periodically for sales by the distributors to the manufacturer-owner; (2) payment only for goods sold; (3) the right of the distributor to return goods to the manufacturer-owner and, in fact, the right of the manufacturer-owner to require the return of goods; (4) liability of the manufacturer for retailer's misrepresentation of merchandise in a tort proceeding; and (5) under certain circumstances, the manufacturer's liability for damage of goods in retailer stocks. See Ralph Cassady, Jr., *Competition and Price Making in Food Retailing* (New York: Ronald Press, 1962), p. 234.

[25] *Simpson* v. *Union Oil Company of California*, 377 U.S. 13. In this case reference was made to *United States* v. *General Electric Company*, 272 U.S. 476 (1926) in which a consignment arrangement that involved the control of

still uncertain, but it appears that consignment selling, when used by the manufacturer as a method of controlling resale prices, faces a difficult future.

3. Alternatively, a manufacturer may simply refuse to sell to distributors who do not adhere to the prices that he suggests.[26] Such an approach may or may not be appropriate depending on the prevalence of price cutting among distributors and how badly a manufacturer needs distributors. The chief problem with this approach is that it necessitates a major policing effort by the manufacturer if the firm uses a large number of distributors, and hence it is impractical for many products. Furthermore, the practice of refusing to sell to distributors who do not adhere to suggested resale prices raises some legal questions for those manufacturers who operate in interstate commerce. In 1918 the United States Supreme Court held, in *United States* v. *Colgate and Company,*[27] that a seller had the right to exercise his own judgment as regards the parties with whom he did business. Under this ruling it was legal for a manufacturer to announce resale prices unilaterally and then refuse to sell to distributors who would not abide by them. In the Beech-Nut case[28] of 1922, however, the Court held that it was illegal for a manufacturer *systematically* to search out offending distributors and refuse to sell to them. In this case, Beech-Nut had set up an elaborate system of price policing whereby the customer-distributors were encouraged to report price cutting by their competitors. The Court held that the system was akin to a price-fixing "combination" as outlawed by the Sherman Act.

A recent case, decided by the United States Supreme Court in 1960, has further complicated the picture by restricting the right of a manufacturer to enforce resale prices. The ruling stated, in general, that a manufacturer may legally refuse to sell to distributors who will not maintain suggested prices, but that additional efforts in this direction by the manufacturer may amount to putting together a "combi-

---

resale prices was upheld by the United States Supreme Court. The difference between the two cases, the Court said, was that the General Electric case involved patented products whereas the Union Oil Company case did not, that the patent laws give sellers the right to exclude others from *making, using, or selling* a patented invention, and that this had been the basis for the decision of the Court in the General Electric case. Apparently this means that if the products involved in the Union Oil case had been patented, the Court would have rendered a different decision.

[26] Refusal to sell is discussed in Cassady, *op. cit.*, pp. 228–32.
[27] 250 U.S. 300.
[28] *Federal Trade Commission* v. *Beech-Nut Packing Company,* 257 U.S. 441.

nation" in violation of the Sherman Act. Specifically, the Court held that Parke, Davis and Company [29] had gone beyond the simple refusal to sell and had unlawfully used other means to secure adherence to resale prices. Parke, Davis had warned price-cutting retailers to stop cutting prices or Parke, Davis would refuse to continue dealing with them. Representatives of Parke, Davis also visited wholesalers and warned them that if they sold to offending retailers their supplies would be cut off. Accordingly, when some retailers persisted in cutting prices, they found that they were unable to buy Parke, Davis products from either that company or from wholesalers.

In sum, although manufacturers who are engaged in interstate commerce have the legal right to refuse to sell to distributors who do not adhere to resale prices, it is not certain what else they can do in order to detect price cutting or to encourage distributors to abide by suggested prices. The Parke, Davis decision restricts the ability of manufacturers to use the refusal-to-sell device as a means of encouraging distributors to abide by suggested prices, but the extent of this restriction is still uncertain.[30]

4. Another way in which a manufacturer may attempt to control resale prices is to by-pass an entire class of distributors when it is found that many or all of them refuse to adhere to suggested resale prices. In such cases the manufacturer must take upon himself the distribution functions. This approach can be a practical solution, however, when the distributors in question are wholesalers. When distributors are retailers this approach is generally not suitable since, in most situations, it is impractical for manufacturers to establish their own retail stores or to sell directly to consumers on a door-to-door basis or by mail.

5. Finally, a manufacturer can attempt to control resale prices by simply announcing to ultimate customers and distributors a "list" price applying to sales to ultimate customers with the hope that distributors will then mark up the product so that it will sell to users at the price announced. The danger in this approach is that, if a list price becomes common knowledge among prospective buyers, it gives the price-cutting distributor an opportunity to charge prices that are

---

[29] *United States* v. *Parke, Davis and Company*, 362 U.S. 503.

[30] Recent antitrust suits filed by the United States Department of Justice indicate that the refusal to sell to distributors who do not adhere to resale prices may be further restricted in the future. See "Antitrust Again Lunges at Fair Trade," *Business Week,* July 4, 1964, p. 20.

lower than list prices and use the announced list price as proof that his price reduction is genuine.

SPECIAL PROBLEMS PRESENTED BY DISCOUNTERS

The rise of discounting at the retail level since World War II has had a significant impact on the marketing of consumer goods. Due in large part to the rapid growth of so-called discount houses, price cutting at the retail level has become widespread.[31] The popularity of discounting, or price cutting, has created some serious problems for manufacturers of consumer goods. Controlling retail prices has become increasingly difficult, and this, in turn, has made it more difficult to select the appropriate type of retailers.

For example, the rise of discounting has made it almost impossible to control retail prices effectively in some lines of consumer goods. The decline in the effectiveness of resale price maintenance laws has contributed to this difficulty. In fact, as we suggested earlier, many manufacturers have found that advertising retail list prices and attaching retail prices to packages have actually encouraged discounting to the extent that they provide the discounter with proof of the legitimacy of his price reduction.[32]

To further complicate the matter, the Federal Trade Commission has recently attacked list prices of manufacturers when they do not coincide with the actual prices charged by retailers on the ground that, when list prices are higher than those actually charged by retailers, they are deceptive in that the consumer thinks he is getting a bargain when in fact he is not. On several occasions in 1961 and 1962 the Commisssion held that neither advertising nor price tags appended to items could carry prices that are not the "usual and customary" retail prices for the product in the trade area involved.[33] It

---

[31] Discount houses and other kinds of retailers are discussed in Chapter 7.

[32] For a discussion of a watch manufacturer's successful attempt to maintain retail prices, see James G. Plunkett, "The Strategy of Price Leadership," *Sales Management,* June 5, 1964.

[33] *Federal Trade Commission* v. *Baltimore Luggage Company* et al., 58 FTC 451 (1961)—petition for writ of certiorari denied in *Baltimore Luggage Company* et al. v. *Federal Trade Commission,* 369 U.S. 949 (1962); *Federal Trade Commission* v. *The Rayex Corporation* et al., 60 FTC 664 (1962); *Federal Trade Commission* v. *The Regina Corporation,* Order to Cease and Desist, Docket 8323, October 31, 1962—decision of Commission upheld in *The Regina Corporation* v. *Federal Trade Commission,* 322 F. (2d) 765 (1963).

is not easy to identify a "usual" or "customary" price in today's world of discounting, however, and this suggests that manufacturers would find it very difficult to make use of suggested prices without running afoul of the Commission's rulings. It is ironic that, although the Commission has discouraged the use of suggested retail prices with these decisions, federal law *requires* that automobile manufacturers place on each new automobile a label that gives the manufacturer's suggested list price. Decisions made in 1964, however, indicate that the Commission has liberalized its position on suggested list prices. As things stand at present, the Commission upholds the general principle that if a manufacturer genuinely believes that his advertised or preticketed price [34] is legitimate and if there are "substantial" sales of his product at that price, he will not be accused of having engaged in a deceptive practice.[35]

Because of the difficulties involved in trying to control retail prices effectively and the uncertainties surrounding the attitude of the Federal Trade Commission, many manufacturers of consumer goods no longer advertise suggested list prices and no longer preticket their merchandise. Instead of announcing specific list prices, their advertisements now contain expressions such as "Priced at less than $_____" or "Nationally advertised at $_____, optional with dealer."

The rise in discounting has also complicated the manufacturer's choice of distributors. The problem is whether or not a manufacturer should allow his product to be handled by retailers who charge less than the suggested retail prices. In the early and mid-1950's, the early days of the current wave of discounting, many manufacturers attempted to keep their products out of the hands of discounters in order to prevent price cutting at the retail level. They were anxious to avoid cheapening the brand in the eyes of the consumer and to avoid alienating other retailers who were not actively engaged in price cutting. However, many manufacturers soon realized that the discounters were beginning to account for a large amount of sales and that not dealing with them resulted in substantial losses in potential sales for the manufacturer. Discounters became difficult to avoid. Today many

---

[34] A preticketed price is a retail price that the manufacturer has appended to his product in the form of a price tag or sticker of some sort.

[35] Federal Trade Commission, *Guides Against Deceptive Pricing*, effective January 8, 1964, pp. 4–5.

manufacturers feel that they are forced to let price cutters sell their products.[36]

When a manufacturer decides to allow discounters to handle his product, he runs the risk of upsetting his relations with the retailers he customarily uses. For example, a manufacturer of power lawn mowers may alienate hardware-store operators if he lets discounters sell his power mowers, too. The hardware dealers may drop his products entirely or refuse to give them much sales support. Assuming that the manufacturer still regards hardware stores as an important element of his marketing system, he has a very difficult decision to make. One way out of this dilemma is to permit the conventional dealer, in our example the hardware stores, to handle the regular brand(s) of the manufacturer's product and to produce another brand, or a private label, to be sold exclusively through price-cutting retail outlets. This procedure helps to avoid ill will among the conventional retailers while at the same time permitting the manufacturer to deal with the discounters.

PROTECTION AGAINST PRICE DECLINES

Manufacturers who make use of outside distributors are sometimes faced with the problem of whether or not to guarantee the prices on their products against decline. The problem arises because losses may be incurred by distributors if a manufacturer should adjust his price downward while they are awaiting delivery of merchandise, or if they have on hand unsold merchandise that was purchased at the previous higher price. Under such circumstances, to the extent that the manufacturer's prices to distributors are reflected in the prices they charge their buyers, the distributors are likely to suffer a loss.

To avoid injuring distributors in this fashion, some manufacturers

---

[36] A problem faced by automobile manufacturers has been the sale of new automobiles by franchised dealers to discount dealers in the southern California area. A federal district court decision upheld the right of General Motors Corporation to prohibit their dealers from making such sales, but this decision has recently been reversed by the United States Supreme Court. See *United States* v. *General Motors Corporation* et al., 34 U.S.L. Week 4383 (U.S. April 28, 1966) (No. 46). Recent legal developments involving the relationship between manufacturers and franchised dealers are summarized in "Is the Franchise System Legal?" *Business Week*, April 3, 1965, p. 66.

agree to guarantee the prices they charge distributors against decline. Such agreements may take various forms. Manufacturers may agree to refund the difference between the old and the new price for all merchandise on order but not yet shipped or delivered at the time the price is adjusted downward. Alternatively, manufacturers may guarantee the price on a certain percentage or on all of the stock the distributor has on hand when the price change is made. Still another possibility is to guarantee all or part of the stock against price decline only for a certain length of time after delivery, such as thirty, sixty, or ninety days. Under any of these arrangements, the manufacturer agrees to send a rebate to the distributor or to credit his account in the amount of the difference between the old and the new price if he reduces the price on a product.

Essentially, guarantees against price declines are designed to eliminate or reduce the price risk involved in the ownership of goods by distributors. But, in addition, these guarantees benefit the manufacturer in certain ways. For one thing they can be used as a competitive weapon to attract business. They can also be used to encourage distributors to buy in large quantities, and to place advance orders. Large advance orders will, in turn, facilitate production scheduling for the manufacturer and enable him to produce for order and not for stock.[37] This is particularly advantageous for a manufacturer who produces a seasonal good. In general, guarantees against price declines are most beneficial to the manufacturer during periods of unstable prices when they may enable him to avoid closing down plants or operating far below capacity.

The chief disadvantage to the manufacturer in any kind of price-guarantee arrangement is, of course, the risk of price change that ordinarily accompanies ownership of goods. The manufacturer is, in effect, assuming the risk of price change that distributors would ordinarily assume. For example, if during periods of economic recession a manufacturer is forced to lower his prices in order to be competitive, he may find these reductions very costly because of the added expense of the guarantee. Manufacturers also run the risk of being

[37] The advantage in producing for order rather than for stock is that there is much less uncertainty involved since the manufacturer knows what and how much to produce and where it is to be made available to his customers. He does not need to plan production for an uncertain demand, nor does he need to worry about carrying inventories of the right quantities in the right places at the right time. In short, the entire production and physical-distribution problem is simplified.

misled about market conditions to the extent that a guarantee stimulates speculative overbuying by distributors. This overbuying may result in the accumulation of surpluses in distributor stockrooms at a later date and thus in a period of slack sales for the manufacturer. There is also the danger of creating ill will among distributors because of disagreements over how much inventory is left in stock when a price reduction goes into effect. Lastly, if a manufacturer knows that a price reduction will result in substantial rebates to distributors, he may hesitate to reduce prices and thus fail to make the price adjustments necessary to maximize sales.

Because of the possible disadvantages associated with guarantees against price declines, particularly those covering distributor inventories, it is probably wiser to guarantee prices only on merchandise that is on order but not yet delivered at the time of the downward price adjustments and to give advance notice of price changes before they take effect in order to give distributors an opportunity to curtail buying and to clear stocks before the new prices become effective.[38]

GEOGRAPHIC PRICING CONSIDERATIONS

IMPORTANCE OF TRANSPORTATION COSTS IN PRICING

Transportation represents a significant percentage of the total cost of marketing in the United States. Although estimates of the actual cost of transportation in the United States are all inaccurate to some degree, they indicate that the nation's freight bill is substantial, and that it is growing. For example, the Transportation Association of America reported that in 1964 a total of $56,079,000,000 was spent on the movement of freight (including intercity and local) in all its forms in the United States. This represented 9 percent of the nation's gross national product in that year.

For some manufacturers, the transportation of goods involves the expenditure of many millions of dollars, but regardless of the amount of money involved in a firm's transportation bill, every manufacturer incurs transportation costs in one way or another and must take

---

[38] This approach is recommended in Phelps and Westing, *op. cit.,* p. 336.

them into account when setting prices on the product manufactured. The way in which this problem is handled can greatly influence the success of a firm's marketing program by helping to determine the scope of the geographic market area the firm is able to serve, the vulnerability of the firm to price competition in areas located near its production facilities, the net margins earned on individual sales of the product, the ability of the firm to control or influence resale prices of distributors, and how difficult it is for salesmen in the field to quote accurate prices and delivery terms to their potential customers.

Every manufacturer who ships his products to customers must decide whether or not he will try to account for these shipping costs in prices and, if so, how he will do this. This same decision must be made regardless of the mode of transportation involved, or whether the transportation facility is internal or external to the operations of the firm. Although there are no freight bills to pay when a manufacturer has his own transportation facilities (private transportation), he still must decide how the costs associated with transportation are to be accounted for in pricing. There are two general ways in which the manufacturer can attempt to account for transportation costs in pricing, the *f.o.b.-origin* [39] method and the *delivered-pricing* method.

F.O.B. ORIGIN

Often prices are quoted "f.o.b. mill," "f.o.b. factory," or "f.o.b. origin." When this is done, the seller quotes to every buyer a price for the products that are ready for shipment at the plant or warehouse. The buyer then selects the mode of transportation, chooses the specific carrier, handles any damage claims that might arise, and pays the freight bills associated with the shipment. This also permits the buyer to pick up the shipment with his own private transportation equipment if he wishes. The net return [40] received by the manufacturer under f.o.b.-origin pricing is the same for all sales of the product that take place under the same circumstances,[41] regardless of

---

[39] F.o.b. is the abbreviation for "free on board."

[40] Net return is sometimes referred to as "mill net."

[41] As we indicated in Chapter 4, the prices charged by a firm can be different for different buyers of the same product because of differences in quantities purchased, trade status of buyers, time of purchase, and uses to which the product is put. In this discussion of geographic pricing, the phrase "under the same circumstances" is intended to mean that the quantities purchased, the trade status of buyers, the time of purchase, and the uses to which a product is put are the same.

where the buyer is located. However, the "total landed cost" to the buyer (price plus transportation costs) will obviously vary under these circumstances depending upon the transportation costs involved, which are largely a function of the distance of the buyer from the point of shipment.[42]

It is sometimes claimed that the use of f.o.b.-origin pricing by competing sellers imposes upon them a geographic market limitation because of differences in their prices and transportation charges. In other words, under these circumstances no one seller is able to invade the home territory of another because the total landed cost to the buyer would be higher than it would be if he purchased from the local seller. An increase or decrease in the f.o.b.-origin price can thus contract or expand each seller's geographic market.

This effect is most evident when the product involved is highly standardized. Some industrial products, such as semifinished steel, cement blocks, and aluminum bars probably fall into this category. Producers of raw materials have the same geographic limitations. For many manufacturers, however, there is sufficient product differentiation, either "real" or psychological, so that f.o.b.-origin pricing does not rigidly confine their markets to a geographic zone based on prices and transportation costs. This is particularly true in the consumer-goods field. Product differentiation makes it possible to sell in distant markets even though the total landed cost to the buyer is higher than it is from some nearer manufacturer because the product involved is somewhat unique and cannot be obtained in its exact same form from other manufacturers. Thus, although f.o.b.-origin pricing definitely makes it difficult to sell in distant markets—unless all competing manufacturers are shipping from the same general area—it does not necessarily impose upon the seller a rigid restriction of the size of the geographic market unless there is practically no product differentiation in the industry in question.

The chief advantage in using f.o.b.-origin pricing is that the firm receives the same net return from every sale of the product under the same circumstances regardless of where the buyers happen to be. This enables the firm to more easily predict future revenues and to make decisions relative to adding new customers or new sales territories since there is no possibility that the firm will ever receive less

---

[42] Although there are many exceptions, transportation rates charged by for-hire carriers generally increase with distance. Transportation costs involved in private carriage also increase as the length of haul increases.

than the expected net return. This is not true of delivered-pricing systems. Another advantage of f.o.b.-origin pricing is that it relieves the manufacturer of the burden of handling the transportation problem; he need not worry about loss and damage claims or any other possible complications that are associated with using for-hire transportation.

As we indicated earlier, the chief disadvantage of f.o.b.-origin pricing is that it may make it difficult to sell a product in distant markets unless there is considerable product differentiation in the industry, or heavy demand for the product, or unless all competing manufacturers are located near one another. If plants that manufacture the generic product in question are geographically scattered, it may be difficult for one manufacturer who is using f.o.b.-origin pricing to penetrate the local market of another because of transportation costs.

F.o.b.-origin pricing also complicates the task of ensuring that distributors sell the product at the same or similar resale prices. Because their landed costs vary depending upon how distant they are from the shipping point, distributors will tend to set different resale prices on the product, assuming that they are all trying to earn about the same margin on the product. This in turn makes it difficult for a manufacturer to advertise a resale price to ultimate customers or to encourage the maintenance of a uniform resale price on his product.

Another possible disadvantage in f.o.b.-origin pricing is that it may mislead the manufacturer into thinking that outbound transportation costs are of no concern to him, although, in fact, they are still quite important to him to the extent that the buyer of a product is concerned with the total landed cost of the product, rather than just the price of the product alone. Consequently, although the manufacturer may avoid dealing with the transportation companies, the matter of transportation costs may affect the purchase decision. Furthermore, the manufacturer's salesmen are faced with the problem of trying to inform prospective buyers what the total landed cost will be on a particular order, which means that a salesman must be able to determine what the specific transportation charges are on a given shipment when for-hire carriers are used. This, in turn, means he must contact the manufacturer's traffic department for the information. The traffic department thus becomes involved in checking freight rates much as it would if the manufacturer were paying the freight bills himself. The outbound transportation problem simply cannot be avoided by means of f.o.b.-origin pricing.

DELIVERED PRICING—ZONE SYSTEMS

Alternatively the price quoted by the manufacturer may include both the price of the product itself and the transportation costs involved in getting the product to the buyer. This is known as *delivered pricing*. Here again transportation may be in the form of either for-hire or private carriage. In either case, the customer is buying both the product and the transportation service from the manufacturer. The invoice in such transactions carries the designation "f.o.b. delivered," or "f.o.b. buyer's warehouse," or some similar phrase. In this case, when for-hire transportation is used, the manufacturer selects the mode of transportation and the particular carrier, handles the damage claims and other paper work, and pays the freight bills.

Under what is known as a *single-zone* delivered-pricing system, the manufacturer sells the product under the same circumstances at a uniform delivered price throughout the entire market area he serves, whether it be a local, regional, or national market. In effect, the seller determines a price for the product and then adds a uniform amount for transportation costs that is charged all buyers who buy under the same circumstances. Clearly, the amount added for transportation costs should reflect the number of buyers the firm expects to serve, as well as their locations, for it is the "average" transportation cost that should be added to the price of the product in arriving at the delivered price.

Under single-zone pricing the manufacturer receives a different net return (delivered price minus transportation costs) depending upon the transportation costs involved in each sale, which, in turn, are largely determined by distance. The buyer, on the other hand, pays the same price (under the same circumstances) as any other buyer, regardless of how far he is from the shipping point. In effect, the nearby buyers pay more for transportation than the actual cost of that transportation, and the more distant buyers pay less for transportation than the actual cost involved.

A variant of single-zone pricing is a *multiple-zone* system of delivered pricing, whereby delivered prices are uniform within each of two or more zones. Here, the differences in delivered prices between the several zones are often based on distance from the point of shipment although other factors, such as competition, may dictate the differences.

Single- and multiple-zone pricing clearly make it easier for the manufacturer to sell his product in distant markets, since distant buyers are not penalized by high transportation costs (particularly under a single-zone system). In fact, they pay less for transportation than the actual cost involved. This is particularly important to those manufacturers who have high fixed costs or excess capacity and, therefore, find that they cannot rely on a small geographic market alone.

A second advantage of single- and multiple-zone pricing is that they help to ensure that distributors will resell the product at a uniform price and perhaps the price that the manufacturer suggests. Because all distributors within a zone who buy under the same circumstances are charged the same delivered prices, they will have the same landed costs, which in turn means that it is possible for them to price uniformly and still earn adequate margins. In short, if a manufacturer wants to advertise a resale price to ultimate customers, affix a resale price to containers, or make use of resale price maintenance legislation, he is far better advised to make use of a zone delivered-pricing system so that he can be sure that his distributors have similar landed costs and can, therefore, price the product at the level he desires.

For the manufacturer single- and multiple-zone pricing also offer the advantage that, once the transportation cost factor has been calculated for a zone, the salesman can simply quote the delivered price to prospective buyers without having to consult his firm's traffic department. The full landed cost to the buyer is a known quantity. Also, when invoices are prepared, there is no need to determine what freight rates apply to a particular transaction. All that needs to be done is to add the previously determined transportation cost factor.

An advantage that is peculiar to multiple-zone pricing, and a reason why it is sometimes preferred to single-zone pricing, is that a manufacturer may find it impossible to arrive at a satisfactory delivered price if he is trying to use just one price for the entire market area served. For example, a manufacturer who is located on the East Coast may find it impossible to maintain one delivered price throughout the entire United States because the high transportation costs for shipments to points in the Far West may raise the average transportation cost factor used in pricing to such a level that the resultant delivered price is noncompetitive. As an alternative, the manufacturer may choose to make use of one delivered price for buyers who are located, say, east of the Rocky Mountains and another, higher delivered price for those buyers located west of the Rocky Mountains.

A related advantage in using multiple-zone pricing is that it may enable a manufacturer to segment his market geographically in terms of price, adjusting delivered prices according to the price elasticity of demand in the different geographic sectors.

Competitive reasons may also lead a manufacturer to use multiple zones. If the degree of competition faced by a manufacturer varies from one geographic area to another, the manufacturer may wish to price differently in the different areas. A multiple-zone system of pricing can help him accomplish this objective.

Among the disadvantages for a manufacturer in using single- and multiple-zone pricing is the fact that the firm does not receive the same net return from each sale. As we pointed out earlier, the net return varies according to the distance of the buyer from the shipping point and the size of the transportation costs involved. If the transportation cost factor(s) has been determined in such a way that it incorporates the overall transportation costs, this difference in net return should present no particular problem. However, if the transportation factor(s) has been determined so that it does not incorporate the overall transportation costs, then the manufacturer may discover that he is paying out more for transportation than he gets back from customers. This is particularly likely to occur if transportation costs are high. Whether or not a firm can successfully absorb freight charges depends, of course, upon the margin of profit it is getting on the product itself. Because of the threat of this hidden freight expense, single- and multiple-zone pricing are most likely to work out satisfactorily for firms that face transportation costs that are low relative to the value of the products involved.

Another difficulty with single- and multiple-zone pricing is that, although the transportation cost factor(s) used in pricing has been designed to provide an overall return to the firm that covers transportation costs, the factor(s) selected may become obsolete as the market for the firm's products shifts geographically. For example, if the firm sells more and more of its output to distant buyers, the transportation cost factor(s) originally selected may no longer yield enough to cover the total current transportation bill. Therefore it is important that the manufacturer continually review the delivered-pricing system and the transportation cost factor(s) used lest it become out-of-date.

Another problem with single- and multiple-zone pricing is that buyers who are located near the manufacturer usually pay more for transportation than the actual costs involved, and this may create ill will; it may even cause them to switch to another manufacturer if this is possible. However, since manufacturers in a given industry tend to use the same systems when pricing geographically, it may be difficult for a buyer to find a manufacturer who could offer him a better price. In any event, one way to overcome possible resentment among nearby buyers is to price f.o.b. origin for customers in the immediate area and to use a delivered-zone pricing system for buyers that are farther away.

Unlike f.o.b.-origin pricing, single- and multiple-zone pricing also mean that the manufacturer, when using for-hire transportation, must choose the mode of transportation, select the carrier, handle the damage claims, and pay the freight bills. These may be a burden on the firm.

One last problem that sometimes arises with multiple-zone pricing is that buyers who are located near the boundary lines of the zones sometimes complain of differences in delivered prices paid by themselves and by other buyers who are nearby but located in another zone.

DELIVERED PRICING—FREIGHT ALLOWED

A manufacturer may quote his prices "f.o.b. origin with freight allowed." Under this arrangement the buyer arranges for and pays for the transportation, but the manufacturer then permits him to deduct the transportation costs from the amount on the invoice. This means that all buyers who buy under the same circumstances are charged the same price, and that the seller receives a varying net return from each sale depending upon the transportation costs involved. In this respect, it is really the same as a delivered-pricing system. The main difference is that the responsibility for arranging for transportation and paying for it is shifted to the buyer, thus permitting him to choose the mode and carrier he prefers. Indeed, in some situations it may enable the buyer to lower the net price he actually pays if the allowance permitted by the manufacturer is based on rates charged by some other, more expensive mode of transportation. For example, because it is traditional and because published rail rates are readily available, the freight allowance is often based on rail rates even though other forms of transportation are actually used.

DELIVERED PRICING—BASING-POINT PRICING

Another form of delivered pricing is called *basing-point pricing*. Under this approach the delivered price on any shipment is calculated by adding together the price of the product at the basing point and the cost of transportation from that basing point to the customer. A basing point is some designated city where the product being priced is produced. It is a basing point if delivered prices are determined by adding together the price of the product at that city and the transportation costs required to move the product from that city to the buyer. This delivered price is used even though the product may in fact be shipped from some other producing point directly to the buyer. The actual location of the firm or plant from which the shipment is made in any given transaction has no effect on the delivered price. One or more basing points can be used in any given transaction, depending upon whether the system used is a *single basing-point system* or a *multiple basing-point system*. The system may be a unilateral company-wide system used only by one firm, such as a firm with several plants located at different geographic points, or it may be an industry-wide system used by all or most firms in a given industry. In the latter case, a given manufacturer may or may not have production facilities at a given basing point. An industry-wide basing-point system can develop as the result of price leadership in which the firms in the industry follow the prices established by a leader(s) that uses a basing-point system. Industry-wide basing-point pricing can also be an accepted industry tradition in which traditional basing points are used. It can also be the result of collusion between the firms involved.

Under a single basing-point system, the firms or plants located at the basing point receive the same net return from each of their sales made under the same circumstances regardless of where the buyer is located, since the delivered price is the sum of the price at the basing point plus transportation charges from that point to the buyer. Firms or plants that are not located at the basing point receive different net returns from different sales, however. The net return received varies because there are differences between actual transportation costs and the transportation cost factor used in calculating the delivered price. If the transportation cost factor used is greater than the actual transportation charges incurred, the seller collects what is termed "phantom freight" or "fictitious freight." If the actual transportation costs from the point of shipment are greater than the transportation cost factor used, the firm is said to be engaging in "freight absorption."

When several points are designated as basing points, the system is called a multiple basing-point system. The basing point that will be used for calculations on a particular sale is usually determined by adding the prices at the various basing points to the transportation costs necessary to ship from those points to the particular buyer in question and then selecting the basing point that provides the lowest delivered price to the buyer. Under multiple basing-point pricing, both the firms or plants located at the basing points *and* the firms or plants not located at the basing points receive varying net returns from different sales. Since any given basing point is sometimes not the "applicable" basing point, plants or firms located at a basing point will sometimes have to absorb freight charges on shipments for which some other basing point is applicable.

A variation of industry-wide basing-point pricing involves the quotation of prices f.o.b. origin but with the understanding that any prices of competitors that result in a total landed cost to a buyer that is less than the buyer would receive from that firm or plant under the f.o.b.-origin method will be matched by the seller. In other words, the manufacturers are willing to absorb freight charges in order to be competitive and, in effect, every firm or plant in the industry becomes a potential basing point. This is because whenever the delivered price associated with a given firm or plant is matched by competitors, that firm or plant has become the basing point for that sale. Such a pricing arrangement is usually referred to as "freight equalization" and is designed to eliminate price as a factor in a buyer's purchasing decision. The practice is limited, of course, by the unwillingness or inability of the manufacturer to absorb freight charges in large amounts.

A *unilateral company-wide* basing-point system can effectively eliminate price competition between the various production facilities of the firm. Since all plants within the firm's production system quote prices according to the basing-point formula, the buyer, no matter where he might be located, pays the same price regardless of which plant the product is shipped from. This also enables the firm to make shipments from plants that otherwise might not receive enough orders to keep them operating at a satisfactory percentage of capacity.

A further advantage of a unilateral company-wide basing-point system is that it simplifies to some degree the task of price quotation in that a schedule of delivered prices to various points throughout the market area need be prepared only for the basing point(s) and not for every production point within the firm's production system.

The manufacturer who makes use of a unilateral company-wide system of basing-point pricing may find that he faces the familiar problem of creating ill will among certain customers who discover that they pay more for transportation than the actual costs involved while other customers pay less for transportation than the actual costs. Indeed, what might at first seem to be the locational advantages of some buyers are turned into disadvantages by the basing-point system. Another possible disadvantage of the unilateral company-wide system of basing-point pricing is the fact that it may result in a considerable amount of freight absorption. Also, as with other delivered-pricing systems, the return to the seller varies on each sale and, for this reason, may be unsatisfactory when compared to f.o.b.-origin pricing. Finally, unilateral company-wide basing-point pricing may embroil the firm in legal complications. (See pp. 216–20 for a discussion of the legality of basing-point pricing.)

When an industry follows a basing-point system of pricing, price competition is eliminated among the competing firms, especially that based on transportation costs. This is a particularly important advantage in industries where the product involved is highly standardized and where price warfare is a possible problem. Industry-wide basing-point pricing also tends to be advantageous to industries that face large transportation costs and high fixed costs or excess capacity, and in which the firms feel they must sell in distant markets in order to secure greater volume without being limited to a relatively small geographic market area by large transportation costs. By eliminating transportation costs as a factor for buyers to consider, any firm or plant in the industry can sell in a much larger geographic market than otherwise. This is especially true for firms or plants located at the basing point(s). In order for an industry-wide basing-point system to be effective, however, experience seems to indicate that the industry should consist of a relatively small number of firms; otherwise, the tendency to deviate from the basing-point formula is great enough to cause the system to break down.

For the reasons discussed above, the industries that have used industry-wide basing-point systems have generally been those that produce a relatively homogeneous product, attach great importance to transportation costs, face high fixed costs or overcapacity, and consist of a relatively small number of firms. The steel, cement, asphalt roofing, sugar, and wood pulp industries are good examples.

The disadvantages in using an industry-wide system of basing-point pricing include the ill will it creates among buyers who find that they are paying transportation costs from production points that are not involved in the particular transaction in question. Since basing-point pricing inherently involves price discrimination, this reaction is to be expected. Buyers may also object that industry-wide basing-point pricing deprives them of a choice as far as price is concerned since they receive the same delivered price regardless of what firm is supplying the product or the location of the point of shipment.

Another objection to industry-wide basing-point pricing, and one that may or may not be generated by buyers, is the fact that basing-point pricing results in a good deal of waste in transportation. Since the delivered price is the same from all producing points, the customer does not care where the product comes from. As a result, there is unnecessary transportation of the product to the extent that a customer could be served by a nearby production point but instead purchases the product from a production point many miles distant. Although this criticism can also be directed to unilateral company-wide systems, it is more frequently directed to industry-wide systems.

Industry-wide basing-point pricing is also said to result in higher and more inflexible prices since there is practically no competitive pressure among the firms in the industry to keep them low or to cause them to change very often.

Finally, as with any kind of basing-point system, industry-wide basing-point pricing may lead to excessive freight absorption on the part of the manufacturer, unsatisfactory, varying returns to the seller, and legal problems.

LEGAL PROBLEMS ASSOCIATED WITH GEOGRAPHIC PRICING PRACTICES

The legality of geographic pricing practices has long been questioned, particularly by agencies of the federal government. The inquiries have dealt exclusively with the various forms of delivered pricing; f.o.b.-origin pricing, by its very nature, is unquestionably legal.

Zone systems   Single- and multiple-zone pricing are subject to the charge of price discrimination. Price discrimination may be considered to be inherent in zone pricing because the net return received by a seller from different sales made under the same circumstances within a zone actually varies depending on the distance of the buyer from the shipping point. The fact that some buyers pay for more transportation than is actually involved on a given transaction, while others pay for less transportation than is involved, is discriminatory on behalf of the latter. In effect, the nearby buyers pay part of the transportation bill for the more distant buyers. Or, to put it another way, nearby buyers are not allowed to exploit their locational advantage under a zone-pricing system. In addition, under a multiple-zone pricing system, buyers located in different zones pay different delivered prices and this, too, can be construed as price discrimination.

Despite the price discrimination inherent in single- and multiple-zone pricing, it has had relatively little legal difficulty. Neither the Federal Trade Commission nor the federal courts have attempted to prevent an individual seller who practices single-zone pricing from maintaining a uniform delivered price. The reason there has been so little criticism of single-zone pricing systems by the Commission and the courts is apparently the fact that, in this instance, they view as discriminatory differences in prices that exist at the point of *destination,* and under single-zone pricing there are no price differences among buyers at the destination point, and hence there is no discrimination. As we have pointed out, there are price differences at the point of *origin* of the product; a seller in effect charges a different price on every sale that has a different freight cost.[43] If the Commission and the courts viewed price differences at the point of origin as discriminatory, as they have with basing-point pricing, then single-zone pricing systems would be of doubtful legality.

Multiple-zone pricing systems have had little legal trouble except in those cases where several producers in an industry, or all the firms in the industry, have adopted similar or identical zone-pricing systems. The Federal Trade Commission has stated that a single firm is free to adopt any geographic pricing system as long as no monopolistic advantage is being maintained through unfair methods of competition.[44] If a multiple-zone pricing system is used by several or all firms in a given industry, then the firms are open to a charge of price

---

[43] Phelps and Westing, *op. cit.,* pp. 358–60.

[44] Federal Trade Commission, *Notice to the Staff: In Re: Commission Policy Toward Geographic Pricing Practices* (Washington, D.C.: U.S. Government Printing Office, October 12, 1948), p. 4.

fixing in violation of section 5 of the Federal Trade Commission Act. In this regard, the Commission has said that when a group of competing firms establish an artificial zone system with identical boundaries and identical price differentials, it is difficult to believe that they could have been achieved and maintained without collusion.[45] This view has been upheld by the federal courts.[46]

Basing-point pricing In sharp contrast to zone pricing, basing-point pricing has had considerable legal difficulty under the Robinson-Patman Act and section 5 of the Federal Trade Commission Act.[47] The Robinson-Patman Act has been applied against unilateral company-wide systems of basing-point pricing and also against industry-wide basing-point systems on the grounds that they involve unjust price discrimination. In addition, the Federal Trade Commission Act has been applied to industry-wide basing-point systems on the ground that they are the result of price fixing among competitors.

When a single firm unilaterally adopts a basing-point system of pricing that it imposes upon its various production plants, or when an entire industry adopts a basing-point system, price discrimination is said to occur much as it might be said to occur under a single-zone or multiple-zone system of pricing. This is because the various firms or plants involved receive varying net returns from the different sales that are made under the same circumstances, depending upon the distance the buyer happens to be from the applicable basing point, and because these varying returns have little or no cost justification. Also, some buyers pay for more transportation than they incur ("phantom freight") while others pay for less ("freight absorption"), and this may be said to be discriminatory in favor of the latter. Finally, basing-point pricing may be said to be discriminatory on the grounds that buyers who are located close to the shipping point are not permitted to exploit their natural locational advantages if the applicable basing point is farther away from the buyer than is the actual point of shipment. In fact, they may be penalized for being close to the shipping point in such a situation in that they must pay more in transportation costs than do buyers who are much farther away from the very same point of shipment.

---

[45] *Ibid.*

[46] *Fort Howard Paper Company* v. *Federal Trade Commission,* 156 F. (2d) 899 (1946). See also *Federal Trade Commission* v. *National Lead Company* et al., 352 U.S. 419 (1957).

[47] See Chapter 4 for a discussion of legislation that affects pricing.

When several or all firms in an industry practice basing-point pricing, the suspicion that price fixing is present naturally arises. Indeed, any industry-wide practice is suspected of being the result of collusive action on the part of the sellers. This means that industry-wide basing-point pricing can be construed as a violation of the Federal Trade Commission Act, which prohibits unfair methods of competition.[48]

Because of these and other criticisms of basing-point pricing, the Federal Trade Commission has attacked the practice for many years. However, it had little success until the 1940's,[49] when, in two cases that reached the United States Supreme Court, the Commission was upheld in its attack on basing-point systems as used by two producers of glucose. These well-known decisions are referred to as the "Glucose" rulings. In *Corn Products Refining Company* v. *Federal Trade Commission*[50] the Supreme Court declared that the single basing-point system used by the Corn Products Refining Company resulted in unlawful price discrimination. The Court ruled that the varying net returns received by the firm bore no relation to the differences in the actual costs of delivery. Such discrimination, the Court continued, is prohibited by the Robinson-Patman Act if it has the effect of reducing competition substantially or of tending to create a monopoly. In this instance, the Court held that the discrimination in the basing-point system of pricing had, in fact, injured competition between candy manufacturers who purchased glucose from the Corn Products Company by giving some candy manufacturers an unwarranted price advantage over others.

In *Federal Trade Commission* v. *Staley Manufacturing Company*[51] the same decision was reached with the additional feature that both the Commission and the Court rejected Staley's defense that it had absorbed freight in order to meet the lower prices of a rival seller (the Corn Products Company). The Court ruled that section 2b of the Robinson-Patman Act, which permits discrimination if it is practiced in good faith to meet a competitor's prices, does not apply to price *systems* but only to individual competitive situations.

The Glucose cases applied to single companies (not industry-wide basing-point pricing) and to single basing-point systems only. But in

[48] Industry-wide basing-point pricing can also be construed as a violation of the Sherman Act.

[49] In 1924 the Commission forced the steel industry to give up the single basing-point system, but the industry then adopted a multiple basing-point system to replace it.

[50] 324 U.S. 726 (1945).

[51] 324 U.S. 746 (1945).

1948 the Supreme Court extended the rule to apply to an industry-wide multiple basing-point system when it upheld the Commission by finding that the system of pricing used was unlawful. The case involved the seventy-four member companies of the Cement Institute.[52] Specifically, the Court held that the multiple basing-point system used by the cement industry involved unlawful discrimination and also unfair competition. The varying net returns received from different sales through the collection of freight differentials bearing no relation to the actual costs of delivery were held to amount to systematic price discrimination between the customers of each producer. The Court further found that such discrimination was practiced for the purpose of eliminating competition between the cement companies and was illegal under the Robinson-Patman Act. The Court rejected the claim of the cement companies that the discrimination was legal under the "good-faith clause" of the Robinson-Patman Act by saying that this clause can be used as a defense only in individual competitive situations and that it does not apply to a general system of pricing. Furthermore, the Court found that the discrimination was not accomplished in good faith to meet a competitor's low price since it was the result of cooperation.

The Court also ruled that the Cement Institute had violated section 5 of the Federal Trade Commission Act by restraining competition in the sale of cement through combinations, understandings, and agreements to employ a multiple basing-point system of pricing. The system of pricing under consideration could be practiced only through concerted action on the part of the competing companies and therefore constituted a conspiracy to maintain identical prices.[53]

Another important case involving basing-point pricing was the 1948 Conduit decision of a United States Circuit Court of Appeals.[54] In this case the court again upheld the Commission and declared that the use of basing-point pricing by an individual company when there is knowledge that competitors also use the system amounts to unfair competition and unlawful price discrimination,

---

[52] *Federal Trade Commission* v. *Cement Institute* et al., 333 U.S. 683.

[53] The Commission had successfully applied section 5 of the Federal Trade Commission Act to basing-point pricing in two other cases. See *U.S. Maltsters Association* v. *Federal Trade Commission,* 152 F. (2d) 161 (1945), and *Milk and Ice Cream Can Institute* v. *Federal Trade Commission,* 152 F. (2d) 478 (1946).

[54] *Triangle Conduit and Cable Company, Inc.* v. *Federal Trade Commission,* 168 F. (2d) 175.

even though no actual conspiracy can be shown. This decision was appealed and resulted in a four-to-four tie vote in the Supreme Court (one Justice did not participate) and thus, in effect, was upheld by that Court.[55]

Immediately after the Cement decision, advocates of basing-point pricing succeeded in getting a bill passed by Congress that would have legalized basing-point pricing by amending both the Federal Trade Commission and Robinson-Patman Acts. This bill was vetoed by President Harry S. Truman in 1950, however. The Federal Trade Commission thereupon modified its stand somewhat on the concurrent use of basing-point pricing by competing firms. In a case decided in 1951 the Commission stated that (1) it was not considering evidence of uniformity of prices, or any element thereof, between two or more sellers at any destination, or destinations, to be in and of itself a violation of law and that (2) it had no intention of prohibiting or interfering with the practices of delivered pricing or freight absorption as such when innocently and independently pursued, regularly or otherwise, in such a way as to promote competition.[56]

Subsequent to the rush of legal activity surrounding basing-point pricing in the late 1940's and early 1950's, there has been little legal action, and thus little to clarify the status of basing-point pricing. In general, it would seem that, at present, industry-wide systems of arriving at identical delivered prices (including basing-point systems) are suspect. However, the Federal Trade Commission appears to be unwilling to apply the decision in the Conduit case, which condemned the concurrent use of basing-point pricing when the practice could be shown to have the effect of restraining competition. In fact, the Commission has indicated that it will not initiate proceedings against the use of delivered-pricing systems except on clear-cut grounds of conspiracy, despite the fact that the Corn Products, Staley, and Conduit cases were not based upon conspiracy charges.[57] As a result, the Commission has limited its intervention to those practices that make it probable, rather than merely possible, that competition will be injured. Furthermore, the Commission seems to have adopted the view that conscious parallelism of action alone is insufficient evidence of

[55] *Clayton Mark* et al. v. *Federal Trade Commission,* 336 U.S. 956 (1949).
[56] *Federal Trade Commission* v. *American Iron and Steel Institute* et al., 48 FTC 123, 154. This case is cited in Vernon A. Mund, *Government and Business,* 3rd ed. (New York: Harper & Bros., 1960), p. 348.
[57] *Ibid.,* p. 350.

conspiracy. "Thus, if recent precedents prevail, the Federal Trade Commission may be less likely to attack some types of basing-point systems in the future, especially if an industry's agreement to employ the method is tacit and if its enforcement machinery is not obtrusive." [58]

This suggests that sellers are free to absorb freight charges in order to get into a market, or to continue to serve a market, as long as they do not do this as part of a collusive scheme with competitors for the purpose of, or with the effect of, restraining competition.

Although many firms and industries discontinued their use of basing-point pricing after the court decisions of the 1940's, basing-point pricing can still be used without interference by the federal government. Several industries are currently employing this kind of pricing. However, in general, a manufacturer should avoid basing-point pricing, if possible, for several reasons. The first is that any kind of basing-point pricing is highly unfair to at least some of a firm's customers because it is inherently discriminatory in its effects. In addition, in industry-wide basing-point pricing all sellers who are using the system quote identical delivered prices, which has the same effect as price fixing. This prevents customers from being able to choose between differently priced products. Second, the unfairness of the system usually leads to dissatisfaction among customers of a firm and a desire to buy the product in question or a substitute from other firms within the same industry (if this is possible), or from another industry. Third, basing-point pricing may lead to excessive freight absorption. Fourth, the possibility of legal complications is ever-present.

Thus, although basing-point pricing offers some advantages to a manufacturer, a firm is better advised as a practical matter to avoid the practice as much as possible. If the manufacturer is anxious to set up a delivered-pricing system, a single- or multiple-zone system is clearly preferable. It must be recognized, however, that sometimes a manufacturer has little choice in deciding on a geographic pricing policy, particularly if the practice is regarded as customary in a given industry. To deviate from the accepted practice in such a case would be highly confusing to buyers, might damage a seller's competitive position, and might even lead to price warfare in the industry.

[58] Merle Fainsod, Lincoln Gordon, and Joseph C. Palamountain, Jr., *Government and the American Economy,* 3rd ed. (New York: W. W. Norton, 1959), p. 590.

DISTRIBUTION-COST ANALYSIS

NATURE AND PURPOSE OF
DISTRIBUTION-COST ANALYSIS

In marketing it is very difficult to measure costs accurately and to relate effort or costs (input) to results (output). As a consequence, management is forced to make decisions about personal selling, advertising, physical distribution, and other aspects of marketing without knowing enough about the exact actual and potential contribution made to sales volume and profit. The result is that in many business firms a large share of the products sold, customers served, territories served, and orders processed account for a relatively small proportion of the sales of the firm. Marketing effort directed at such products, customers, and territories is not only wasteful in itself, but also wasteful in the sense that it is not being directed toward more profitable products, customers, and territories.

In this regard, the study of distribution costs by individual business firms has been of increasing concern to business management in recent years. There has also been a growing interest in distribution-cost analysis (sometimes called marketing-cost analysis) because marketing costs are growing relative to other costs of doing business and also because of the limitations imposed by the Robinson-Patman Act relative to price discrimination. The development of operations-research techniques and electronic data-processing equipment has encouraged this trend.

Although distribution-cost analysis can be used by almost any business firm, it appears to be of more importance to manufacturers because the problems of identifying and measuring distribution costs and of measuring the effectiveness of marketing effort seem to be somewhat more complex for manufacturers than for other business firms.

Distribution-cost analysis, which involves a detailed study of a firm's entire distribution-cost structure, is designed to identify and measure distribution-cost elements, to determine the productivity of different sales segments, such as products, customers, territories, and sales-order sizes, and to eliminate or reduce the losses involved in the unprofitable sales that result from misallocation of marketing effort. In other words, distribution-cost analysis is one method of measuring whether marketing effort and expenditures are used where they will be most productive for the firm and hence generate the greatest net profit. By using distribution-cost analysis, the manufacturer hopes to find out exactly what the several parts of the marketing effort of the firm contribute to the costs of the firm, the sales of the firm, and the profits of the firm. Usual accounting techniques are somewhat inadequate for this purpose because the present accounting techniques used to record the results of marketing effort are insufficiently detailed, and their figures are distorted by arbitrary cost allocations.[59] Although developments in managerial accounting are changing this situation, there is no question that the development of methods of measuring and controlling distribution costs have lagged behind the methods of production-cost accounting.

The first step in distribution-cost analysis is usually to determine what expenditures should be considered as distribution or marketing costs. This is sometimes difficult to do because of the difficulty of distinguishing between production and distribution costs. After this is done, the next step, at least according to one approach, is a two-fold process:

1. The marketing expenditures of a particular firm that are usually accounted for on a "natural" expense basis are reclassified into "functional-cost" groups. These functional-cost groups bring together all the costs associated with each marketing activity performed by that firm.

2. The functional-cost groups are "allocated" to products, customers, territories, and other segments of sales on the basis of measurable factors. These measurable factors or bases of allocation are product, customer, territory, etc., characteristics which bear a "causative" relationship to the total amounts of the functional-cost groups.[60]

Charles H. Sevin points out that the functional classifications used are selling costs, advertising costs, sales-promotion costs, transporta-

[59] William J. Baumol and Charles H. Sevin, "Marketing Costs and Mathematical Programming," *Harvard Business Review*, September–October, 1957, p. 53.
[60] Charles H. Sevin, *Marketing Productivity Analysis* (New York: McGraw-Hill, 1965), pp. 12–16.

tion costs, storage and shipping costs, and order-processing costs. The objective is to charge each segment of sales with the cost of its share of the activity of each functional-cost group, that is, the cost of the portion of the marketing effort that it is "responsible" for. To put this another way, the manufacturer's overall distribution costs must be allocated to the specific sales segments for which they are incurred. Thus, the sale of 1,000 boxes of a product to retail grocery chains in a given state may require X dollars worth of salesman time, Y dollars in physical distribution costs, and Z dollars in advertising expenditures. By properly allocating cost and profit information, it is hoped that the profits or losses derived from this segment of the business can be determined.

Product, customer, and territory characteristics (or characteristics of other segments of the business) that may be used as bases for allocation of costs to products, customers, and territories include such things as the selling time devoted to each product or customer, media costs for advertising expenditures on a given product, transportation rates for given products, warehouse space required by an average inventory of a product, and the number of shipping units to certain customers.[61]

In distribution-cost analysis it is possible to distinguish between three separate classes of cost.[62]

Common fixed distribution costs are costs that are incurred in common for different sales segments, and that do not vary in size with the volume of sales in any one sales segment. An example is expenditures on institutional advertising of the company name (rather than advertising of any individual product or service), which presumably influence sales to some extent in all sales segments. Although firms often attempt to allocate such expenses to sales segments, such costs can be excluded from distribution-cost analysis since the "contribution" to fixed cost after deduction of variable and separable costs (as these are defined below) may be what is important in respect to decisions on individual sales segments.

Variable distribution costs are those that vary with sales and can be allocated to sales segments. An example of this category is the additional transportation cost associated with increased sales. Varia-

---

[61] *Ibid.*, pp. 12–31.
[62] This discussion of different kinds of costs is based on Baumol and Sevin, *op. cit.*, pp. 54–55.

ble costs are, of course, included in distribution-cost analysis and are allocated to particular sales segments.

Separable fixed distribution costs are fixed marketing costs that can be allocated to specific sales segments. For example, the time and effort a sales manager spends on specific sales segments should be allocated to sales segments, even though his salary is a fixed cost element. Similarly, the floor space in a warehouse containing finished goods whose rental is fixed should be allocated among the different products in terms of the space used by each. Separable fixed distribution costs are very important in distribution-cost analysis since one purpose of the analysis is to show where a firm's marketing effort can be used most effectively. It is clear, for example, that a sales manager should devote his time to a sales segment that yields $50 per hour of his time rather than to another segment that yields only $30 in return for an hour of his effort.

The approach to cost allocation outlined above is one version of the "contribution" method of distribution-cost analysis (sometimes called the "marginal" method). Its name derives from the fact that it does not attempt to allocate common fixed distribution costs but emphasizes instead the contribution over variable costs and separable fixed costs made to common fixed costs by different sales segments. A less satisfactory version of the contribution approach does not attempt to allocate either common fixed distribution costs or separable fixed distribution costs.

A different approach from the contribution method is to follow the "net-profit" system, which attempts to allocate all indirect expenses among the segments being analyzed. Proponents of the net-profit approach contend that the purpose of a distribution-cost study is to determine the net profitability of the segments being studied and that the contribution approach does not fulfill this purpose.[63]

One important advantage of the contribution method is that it avoids arbitrary allocation of common fixed costs and emphasizes the contribution over allocated expenses made by different sales segments. It is also easier to carry out than the net-profit approach. However, it does not satisfy the accountant's standard of complete

[63] William J. Stanton, *Fundamentals of Marketing* (New York: McGraw-Hill, 1964), p. 690. Discussions of various systems that may be used to allocate distribution costs are found in J. Brooks Heckert and Robert B. Miner, *Distribution Costs*, 2nd ed. (New York: Ronald Press, 1953), pp. 31–34 and Chapter 12, and Donald R. Longman and Michael Schiff, *Practical Distribution Cost Analysis* (Homewood, Ill.: Irwin, 1955), pp. 358–79.

breakdown of costs, on the basis of which the net profitability of sales segments can be established.

Either of these two basic approaches can be appropriate depending upon the purpose of the analysis. In order to justify cost differences under the Robinson-Patman Act, for example, all costs must be allocated equally. Budgeting decisions might also require such an approach. However, for short-run decisions of various kinds management needs to know the contribution made by specific sales segments, and some variety of the contribution approach can best provide this sort of information.

Regardless of the method used, once the cost allocations have been made, it is possible to compare the costs of various phases of the marketing effort against sales results, thereby indicating how productive each phase of the marketing effort has been and which products, customers, and territories are most profitable for the firm. Distribution-cost analysis can also be used to locate costs that should be reduced. It provides management with a means of finding out, or estimating, what would happen to marketing costs and productivity if effort were channeled more in one direction. In other words, it gives management an idea of how changes in total costs for each sales segment are related to changes in volume in that segment. Under the contribution method, the guiding principle is that effort should be reallocated as much as possible to those segments of sales where an additional unit of marketing effort will yield the highest contribution to net profits and overhead, after deduction of variable costs and separable fixed costs.[64] The specific kinds of decisions for which distribution-cost analysis can provide useful data include the following:

1. The selection of channels of distribution
2. The selection of specific target customers
3. The determination of which products are to be added and which are to be continued or dropped
4. The determination of how sales effort should be directed for specific products or for specific customers and territories
5. The determination of the proper order size to accept or reject
6. The determination of what services are to be offered
7. The selection of sales territories
8. Pricing

[64] Baumol and Sevin, *op. cit.*, p. 56.

In short, distribution-cost analysis can direct the attention of management to unhealthy situations in the areas specified so that management, through further analysis, can then determine what action to take.[65]

THE CONTRIBUTION OF DISTRIBUTION-COST ANALYSIS TO PRICING

To the extent that distribution-cost analysis helps to measure what distribution costs are and what they can be expected to be in the future, it can be of great assistance in pricing since costs can often be a very important consideration in pricing, as we indicated in Chapter 2. Indeed, when used in conjunction with studies of demand, competition, nondistribution costs, and other factors, distribution-cost analysis can contribute greatly to successful pricing.

In addition to measuring costs, distribution-cost analysis is also designed to evaluate the profitability of different sales segments, such as different products and customers. This phase of distribution-cost analysis provides information as to what sales segments are profitable at existing or past prices and what ones would be profitable at certain hypothetical prices (assuming, of course, that price itself does not affect demand). In this case, then, distribution-cost analysis is like break-even analysis in that this aspect of distribution-cost analysis provides information on the probable results of different alternative prices.

Distribution-cost analysis can also be used to determine when a price adjustment is required although, like break-even analysis, it does not tell the price maker what prices are feasible in the market place, given the nature of demand and other pricing considerations. For example, distribution-cost analysis may indicate that certain distributor-customers or certain sizes of orders are unprofitable and that a price change may be used either to make such sales segments profitable or to discourage the further existence or growth of such sales segments. Distribution-cost analysis can also be the basis for pricing in such a way as to encourage the continuation or growth of profitable segments, such as where price and margin adjustments are initiated for the benefit of certain classes of distributors who are highly profitable to the manufacturer. It should be emphasized, how-

[65] Phelps and Westing, *op. cit.,* p. 820.

ever, that distribution-cost analysis does not tell the price maker what prices should be or are feasible.

Another way in which distribution-cost analysis can be of assistance in pricing is that cost data generated by such analysis can be used in defense of differential pricing practices in the event that the company should be prosecuted under the Robinson-Patman Act. One of the chief reasons for the failure of the cost defense in so many Robinson-Patman Act cases has been the inability of the accused firms to provide cost data in support of their pricing systems. (See Chapter 4.) Of course, a cost analysis is no guarantee that a given pricing structure can be justified successfully before the Federal Trade Commission and the courts, but it at least provides the firm with some cost data on the basis of which to build a defense.

In addition to analyzing their own distribution costs, manufacturers should also encourage their distributors to engage in distribution-cost analysis. If a manufacturer has an accurate idea of the distributor's costs, it may alert him to the need for alteration of the margins offered to distributors and this in turn may enable him to modify his price structures in such a way as to obtain the desired degree of distributor support. Furthermore, the information gained from such cost analysis may help distributors realize that the gross margins they are earning are adequate, and this may increase their willingness to give promotional support to the manufacturer.[66]

Selected References

The following publications contain considerable material on pricing, much of which is applicable to pricing by manufacturers: Jules Backman, *Price Practices and Price Policies* (New York: Ronald Press, 1953); A. D. H. Kaplan, Joel B. Dirlam, and Robert F. Lanzillotti, *Pricing in Big Business* (Washington, D.C.: Brookings Institution, 1958); Backman, *Pricing: Policies and Practices* (New York: National Industrial Conference Board, 1961); and Alfred R. Oxenfeldt, *Pricing for Marketing Executives* (San Francisco: Wadsworth, 1961). Much of the material on pricing that is found in general marketing books and in books on managerial economics pertains to manufacturers. Pricing by small manufacturers is discussed in W. Warren Haynes, *Pricing Decisions in Small Business* (Lexington, Ky.: University of Kentucky Press, 1962), and Lanzillotti and Gordon O. Parrish, *Pricing, Production, and Marketing Policies of Small Manufacturers* (Pullman, Wash.: Washington State University Press, 1964).

[66] Warshaw, *op. cit.,* p. 53.

Product-line pricing is discussed in Joel Dean, *Managerial Economics* (Englewood Cliffs, N.J.: Prentice-Hall, 1951), Chapter 8.

Pricing of new products has been the subject of several publications. See, for example, Dean, "Pricing a New Product," *The Controller*, April, 1955; Oxenfeldt, *Pricing for Marketing Executives*, pp. 77–82; Stephen J. Welsh, "A Planned Approach to New Product Pricing," in American Management Association, *Pricing: The Critical Decision*, AMA Management Report No. 66 (New York: American Management Association, 1961); and G. Clark Thompson and Morgan B. MacDonald, Jr., "Pricing New Products," *Conference Board Record*, January, 1964.

The life cycle of products and the pricing of mature products are treated in Dean, "Pricing Policies for New Products," *Harvard Business Review*, November, 1950.

Methods manufacturers might use to control resale prices charged by distributors are discussed in Ralph Cassady, Jr., *Competition and Price Making in Food Retailing* (New York: Ronald Press, 1962), pp. 222–36.

Geographic pricing practices are usually discussed in general marketing texts such as Theodore N. Beckman and William R. Davidson, *Marketing*, 7th ed. (New York: Ronald Press, 1962), pp. 727–38, and in texts dealing with government regulation of business such as Vernon L. Mund, *Government and Business*, 3rd ed. (New York: Harper & Bros., 1960), Chapter 15. See also Fritz Machlup, *The Basing Point System* (Philadelphia: Blakiston, 1949); George W. Stocking, *Basing Point Pricing and Regional Development* (Chapel Hill, N.C.: University of North Carolina Press, 1954); and Backman, *Price Practices and Price Policies*, Chapter 7.

Distribution-cost analysis has been the subject of several good publications. A recent book on the subject is Charles H. Sevin, *Marketing Productivity Analysis* (New York: McGraw-Hill, 1965). Two older books are J. Brooks Heckert and Robert B. Miner, *Distribution Costs*, 2nd ed. (New York: Ronald Press, 1953) and Donald R. Longman and Michael Schiff, *Practical Distribution Cost Analysis* (Homewood, Ill.: Irwin, 1955). General marketing texts sometimes also contain some discussion of distribution-cost analysis. See William F. Stanton, *Fundamentals of Marketing* (New York: McGraw-Hill, 1964), pp. 685–96 and Kenneth R. Davis, *Marketing Management* (New York: Ronald Press, 1961), pp. 290–300. Good articles on the subject are William J. Baumol and Sevin, "Marketing Costs and Mathematical Programming," *Harvard Business Review*, September–October, 1957, and Sevin, "Measuring the Productivity of Marketing Expenditures," in Wroe Alderson and Stanley J. Shapiro, eds., *Marketing and the Computer* (Englewood Cliffs, N.J.: Prentice-Hall, 1963).

7

PRICING BY DISTRIBUTORS

THE NATURE OF THE PRICING DECISION OF DISTRIBUTORS

Distributors have a somewhat different pricing problem than that of manufacturers. Whereas a manufacturer has a high degree of control over the nature of his product and also its price, the distributor usually does not have control over the nature of the product (unless he has a private label), and his pricing decision is greatly influenced by the price the supplier charges for a product and perhaps also by the supplier's attempts to control resale prices. Furthermore, manufacturers generally have more discretion or latitude in pricing than distributors do because their products are differentiated, because they are generally larger in size, and because there are often a small number of firms in the industry. Nonetheless, for the distributor pricing is an important phase of the marketing effort, and it can be a difficult problem. In this chapter we will attempt to point out some of the basic characteristics of distributor pricing, some of the basic pricing problems distributors face, and the kinds of decisions that they must make. We will also make some recommendations concerning how such tasks should be handled.

THE NATURE OF COMPETITION

The market structure within which distributors compete against one another varies according to the kind of wholesaling or retailing involved and the geographic area in which competition takes place. The number of competitors involved in any particular kind of wholesaling or retailing may vary, as may the relative sizes of the competitors. Thus, the competitive situation of the distributor may vary from one similar to oligopoly to one approaching pure competition.

Competition between wholesalers and between retailers differs from competition between manufacturers, however. Manufacturers often compete against other manufacturers of the same or similar products over very large geographic areas, and they do so primarily on the bases of product differentiation and price. Distributors, on the other hand, compete against other distributors of their kind who handle any of the same products, but they do so generally within a somewhat limited geographic area, particularly in the case of retailing. Competition among distributors is based on price, location, services offered to the customer, and the nature of the products carried.

Location   Location is a critical competitive factor for distributors because nearness to buyers determines to a great extent their ability to attract customers. For wholesalers, nearness to buyers (who may be retailers, other wholesalers, or, in the case of some industrial goods, manufacturers and primary producers) directly affects transportation costs and hence total landed costs to buyers. Since wholesalers typically purchase goods in large quantities and sell goods in relatively small quantities, inbound shipments may be made under carload or truckload rates, whereas outbound shipments must often be made at higher less-than-carload or less-than-truckload rates. This is true even if the wholesaler maintains his own fleet of vehicles for outbound shipments. Thus, the closer the wholesaler is to his market, the lower is the price he can offer the buyer in terms of total landed cost. As a result, wholesalers (including branches of large wholesalers) generally confine their efforts to relatively small geographic areas.

Location is also one of the most important factors in the success or failure of retail stores. If a store is not located where it can generate sufficient customer traffic, it will fail. This is true regardless of the kind of merchandise being sold—convenience, shopping, or specialty goods—although it is relatively more important for the first two kinds of goods than it is for specialty goods. For example, retailers of convenience goods must locate their stores close to customers because, by definition, purchasers of convenience goods will not exert much effort to make such purchases. Retailers of shopping goods ordinarily must locate near other retailers who carry similar merchandise in order to give customers an opportunity to "shop." Witness the fact that regional shopping centers usually contain at least two department stores.

Services   Another factor that is becoming increasingly important as a determinant of success for wholesalers is the services they offer. Such services include satisfactory delivery times, credit extension, promotional assistance, and advice on accounting. Services of this type tend to play a more important role when a wholesaler is selling to other distributors than when he is selling industrial goods to a manufacturer or a primary producer. The increasing importance of services is evidenced most clearly by the considerable assistance offered retailers by wholesalers in the handling of some lines of consumer goods. In some cases the wholesaler will even enter into contractual arrangements with retailers by forming groups, such as voluntary chains.[1] Some buyers, however, prefer to forego such services in return for lower prices.

For retailers, services to customers have always been and still are an important determinant of success despite the recent rise of limited-service discounters in some lines of merchandise. In fact, discounters are finding it increasingly difficult to avoid offering certain services because consumers often demand them, even from discounters. Services such as credit extension, free delivery, personal sales help, return privileges, and guarantees are important to many consumers. Here again, however, there are some consumers who are happy to do without the services in exchange for lower prices. It should also be noted that the overall reputation of a store for reliability and trustworthiness, another important competitive factor, can be influenced by the services provided.

The nature of products carried   Distributors must be buyers before they can be sellers, and the ability to buy wisely is crucial since the nature of the products carried is an important competitive factor. The general quality of the merchandise a distributor carries is what distinguishes one distributor from its competitors. Although quality

---

[1] A *voluntary chain* is a contractual arrangement between a wholesaler and a number of retailers. The wholesaler may agree to furnish retailers with sales-promotion and advertising assistance and to provide advice on management, set up accounting systems, help select store sites, extend credit, provide uniform store signs, and furnish private-label merchandise. The retailers may agree to cooperate with the wholesaler in sales-promotion programs, for example, and to concentrate a certain percentage of their purchases with the wholesaler.

of merchandise serves to differentiate a firm from its competitors, it also tends to determine which distributors will be its close competitors. Also of importance is the assortment of merchandise carried by a distributor. The customer of a distributor, whether he be another distributor or a final customer, is often more interested in the range of products carried than he is in any individual product or brand.

In sum, like other firms in the American economy, distributors attempt to achieve product differentiation in order to attract buyers by offering something not offered by other firms. However, instead of attempting to differentiate an individual *product* in the eyes of potential customers, as the manufacturer does, the distributor is more interested in attempting to differentiate the *firm* in the eyes of potential customers by pointing out the superiority of his location, services, merchandise, and price.

Because of the variety of ways in which distributors may be differentiated from one another, one is likely to encounter direct competition between very similar firms that are close to one another geographically, and at the same time indirect competition between firms that are dissimilar and far apart geographically. As a rule, however, only a small number of distributors will be in direct competition with one another, especially in retailing. As Ralph Cassady, Jr., points out:

> Actually, as a result of differing service requirements, the importance of the spatial element, and product preferences, consumers consider only a few stores as completely satisfactory substitutes for one another. The balance of the establishments, as a result of geographical distance and dissimilarity of offerings, are at best only imperfect substitutes for one another.[2]

INFLUENCE OF SUPPLIERS

One important characteristic of pricing by distributors is that it is very much affected by prices charged by and resale prices recommended by producers or by other distributors from whom the product

---

[2] *Competition and Price Making in Food Retailing* (New York: Ronald Press, 1962), pp. 57–58. The influence of custom, consumer expectations, and social pressure on retail competition is discussed in Stanley C. Hollander, "Social Pressure and Retail Competition," *Michigan State University Business Topics*, Winter, 1965.

is purchased. Wholesalers and retailers often mark up merchandise by traditional percentages. In such a situation, the prices charged by a distributor are directly determined by the prices charged by the supplier. In effect, the distributors fall back on the judgments of suppliers relative to pricing. Suppliers also influence the resale prices of distributors by suggestion. The degree of influence here depends upon how much independence the distributors wish to exercise in pricing, that is, the extent to which they wish to establish price policies that are independent of those recommended by their suppliers. Since the distributor usually owns the goods to be priced, he has the right to price them as he wishes.[3]

A distributor's decision concerning whether or not to price independently of suppliers will be influenced to some extent by the degree of control over resale prices exercised by the supplier (who is usually the manufacturer). If a manufacturer makes use of resale price maintenance legislation to force compliance with suggested resale prices, for example, a retailer may have little choice but to go along.[4] However, with the general decline in the use and effectiveness of resale price maintenance legislation in recent years and with the difficulty manufacturers have had in attempting to influence or control resale prices through other methods, it appears that wholesalers and retailers now have more freedom in pricing.

Another factor that influences a distributor's decision on this matter is whether the supplier has granted him limited or exclusive distribution rights. Where such distribution rights have been granted, the distributor is likely to prefer to go along with the supplier on pricing.

Another consideration is the number of individual products to be priced. The sheer size of the pricing job for some wholesalers and retailers makes it difficult for them to set their own price on each product. It is far easier merely to adopt the prices suggested by suppliers. Indeed, this is the main reason why some distributors, particularly wholesalers, do not usually exhibit independence in pricing.

When a distributor decides to follow the resale prices suggested by the supplier, he must recognize that he is accepting certain risks. Since suggested prices cannot take into account the different operating costs of different distributors or different market conditions or characteris-

[3] However, a distributor does not always own the goods he sells, as for example when a manufacturer sells to distributors on a consignment basis or when retailers obtain merchandise from "rack" jobbers who retain title to the goods.
[4] Resale price maintenance or "fair-trade" laws are discussed on pp. 261–68.

tics, a wholesaler or a retailer who enjoys better than average efficiency may be able to sell a given product for less than his less efficient competitors and still make the same dollar gross margin (price minus landed cost). Furthermore, a distributor who serves a market that is unwilling or unable to pay a suggested resale price will find it impossible to sell the product at such a price. In either situation, the distributor may find it wise to set his own prices on the products in question.

Not only can suppliers influence the pricing of distributors, they can also influence competitive relationships between distributors through their pricing policies, if they, subject to legal restraints, discriminate between distributors on the basis of quantities purchased or trade status. Clearly, this will influence competition between distributors.[5]

MULTIPLE PRODUCTS

We have mentioned that, unlike most manufacturers, a distributor must usually price hundreds or thousands of different products, and, as a consequence, he sometimes fails to exercise much independence in pricing because of the great time and effort that would be required to consider in detail costs, demand, and other factors for each product. It is also true that, since each of the thousands of products has different characteristics in terms of rate of turnover, space required, and ease of selling, the distributor finds it very difficult to allocate his costs accurately to individual products beyond their initial invoice and transportation costs.

For these reasons, those distributors who decide to exercise independence in pricing, often use various formula-type approaches to pricing, whereby products are handled by groups rather than individually. Furthermore, because they are uncertain about the internal factors that influence costs, distributors tend to rely heavily upon external factors as pricing guides, particularly the prices of competitors and the nature of demand.

In addition, the distributor may find that his products are substitutes for one another, or that they are related complementary products, or that they are entirely unrelated. In other words, the pricing of

[5] Discount systems are discussed in Chapter 8.

any one product may have an impact on the prices and sales of other products. In Chapter 6 we discussed the various factors and alternative policies that should be considered by a manufacturing firm that sells multiple products. These same factors are generally applicable for distributors as well.

PRICING BY WHOLESALERS

A ONE-PRICE POLICY VERSUS VARYING PRICES

As was pointed out in Chapter 6, a one-price policy is the practice of charging uniform prices so that all buyers who purchase the same quantities of a product under substantially similar circumstances pay the same price. Varying prices, on the other hand, exist when different prices are charged different buyers of the same quantity of goods under similar circumstances, depending upon competitive factors or the bargaining ability of the buyer.

In general, wholesalers [6] in the United States have not adopted the one-price policy to the degree that retailers have. One reason wholesalers prefer varying prices is that in wholesaling individual transactions tend to be far more important than they are in retailing. Purchases are often made in very large quantities, and experience shows that small adjustments in price can be an effective means of attracting buyers.[7] Furthermore, customers of wholesalers are generally more conscious of price differences than are customers of retailers.

Nonetheless, there has been a tendency in recent years for wholesalers to move toward a one-price policy. The Robinson-Patman Act, which prohibits unjust price discrimination in interstate commerce, has undoubtedly had a great deal to do with this trend, as have the disadvantages of varying prices, including the higher cost of selling because of the higher caliber of sales personnel required, the time involved in price bargaining, the need to delegate pricing author-

[6] In this and the following discussion, the term *wholesaler* refers to middlemen at the wholesale level who take title to the goods they sell and to those agent middlemen (who do not take title) who have control over prices.

[7] Theodore N. Beckman, Nathanael H. Engle, and Robert D. Buzzell, *Wholesaling,* 3rd ed. (New York: Ronald Press, 1959), p. 405.

ity, the ill will created among certain customers, and the fact that varying prices encourage price cutting by salesmen. The use of varying prices also creates procedural problems in order-handling and accounting, a difficulty of paramount importance to wholesalers who handle so many different products. The whole problem of maintaining records is greatly complicated by the introduction of an additional factor that must be carefully controlled.[8]

A one-price policy also offers positive advantages. For one thing, the selling function is simplified. The policy is also fairer to buyers, and this encourages the buyer to place more confidence in the seller. Finally, a one-price policy permits both salesmen and customers to concentrate on product quality and service rather than on price.

In short, a one-price or uniform pricing policy is no longer uncommon among wholesalers, and it would seem that, given the clear-cut advantages of this policy, wholesalers should attempt to follow it whenever possible.

COSTS AND MARGINS

The success of any pricing decision depends to some extent upon costs.[9] The large number and variety of products carried by wholesalers make it difficult for them to allocate costs to specific products accurately. The only costs of which a price maker in a wholesale firm can be certain are invoice costs and transportation charges (landed costs). All other costs must be allocated to specific products on an arbitrary basis.[10]

Some wholesalers approach the pricing problem from the cost side and attempt to earn a reasonable return over all costs chargeable to a given product. Because of the difficulty in cost allocation, the cost ap-

---

[8] *Ibid.,* pp. 407–08.

[9] The relationship between costs and pricing was discussed in some detail in Chapter 2; this discussion applies to wholesaling as well as to any other kind of business. To recapitulate, the proper role of costs is to establish a floor below which a firm should not go in setting a price. For purposes of pricing, the important costs are the variable costs. It is not necessary that every item carried by a wholesaler cover fully distributed costs. In some cases, it may be sound pricing policy to charge prices that cover only variable costs, not fully-distributed costs.

[10] Costing techniques designed specifically for wholesalers are discussed in texts on wholesaling. See, for example, Richard M. Hill, *Wholesaling Management* (Homewood, Ill.: Irwin, 1963), pp. 437–63.

proach frequently results in the addition of a predetermined percentage margin to the landed cost of a product, a margin that is assumed to cover all costs and provide a margin of profit. The obvious drawback of this approach is that it ignores the demand factor. For example, wholesalers who follow this policy often apply "average" markups or margins to groups of products, perhaps by department, rather than compute separate markups for each product. The margins applied are often the result of customary trade practice.[11] The use of average or customary group or departmental margins does not allow for differences in the price elasticity of demand, degree of competition, and other factors associated with different products. It also ignores the fact that different products involve different costs.

Other wholesalers first attempt to estimate what prices customers will be willing to pay for particular products, and then they deduct estimated costs from this figure in order to determine what their profit will be on the sale of the product. The price the market will pay is, in turn, often determined by the prices charged by direct competitors for identical or similar goods. This approach, which concentrates on the prices customers can be expected to pay, is superior to the cost-dominated approach because it recognizes the market side of the problem.

DISTRIBUTION-COST ANALYSIS

Wholesalers seldom attempt to determine the dollar distribution (marketing) costs and the dollar profit (or loss) contribution of each of their products, customers, and sales territories. Those wholesalers who have made distribution-cost and profitability analyses, however, have discovered that there are extremely wide variations in the distribution costs and profits (or losses) from one segment of a wholesaling firm to another, and that subjective estimates of the relative profitability of the various segments are grossly unreliable.[12] This suggests that most wholesalers could benefit greatly from distribution-cost analysis. The methods that wholesalers should use in such an analysis are similar to those discussed in Chapter 6.[13]

[11] Beckman, Engle, and Buzzell, *op. cit.*, pp. 413–14.
[12] Charles H. Sevin, *Marketing Productivity Analysis* (New York: McGraw-Hill, 1965), pp. 11–12.
[13] See *ibid.*, particularly Chapter 2.

PROTECTION AGAINST PRICE DECLINES

The pros and cons (from the manufacturers' point of view) of guaranteeing prices against declines were discussed in Chapter 6. Wholesalers also must decide whether or not to give such guarantees to their customers. This is especially true for wholesalers who distribute their own private labels. In addition to those factors already discussed, which apply generally to wholesalers as well as to manufacturers, wholesalers should take into consideration whether or not they themselves receive price protection from their suppliers before they decide to grant others such price guarantees.

GEOGRAPHIC PRICING CONSIDERATIONS

Although the cost of shipping goods to customers can be an important pricing consideration for wholesalers, the geographic market areas served by many of them are so small that differences in the cost of shipping goods to customers are negligible. For example, it is not uncommon for wholesalers to limit their trading areas to a single city or to a metropolitan area. In such situations most wholesalers follow a policy of single-zone delivered pricing as defined in Chapter 6.[14] Wholesalers who serve fairly large geographic markets, however, should consider using f.o.b.-origin or multiple-zone delivered pricing and perhaps freight-equalization pricing, instead of single-zone pricing. These approaches to geographic pricing apply for wholesalers as well as for manufacturers.

PRICING BY RETAILERS

PRICE AND THE CHANGING RETAIL STRUCTURE

Retail prices are of particular importance because these are the prices that are paid by the ultimate buyers of consumer products. Consequently, the prices attached to products at the retail level are

---

[14] Hill, *op. cit.*, p. 164.

extremely important to the retailer, the wholesaler, and the producer. Retailing is historically one of the most volatile phases of American marketing. Great changes have taken place in the retail system at frequent intervals, and price has often played a leading role in such changes because the appearance of a new kind of retailing is usually accompanied by some sort of price appeal.

When department stores were first introduced, during the Civil War, they attempted to beat the competition by offering lower prices. Chain stores, which began in 1859 but the growth of which came primarily after World War I, also stressed low prices. The same approach was used by the new mail-order houses of the 1870's and 1880's. Similarly, the early supermarkets of the 1920's and 1930's were barren structures that offered no customer services, and low prices were their main appeal. More recently, the discount houses have stressed low prices.

Although the initial appeal of many forms of retailing has been low prices, at least in part, retailers have usually found it necessary to "trade up" after awhile by adding more customer services, improving their store facilities, and improving product quality and assortment. This was primarily necessitated by competitive factors. As retailers of a particular kind, say supermarkets, began to compete against one another as well as against older forms of retailing, it became necessary to offer to the public more than just low prices and to spend more on promotion in order to attract patronage. As a result, the new retailers' costs rose, making it more and more difficult for them to offer low prices. This provided an opportunity for still another retail innovation to emerge by offering lower prices.[15]

But this does not mean that price alone determines the success or failure of a particular kind of retailing institution. There appears to be room in the retailing structure for many kinds of retail stores, some of which stress low prices and others of which do not. Indeed, competition between retailers involves many nonprice elements such as location, credit terms, delivery service, return privileges, assortment and quality of merchandise carried, and caliber of sales personnel.

[15] The patterns involved in the changing retail structure are discussed in Malcolm P. McNair, "Significant Trends and Developments in the Postwar Period," in A. B. Smith, ed., *Competitive Distribution in a Free High-Level Economy and Its Implications for the University* (Pittsburgh: Pittsburgh University Press, 1958), and Stanley C. Hollander, "The Wheel of Retailing," *Journal of Marketing,* July, 1960.

ONE-PRICE POLICY VERSUS VARYING PRICES

Unlike retailers in many other parts of the world and unlike many wholesalers in the United States, American retailers in the twentieth century have generally followed a one-price policy. Instead of bargaining or haggling over prices on each individual sale, retailers usually attach a price to merchandise so that all buyers who purchase a particular product under similar circumstances pay the same price. In fact, retailers in the United States generally make use of a "single-price" policy in that they charge all customers the same price for a product, even though the quantities purchased or other factors that may alter the circumstances surrounding each sale are dissimilar.

There are important exceptions, of course. If trade-in allowances are offered by retailers, for example, it usually means that a one-price policy is not being followed since the amount of the allowance given by the retailer alters the price being paid. Retailers sometimes give special discounts to certain groups, such as members of certain labor unions or other organizations. Some retailers advertise that they will meet the lower prices of competitors if a customer can show that a competitor has offered a lower price. In such cases, a one-price policy is not being followed since only the customers who can show that a competitor has a lower price receive the corresponding low price. Outright bargaining is found in some forms of retailing, such as in the sale of automobiles or used merchandise. Such retailers do not even pretend to follow a one-price policy but instead bargain openly with customers. It is probable that all retailers occasionally depart from the one-price policy.[16]

Nonetheless, most retailers try to follow a one-price policy because it offers certain basic advantages and avoids some of the disadvantages inherent in a varying-price policy. These factors were discussed in relation to manufacturers in Chapter 6, but perhaps a brief summary is in order to indicate how these factors apply to retailers. For them, the basic problem with varying prices is that pricing authority may have to be delegated to sales clerks. This means that management loses some control over pricing and that a higher caliber and more expensive sales force is required. Furthermore, price bargaining is a very

---

[16] Deviations from the one-price policy are discussed in Hollander, "The 'One-Price' System—Fact or Fiction?" *Journal of Retailing*, Fall, 1955.

time-consuming process and this, in turn, increases the cost of selling. This drawback is particularly important for retailers since they usually sell in very small quantities to many different customers, in contrast to manufacturers and wholesalers who sell large quantities of product at infrequent intervals. Another difficulty with varying prices at the retail level is that it encourages price reductions since sales clerks may choose to cut prices whenever they have difficulty making a sale.

When a retailer uses varying prices, ill will may also be created among certain customers. The ease with which this can occur is illustrated by the fact that retailers often receive complaints from customers immediately after they announce a sale price on certain merchandise because the customers recently purchased the merchandise in question at the presale price. A one-price policy encourages customers to place more confidence in the retailer. Therefore, unless a retailer does not care about developing a permanent clientele, the ill-will factor can be an important drawback of varying prices.

Furthermore, if varying prices were widely used by American retailers, retailing would be less efficient than it is now and large-scale retailing would be impossible. More time would be required for each sale; more sales people would have to be hired; economies of scale would be extremely difficult to achieve; and to the extent that owners of retail stores hesitate to delegate pricing authority to sales clerks, they would tend to prefer to have smaller stores that they could supervise personally in order to keep control of the pricing function.

In contrast, a one-price policy is easier to administer than is a varying-price approach, and it makes the selling job less complicated by relieving the sales clerk of the responsibility for pricing. This not only saves selling time but also permits sales people to concentrate on the product and its attributes rather than on price. In addition, a one-price policy is fair to all buyers and is more likely to ensure good will among buyers. Laws against price discrimination have not been extended to retail transactions and hence the retailer faces no legal problems in using varying prices.

DETERMINATION OF THE LEVEL OF PRICES

Like a manufacturer, a retailer may decide to price "at the market," "below the market," or "above the market." His decision will affect all other pricing decisions and, perhaps, the use of other marketing tools. More important, however, it determines the general character of the retail operation and its image in the eyes of consumers.

Pricing at the market   When a retailer prices at the market he is attempting to match prices of direct competitors who handle the products in question. This approach to pricing is probably most suitable if the retailer feels that there is little in the way of location, customer services, or product quality and assortment that distinguishes his store from competing establishments. It should be noted that only the prices of *direct* competitors—those who are very similar in character and who are very close geographically—need be matched. It is becoming increasingly difficult for a retailer to identify his close competitors since more and more retailers are starting to carry lines of merchandise that traditionally they did not carry. Even though direct competitors are identified and the retailer has decided to match their prices, he should remember that only those products that are identical and can be compared by customers are candidates for price matching. Food products sold in supermarkets offer good examples of such price matching. Actually, given the variety of ways in which retailers can differentiate themselves from one another, competition between retailers often is not sufficiently direct to require identical prices. Only a few retail stores are completely satisfactory substitutes for one another.

There are other reasons, in addition to the lack of differentiation, that lead retailers to price their goods at the market. For some products customer expectations make identical prices among competing retailers a necessity. For example, this is the case with many products that traditionally have been priced the same by competing retailers. Price matching is also likely to occur on products over which manufacturers have exercised control or great influence with regard to the resale prices charged by retailers. Other factors that encourage price matching are the desire to avoid starting a price war with competitors and the uncertainty concerning the nature of demand for a product.

Pricing below the market   When a retailer decides to price below the prices of competitors on all or some of the products he carries, he is assigning a very important role to price. This approach is in contrast to the policy of pricing at the market, in which price is treated as a neutral marketing element. Pricing below the market has been used frequently by retailers in the past and is receiving a great deal of attention in today's economy because of the popularity of discounting. Clearly, pricing below the market is only advisable if the retailer is able to obtain satisfactory dollar profits, even though he is receiving a low margin on every unit of merchandise sold. This is particularly true if the policy is to be applied to all or most of the merchandise carried.

A retailer may feel he can price below the market profitably if he has lower costs than his competitors (as is true of some discount houses) or if the products he carries are of lower quality than similar products carried by competitors. Another factor that may cause a firm to follow this policy is a philosophy of high volume and low margin per unit of merchandise sold.

As we pointed out in Chapter 6, one of the most important determinants of success for a policy of pricing below competitors is the price elasticity of demand for the products in question.[17] It is usually assumed that most consumers are very price conscious and that their demand is sensitive to price adjustments. However, when low prices are offered to consumers, they are usually accompanied by fewer customer services and a poorer assortment of merchandise, and these negative factors may offset the attractions of a lower price. The success of discount houses in the post–World War II period, however, apparently supports the conclusion that many consumers react favorably to price adjustments.

Pricing below the market may lead to retaliation by direct competitors, thus leaving the initiating firm with lower total revenue and no price advantage. The other problem with pricing below the market is that low prices may tend to cheapen a manufacturer's product in the eyes of ultimate customers. However, it does not necessarily follow that such a policy will cheapen the retail store itself in the eyes of consumers particularly if only some of the products carried are priced this way. In fact, even if a retailer adopts a low-price policy on all the merchandise he carries, the store may not encounter any image problems. Consumers may regard the store favorably as a place where real bargains can be found. This reaction is most likely to occur if the store stocks primarily well-known manufacturers' brands, since low prices on such merchandise are readily recognized and appreciated by the buyer. However, if the products in question are unknown brands

[17] For a discussion of techniques retailers might use in estimating the price elasticity of demand, see David J. Rachman, "How Manufacturer Pricing Methods Are Adapted to Retailer Use," *Journal of Retailing,* Spring, 1960.

of manufacturers or private labels of the retailer or a wholesaler, the consumers may suspect that the store is selling low-grade merchandise at prices that reflect their quality, and the store may acquire a reputation for cheapness and poor quality.

Sometimes retailers temporarily price selected products below the prices of competitors, particularly those products that are being promoted in some way. Various products are given this special price treatment at brief intervals. As a result, some stores will offer lower prices on certain products and other stores will offer lower prices on other products at any one time, but on the average they may be almost identical. This is probably more prevalent in food retailing than elsewhere.[18]

Pricing above the market   It is usually impossible for a retailer to price his goods much above the prices charged by direct competitors unless he enjoys substantial product or firm differentiation that will attract consumers despite the higher prices. Without such differentiation, the retailer who follows such a policy can only hope to attract those consumers whose ignorance or haste leads them to pay higher prices than they could obtain elsewhere. Differentiation can be based on location, customer services, product quality and assortment, and general reputation and prestige of the store.[19] Retailers who price above the market are, in effect, indicating that they believe consumers are attracted to their store by considerations other than price. In fact, it is entirely possible for two nearby stores that are in direct competition with one another to have different prices and still succeed because of these nonprice considerations.

On the other hand, regardless of the degree of differentiation a store enjoys, it cannot escape price competition entirely. Although a store's location, services, prestige, and other factors may enable it to sell its goods at somewhat higher prices, it will lose some customers if this price difference becomes too broad. In fact, according to Delbert J. Duncan and Charles F. Phillips, any price differences will cause a store to lose some customers, since there are some who have little re-

---

[18] For an analysis of price making in food retailing, see Cassady, *op. cit.*

[19] Other ways in which a retail store can be differentiated are on the basis of unusually attractive store atmosphere, exclusiveness of merchandise lines, special promotional attractions such as premiums or trading stamps, and service at hours when most other stores are closed. See William R. Davidson and Paul L. Brown, *Retailing Management,* 2nd ed. (New York: Ronald Press, 1960), p. 388.

gard for a store's services or prestige or other elements of differentiation. Customers are particularly likely to be driven elsewhere by higher prices when the product in question is well-known branded merchandise that can be compared easily from store to store.[20] On the other hand, the higher prices may, in turn, attract other customers who appreciate such factors as location, services, and product quality and assortment, which are offered by the store, and who feel that these factors justify the higher prices.

A retailer might decide to price his goods above the market if he has higher costs than those of competitors, if he is attempting to establish a prestige reputation, if his products are better than similar products carried by competitors, or if the firm prefers to operate on a high-margin, low-volume basis. Furthermore, if the product involved is a private label, higher prices are possible since private labels are not directly comparable to merchandise carried by competitors. (However, private labels often carry *lower* prices than manufacturers' brands.) Another factor that can persuade a retailer to price above the market is the possession of exclusive right to distribute a well-known manufacturer's brand in the area. In such a situation, although competitors may carry similar products, direct price comparison on the brand in question is not possible.

PRICE LINING

As we indicated in Chapter 6, a seller who practices price lining does not attempt to sell products or services at all possible prices but, instead, confines his efforts to products or services that are sold at a limited number of prices. A retailer who practices price lining may limit his stock to two or three price categories for each kind of merchandise, which in his opinion reflect the "good," "better," and "best" categories of merchandise carried.

Price lining is widely practiced by American retailers. It simplifies to some extent the pricing task for a retailer, since once the price lines are chosen he has only to select the merchandise that is appropriate for each price line. However, because products that are sold in

---

[20] *Retailing Principles and Methods,* 6th ed. (Homewood, Ill.: Irwin, 1963), pp. 459–60.

any given price line may have been purchased at different landed costs, the retailer will earn different gross margins on different products within the same price line.

In general, price lining offers the same advantages to a retailer that it offers to a manufacturer. Price lining is especially advantageous for the retailer who carries mostly shopping goods and thus, of necessity, a wide assortment of merchandise. Price lining simplifies his inventory control problems as well as his customers' buying decisions by reducing the number of prices and groups of products from which to choose. Price lining also makes the sales-training process much easier in that sales clerks do not need to become acquainted with a vast number of different prices. In addition, price lining helps the retailer avoid frequent price changes. Finally, the practice also facilitates the buying task in that the retailer does not have to consider buying merchandise that clearly does not fit into his established price lines.[21]

Price lines do have some drawbacks, however. They may be difficult to maintain during periods of rapidly rising costs if the firm is still to receive adequate gross margins. There is also the risk that the price lines selected will not be suited to customer preferences. Finally, price lining results in inflexible prices and, to a great extent, reduces the effectiveness of price as a marketing tool since individual prices cannot be adjusted to reflect the different conditions surrounding each product.

Price lines are usually selected on the basis of past experience with the prices at which most sales of the merchandise in question are made. However, retailers sometimes merely select the price lines they want to use without reference to past experience. In any event, the price lines offered by direct competitors always warrant consideration.

Like the manufacturer who practices price lining, the retailer must be sure that the difference between price lines is sizable enough to be meaningful to customers if he is to reap the advantages of price lining. On the other hand, the space between lines cannot be so wide that they are out of proportion to the quality differences in the products or so wide that customers might prefer some intermediate price(s).

---

[21] Some additional advantages of price lining to a retailer are discussed in E. B. Weiss, "What Manufacturers Should Know about Price Lining Policies and Practices of Stores," *Printers' Ink,* February 6, 1948.

COSTS AND MARGINS

As is often the case with wholesalers, many retailers find that, because of the large number and variety of products carried, it is difficult to allocate costs accurately to specific products. Landed costs are the only costs that can be treated with certainty; other costs must be allocated to particular products on an arbitrary basis.[22] Furthermore, retailers are usually more interested in the overall gross margin of the entire store or of a major department than in the gross margin earned by any single product. Consequently, they may not feel that it is crucial to know the exact costs connected with a particular product. For these reasons, retailers often rely on average cost concepts as guides in pricing.[23]

The decision the retailer makes concerning whether he should price at the market, below the market, or above the market is one of the main determinants of the overall gross margin he earns. Only after careful study and planning can the retailer determine the optimal overall target gross margin for his store. Such research and planning might include the establishment of a realistic sales-volume goal, the determination of the amount of operating expenses required to attain that sales volume, an estimate of the total reductions, such as markdowns, discounts to employees, and stock shortages, and the establishment of a net profit goal.[24] Once a retailer has selected the target overall gross margin for his store, he must translate this figure into an average markup (the amount that must be added to landed cost to yield the selling price). Notice that the average markup needed differs from the target gross margin because the initial markup must allow for future markdowns, pilferage, and merchandise sold to employees and other groups at a discount, and hence must be greater than the gross margin earned.

Although a retailer may be able to determine the overall gross

[22] Costing techniques that can be used by retailers are discussed in texts on retailing. For example, see Davidson and Brown, *op. cit.*, Chapter 28.

[23] Malcolm P. McNair and Eleanor G. May criticize the gross-margin approach and the emphasis on percentages of sales concepts in retailing. They suggest that the emphasis in measuring retail success be on dollar contribution and return on investment. See "Pricing for Profit," *Harvard Business Review*, May–June, 1957.

[24] Davidson and Brown, *op. cit.*, pp. 389–90.

margin he needs and the average markup that will achieve that gross margin, it is usually impossible for him to apply this average markup to all the merchandise he carries because these goods differ in price elasticity of demand, degree of competition, costs of handling and selling, rate of turnover, susceptibility to large markdowns (such as with fashion merchandise or perishable goods), the degree of control over price exercised by suppliers, and other factors. One possible solution is to apply markups to groups of products or to entire departments. This practice is widely followed by retailers who carry a very large number and variety of products and therefore find it impractical to price products individually. According to this approach, the markup applied to each group reflects the general characteristics of the products in the group, such as price elasticity of demand and degree of competition.

The application of a separate markup to each product group is only a partial solution to the problem; even the group approach cannot account for variations in price elasticity of demand, degree of competition, and costs of handling and selling within the group. It also fails to recognize the demand side of the pricing problem. Consequently, wherever practical the best approach is to price individual products.[25]

DISTRIBUTION-COST ANALYSIS

Although most retailers are not interested in making distribution-cost and profitability analyses of customers and sales territories, they *should* be interested in methods they can use to determine the profitability of the various products they carry. Nonetheless, many retailers have no idea of the operating costs and net profits or losses associated with each of the many products they carry.[26] This suggests that retailers should make greater use of cost and profitability analysis.

A distribution-cost and profitability analysis of a retail operation involves the same general approach that manufacturers might use. Costs are identified and classified into functional-cost groups, which might include "selling-space costs" (the costs of space for merchan-

---

[25] Pricing by retailers so that different percentage margins are earned on different products is cited by Richard N. Holton as a form of price discrimination. See "Price Discrimination at Retail: The Supermarket Case," *Journal of Industrial Economics*, October, 1957, p. 18.

[26] Sevin, *op. cit.*, pp. 34–35.

dise display and storage), inventory costs, "movement costs" (the costs of customer- and service-area space and clerk time), and "sales-volume costs," such as the expense of trading stamps. Those indirect costs that can be allocated and direct costs, such as the expense of special wrapping materials, are then allocated to the various products carried by the store. If the contribution approach to profitability analysis is then applied, the total allocated costs of carrying each product are subtracted from its dollar gross margin, and any excess represents the product's "contribution" toward the remaining expenses of running the store and is also a measure of its relative profitability.

Notice that it is the dollar amount, rather than the percentage rate, of the excess of margin over cost that is used as a basis for comparison. Those products that show the largest dollar amounts over allocated costs are the most profitable. Those products that contribute the smallest excess of dollar gross margin over allocated costs are relatively unprofitable. Some unprofitable products may actually show a negative dollar amount after costs are deducted from margins. Such comparisons can be made for all products in the store, for the products within a single department, for groups of similar products, or for different brands of the same product.[27]

Distribution-cost analysis is also a valuable pricing guide. It helps to identify and measure distribution costs and thereby enable the firm to price more intelligently; it provides information on the probable results of alternative prices; it helps to determine when price adjustments are required by pointing out which products are profitable and which are unprofitable; and it can provide tangible evidence that can be used to persuade suppliers to make price and margin adjustments.

MARKDOWNS

Whatever prices a retailer attaches to his goods, and regardless of the pricing method used, it is important to realize that these prices are only tentative and may be raised or lowered in response to changes in market conditions or other factors. Prices established by retailers should always be subject to change in the form of additional markups or markdowns, particularly the latter. Indeed, markdowns—

---

[27] This discussion of distribution-cost analysis is based on that presented by Sevin in *ibid.,* Chapter 3, particularly pp. 43–48.

reductions made in the original prices attached to products—are a characteristic feature of retail pricing.

Reasons for markdowns   There are many possible reasons for marking down the price of merchandise. Markdowns are often adjustments made to correct errors in pricing. A retailer may find, for example, that lower prices are required to encourage larger sales of merchandise that did not sell well enough at the original price because the price was too high. In fact, one test of a good price is whether or not a subsequent markdown proves necessary. This points up the importance of establishing correct prices initially since the greater the amount of merchandise that can be sold at the initial price, the greater the profit is likely to be.[28]

Another important cause of markdowns is mistakes in buying merchandise, such as poor choices of merchandise, incorrect estimates of the quantities required, or poor timing of purchases. Markdowns might also be made by the retailer if suppliers reduce prices or if a line of merchandise is to be discontinued.

Markdowns may be necessary, too, under any of the following possible circumstances:

1. If the retailer has failed to push a product adequately.
2. If merchandise has been damaged while in the store.
3. If some merchandise is left over at the end of a season or fashion cycle.
4. If the retailer desires to use price reductions as a promotional device.
5. If the retailer has followed an excessively liberal return policy, thus accumulating a large quantity of returned merchandise that is difficult to sell at regular prices.
6. If the retailer is faced with a price cut by direct competitors.

Markdowns may even be a basic part of the store's overall pricing policy. For example, a retailer may price his goods at a relatively high level initially with the intention of reducing them substantially at a later time and promoting such reductions vigorously. In other situations, markdowns may be regularly scheduled to permit periodic spectacular store-wide sales.[29]

---

[28] Q. Forrest Walker, "Some Principles of Department Store Pricing," *Journal of Marketing,* January, 1950, p. 532.

[29] The use of markdowns as a part of overall policy is discussed in Oswald Knauth, "Considerations in the Setting of Retail Prices," *Journal of Marketing,* July, 1949.

It should be noted that some retailers make the mistake of marking down merchandise whenever it does not sell satisfactorily, instead of trying to determine the cause of the slow sale and attempting to correct it without resorting to price adjustments. By so doing, the retailer may be needlessly foregoing profits.

Timing of markdowns Some retailers try to avoid marking prices down as long as possible, perhaps until a periodic special-clearance sale is held. Other retailers believe that it is best to reduce prices on merchandise as soon as it is determined that it is not selling well at the original prices. The proper timing of markdowns varies with the kind of merchandise involved and the cause of the markdown.

One advantage in delaying markdowns as long as possible is that the merchandise is given a longer period of time in which to sell at its original price, and the retailer may discover that fewer markdowns are needed. Another is that it enables the store to concentrate its markdowns within the framework of one well-promoted sales event that may attract a large number of bargain hunters and, therefore, increase the chances of successfully clearing out the merchandise. This is particularly useful for "exclusive" stores that are anxious to avoid attracting bargain hunters regularly; in this way such buyers will be attracted to the store only during the period of the special sale. To some extent the policy of confining markdowns to periodic sales events also avoids creating ill will among customers who dislike frequent price reductions that make them uncertain as to when to buy. Frequent price adjustments may also cause customers to lose confidence in the regular prices of the retailer.

On the other hand, taking markdowns as soon as a problem is recognized offers the possible advantage that smaller markdowns will be required to move the merchandise. In an extreme case this may ensure that the goods will be sold before they become completely unsalable since there is time for further markdowns if the initial one is unsuccessful. Another advantage of early markdowns is that it clears the shelves of slow-moving merchandise and makes room for new and, hopefully, faster selling merchandise. It also provides the cash needed for new purchases.

Although it is unlikely that any retail store follows either one of these alternatives to the exclusion of the other, there seems to be a tendency for retailers to prefer early markdowns. For example, some department stores are now making use of computers to detect which products are slow moving so that markdowns can be taken as soon as possible. Early identification of slow-moving merchandise makes it possible for one to take full advantage of early markdowns.

Size of markdowns   Once a retailer decides to reduce the price on an item of merchandise, he must next decide how large that markdown will be. The only generalization he can use as a guide is that markdowns must be large enough to encourage better sales. Or, to state it somewhat differently, a markdown must be large enough to be recognized and appreciated by potential customers. Thus, it follows that a fairly large markdown made at one time will usually be more effective than a small markdown or a series of small markdowns. On the other hand, of course, markdowns should not be so large that they needlessly reduce the revenues of the firm.

Exactly how sizable a markdown should be in any particular case depends upon the circumstances surrounding the sale of the product, such as price elasticity of demand, degree of competition, quantity of merchandise on hand, the original price, the reason for the markdown, and costs. It should be noted, however, that as a general rule the more desperate the situation is, the less consideration should be given to costs. The important thing is to move the merchandise rather than to try to recover full costs.

One rule of thumb used by some retailers is that price should be reduced at least 15 percent in any markdown. Some retailers that use price lines claim that as a general rule a price reduction should represent a drop of at least one full price range. Still another rule used by retailers is that the initial markdown should be designed to move at least 25 percent of the stock on hand. In practice, there is considerable variation in the percentage markdowns customarily applied to different types of merchandise. Consequently, this is one type of pricing decision that demands considerable judgment on the part of the price maker.

LEADER AND BAIT PRICING

We have said that one of the reasons a retailer might mark down the price of merchandise is for promotional purposes. Such price reductions can be made on a selective basis or on a store-wide or department-wide basis. Leader and bait pricing are forms of selective price reduction.

Leader pricing   The practice of temporarily reducing the price of a product, usually a well-known brand, below its customary level and relying on this "leader" to attract customer traffic into a store with the hope that customers will also purchase other merchandise is referred to as leader pricing.[30] If the price is reduced below cost, particularly below landed cost or below invoice cost, the product involved is usually termed a *loss leader*.

The ideal characteristics of a price leader are the following:

1. It is well known, widely used, and appeals to many consumers.
2. It is priced low enough so that more than a few persons can buy it.
3. It is not so low in price that reductions will arouse no interest.
4. It is not usually bought in large quantities and stored.
5. It enjoys a high price elasticity of demand.
6. It does not compete closely with other products in the retailer's assortment of merchandise (in which case it would destroy sales opportunities instead of creating them).[31]

Because leader pricing is primarily designed to draw customer traffic into the store and to sell other merchandise in addition to the leader, the sales of the leader itself are not of primary importance. However, it does seem to follow that the more that is sold of the leader, the more that is likely to be sold of other products.

The obvious danger in the use of price leaders is that the policy may trigger retaliation from direct competitors, thereby yielding no real benefit to the initiating retailer. There is also the possibility of starting a price war. Another problem with leaders is that some or all customers may purchase only the leader(s) and thus defeat the purpose of the promotion. In addition, as we will discuss in another section of this chapter, manufacturers frequently object to retailers who use their brands as leaders. In such situations leader pricing may even result in legal difficulties.

Bait pricing The practice of announcing lower than customary prices for certain products, usually well-known brands, with the purpose of attracting customers into a store so that they will purchase other merchandise is termed *bait pricing*. The chief difference between leader and bait pricing is that in the latter the retailer hopes *not*

---

[30] An excellent discussion of leader pricing as practiced by retail supermarkets is found in Cassady, *op. cit.*, pp. 167–77.

[31] Roland S. Vaile, E. T. Grether, and Reavis Cox, *Marketing in the American Economy* (New York: Ronald Press, 1952), p. 447.

to sell the bait product. Indeed, he usually makes it difficult or impossible for a customer to buy the bait product. This can be done by trading the customer up, by trying to persuade him to switch to other products or brands, or by stocking only a very small quantity of the bait product so that it is soon out of stock. In an extreme case a retailer may carry no stock of the bait product at all.

Bait pricing is unethical and unfair to the consumer. The Federal Trade Commission considers advertising a product that a seller does not, in fact, intend to sell a deceptive practice and advises that such sellers may be prosecuted. Furthermore, several states have enacted statutes that attempt to prohibit bait advertising.

FICTITIOUS PRICING

The practice of advertising or otherwise announcing prices as reductions from the usual or customary prices when such prices are not, in fact, reductions at all or are lesser reductions than claimed is termed *fictitious pricing*. Phrases such as "formerly $————," "made to sell for $————," "reduced from $————," "regularly priced at $————," "manufacturer's suggested price $————," "nationally advertised at $————," "you save $————," and "originally priced at $————" are used in fictitious pricing. Since genuine price reductions are announced in this fashion, too, these phrases do not, in and of themselves, indicate that the price reductions quoted are fictitious.

Although fictitious pricing has probably always existed to some degree at the retail level, it appears that the practice has become much more widespread because of the increasing popularity of discounting in the post–World War II period. In some cases, manufacturers have been known to cooperate with retailers in the practice by providing fictitious price lists or price tags from which "discounts" could be offered to the public. Indeed, all manufacturers who advertise or otherwise announce list prices to the public encourage fictitious pricing intentionally or unintentionally if the announced list prices are above the usual or customary prices at which the product generally sells.

Fictitious pricing is practiced because retailers assume that the consumer is interested in a bargain and that, therefore, claimed price reductions or discounts can attract patronage. Although consumers are probably not so gullible that they believe every claimed price reduction, they are sufficiently gullible to have unintentionally encouraged many retailers to practice fictitious pricing. Fictitious pricing works primarily because consumers are ignorant of the comparative offerings and prices available to them in the market place. Consumers are ignorant because they are generally not willing to spend the time or exert the effort required to become more informed about prices and because the task of comparing prices and merchandise offered by different retailers is a formidable one. Indeed for little known products or products that are only carried in a few stores, price comparisons may be virtually impossible. Even if the product involved is well known and widely distributed, the task of comparing prices asked by many different retailers for the same merchandise can be laborious, time consuming, and often impractical.

The effect of fictitious pricing is to cheat consumers who make purchases under the impression that the price reductions are genuine. It matters not whether the price paid is similar or identical to the usual price or whether it is above or below such usual price. The consumer is cheated because he is led to believe that he is getting a given price reduction when actually he is not.

Manufacturers whose products are vulnerable to fictitious pricing, are affected by it whether or not they cooperate in the practice. On the one hand, it may increase the sales of their products, and, on the other hand, if consumers become aware of the fact that they have been victimized by fictitious pricing, it may cause ill will toward the manufacturer, particularly if consumers think that the manufacturer had a part in the scheme.

In general, widespread fictitious pricing could reduce the faith of the public in the marketing system, and the advertising function in particular, and thereby weaken or destroy the effectiveness of the marketing system.

Clearly, fictitious pricing is an undesirable practice. The problem is how to stop it. Government intervention is one possibility. Since the late 1950's the Federal Trade Commission has attempted to bring a stop to fictitious pricing in interstate commerce and has listed in its publications what it considers to be various forms of illegal, deceptive price comparisons used by advertisers.[32] Furthermore, as we pointed out in Chapter 6, the Commission has attacked the list prices of man-

---

[32] Federal Trade Commission, *Guides Against Deceptive Pricing*, effective October, 1958, and *Guides Against Deceptive Pricing*, effective January 8, 1964.

ufacturers when they do not represent actual retail prices. The Commission's *Guides Against Deceptive Pricing* have been widely circulated among business firms and have produced good results in discouraging the practice among businessmen. Furthermore, several states have enacted legislation aimed at prohibiting false statements in advertising, and this legislation usually can be invoked against the advertising of fictitious price reductions.

The problem with trying to stop fictitious pricing through legal means is that of enforcement. The sheer volume of prices and advertisements carrying price information is so great that it is literally impossible for a federal or state agency to police the activity. As a result, only a handful of offenders are identified and prosecuted.

To some extent, Better Business Bureaus and local chambers of commerce can be effective in discouraging the use of fictitious pricing by exerting pressure on local businessmen. The advertising media can also cooperate in this respect by refusing to carry advertising of fictitious price reductions.

However, probably the most effective way of stopping fictitious pricing is to make consumers more aware of the problem. If they could be persuaded to make a greater attempt to be sure that they are not being deceived, and if they were more willing to report infractions to legal authorities, Better Business Bureaus, or chambers of commerce, the practice of fictitious pricing could be reduced substantially.

Indeed, from the retailer's standpoint, engaging in fictitious pricing is bad business for, even leaving aside ethical considerations, it can create a great deal of ill will among customers and possibly bring on bad publicity and even legal action. Furthermore, if the problem of fictitious pricing remains serious or becomes more serious than it is now, it could bring about additional and extremely restrictive legislation that could curtail considerably the pricing discretion presently enjoyed by retailers.

DISCOUNT HOUSES

A wide variety of different kinds of stores that generally sell, or claim to sell, all or most of their merchandise at prices that are lower than the usual retail prices charged for such merchandise are termed *discount houses*. Such stores range from small open showroom and catalog order offices to full-line, limited-service, promotional stores that are, in effect, discount department stores. Specifically, the types of establishments that commonly refer to themselves as discount houses include the following:

1. "Open showrooms" maintained by manufacturers and whole-salers, where sales are made to the consuming public at less than "regular" retail prices.
2. "Brokerage buying arrangements" that are typically small bus-inesses with access to sources of supply and that operate on a "cost-plus" basis (usually 10 to 25 percent).
3. "Closed-door discount houses" that cater to a membership group and feature prices below "regular" retail prices.
4. "Open discount houses" that are geared for a high-volume, low-markup, limited-service type of operation. These houses usually carry hard lines where brand names are important to the custo-mer and readily identifiable.
5. "Discount department stores" that operate on a very large scale and carry a wide variety of merchandise under one roof, usually on a self-service, supermarket-like basis.[33]

Of the categories listed above, the discount department stores have exhibited the most spectacular expansion in the past decade and are today the most important form of discounting in American retailing. Most of the discount department stores are units in chain-store sys-tems.

Discount stores are able to offer low prices on the merchandise they carry because of low operating costs based on little or no cus-tomer service, spartan physical facilities, and minimum inventories. The willingness to take a small margin on every unit sold is also im-portant. Large-scale discounters are also able to take advantage of discounts granted for large quantity purchases. They also benefit from large volume sales at a fast rate of turnover.

As we mentioned earlier, discount retailers have always existed in one form or another in American retailing. Chain stores, mail-order houses, and several other types of retailing that were once innova-tions based their initial appeal on low prices. However, retailers who specifically referred to themselves as "discount houses" seem to have

[33] William R. Davidson and Alton F. Doody, "The Future of Discounting," *Journal of Marketing,* January, 1963, p. 36.

first emerged as a marketing power in the late 1930's. At that time, discount houses were often back-alley, secretive organizations. Many were "closed" [34] and served only specific groups of consumers, such as clergymen, school teachers, government employees, and members of certain labor unions. The early discounters usually carried a very limited assortment of merchandise; it was often distress merchandise. A primary reason for the emergence of these early discounters at that time was the advent of resale price maintenance or "fair-trade" legislation of the 1930's. This legislation provided retailers who complied with fair-trade prices with relatively large margins on merchandise that was fair-traded and this, in turn, meant that discounts, although technically illegal, could be given profitably and that discounters had proof for customers that the discounts they offered were valid. Thus, although fair-trade laws had the objective of preventing price cutting, they actually stimulated it. However, discounting below fair-trade prices was technically illegal and could not be done as openly as it was in later years.

In the post–World War II period, a buyers' market returned as production again caught up with consumer demand, and effective enforcement of resale price maintenance broke down, thus eliminating to a great degree legal barriers to discounting below fair-trade prices. For these reasons, discounting grew rapidly and became more open in character. The merchandise carried by the early postwar discount houses was primarily hard goods, particularly well-known household appliances. Since then, discount houses have expanded the scope of their operations so that many of them, particularly the full-line discount department stores, carry soft goods such as clothing, as well as hard goods. In addition, many discounters have moved into the supermarket business, usually for the purpose of attracting customer traffic to the other part of their discount operations. In some cases the entire food department is operated as a giant price leader designed primarily to attract customer traffic.[35] Some discount houses operate their food departments themselves; others turn the operation of the food department over to a lessee.

---

[34] Discount department stores may be "closed" or "open." A "closed" store is open only to "members" who have qualified for membership in some way, perhaps by the fact that they are government employees or members of a particular labor union. "Open" stores serve the public in general.

[35] This kind of operation is not peculiar to discount houses. Some "conventional" department stores have done the same thing.

Discounting is here to stay. One indication of this is the fact that the so-called conventional retailers have ventured into discounting themselves by opening new discount stores. Such retailers include variety-store chains, department-store chains, department-store ownership groups, supermarket chains, drug chains, and mail-order houses.

It is difficult to determine just how many discount houses there are or what their total sales volume is since government statistics do not as yet provide a separate classification for discount houses. Many conventional retailers refer to themselves as discounters when, in reality, they are not; this further complicates the task of gathering meaningful data. In addition, there are many varieties of discount houses, and there is some disagreement as to what constitutes a discount house. Charles E. Silberman reports that the sales of one type of discount operation, full-line discount department stores, were $4 to $4.5 billion in 1961. He estimates that the annual sales of these stores will reach $20 billion by 1970.[36] Whatever the actual figures are, it is clear that discount houses, in all their forms, now account for a substantial share of retail sales volume.

This raises the question: How low are discount-house prices and how legitimate are the bargains they offer to the consumer? Discounters claim that their prices are from 10 to 30 percent below those of conventional retailers, and that their average markup on sales (expressed as a percent of selling price) is between 18 and 25 percent, as against 35 to 40 percent for many other retailers.

Although many discount houses offer genuine price advantages to the consumer, other discount houses are doing nothing more than selling low-quality merchandise at what only appear to be lower than average prices. According to Silberman: "To be sure the merchandise varies widely from store to store, and some alleged discount houses —like some conventional stores—are in reality 'schlock' operations offering manufacturers' 'seconds' at inflated prices." [37] When the merchandise in question consists of well-known, advertised brands, the consumer is in a better position to judge the validity of the "bargain" he is offered than if the merchandise is some kind of soft goods, such as undershirts or sheets, and the brands carried are not very well known. In the latter case it is more difficult to make price compari-

---

[36] "The Revolutionists of Retailing," *Fortune,* April, 1962, pp. 100 and 265.
[37] *Ibid.,* pp. 101–02.

sons. However, most of the larger full-line discount department stores seem to carry first-line merchandise and price their soft goods lower than soft goods in conventional stores are priced.

At present, discount houses seem to be going through a period of "trading up." As they have begun to compete against one another as well as against conventional retailers, discounters have found that they must offer more than just low prices to the public. Therefore, they have been adding more customer services, such as credit and free alterations, and have been improving their store facilities and the quality and assortment of the merchandise carried. Inevitably, such steps will increase their costs and make it more difficult for them to keep their prices low. That such trading up has occurred in the past in connection with other retailing innovations was pointed out in an earlier section of this chapter.

The advent of discount houses has had a tremendous effect on American retailing. The success of discounting probably means that the traditional retail margins on some lines of merchandise were too high, and that these margins will probably be lower in the future. Indeed, it appears likely that pressures from discount-house competition have permanently lowered the level of gross margins on some kinds of goods.[38] Discount selling has also increased the importance of price as a marketing tool at the retail level and has encouraged many non-discount-house retailers to do some "discounting," or at least claim to do it, even though technically they are not discount houses.

Discount houses have probably had a greater impact on conventional department stores than on any other kind of retailer—although they have had an impact on all retailers of clothing, household items, and food—because discount houses usually carry merchandise that competes directly with that carried by conventional department stores. The result has been that conventional department stores have begun to change their methods of operation. Some have begun operating their own discount or budget departments alongside their conventional full-service departments. Others have tried to cope with this problem by pledging to meet any price of a competitor. Still others have increased their emphasis on higher-price fashion merchandise,

---

[38] Theodore N. Beckman and William R. Davidson, *Marketing,* 7th ed. (New York: Ronald Press, 1962), p. 250.

dropped some of the lines of merchandise that were also sold by discounters, and offered more rather than fewer services.[39]

The proper course of action for any retailer who faces strong competition from discount houses varies according to the circumstances of the situation. Retailers who find themselves in direct competition with discount houses must examine their own operations in order to determine what actions will enable them to compete more effectively with this new threat. The long-run result of such self-appraisal will probably be increased efficiency, which will ultimately benefit the consumer through better retailing and lower prices.[40]

RESALE PRICE MAINTENANCE LAWS

Resale price maintenance or "fair-trade" laws, which have been passed by most states, provide that manufacturers or other owners of brand names (and, in some states, their distributors) may fix the minimum or actual (depending upon the law under discussion) wholesale and retail prices at which distributors sell their products. Since the fixing of *retail* prices by *manufacturers* has been the most important and well-known form of fair-trade pricing, we will confine our discussion to that area of price fixing, passing over the fixing of wholesale prices by manufacturers or the fixing of retail prices by brand owners (such as wholesalers) who are not manufacturers.

Resale price maintenance laws apply only to branded merchandise that is in fair and open competition with other commodities of the same general class produced or distributed by others. Those resale price maintenance laws that have proved most effective have included a "nonsigner" clause, which provides that, if a manufacturer is able to persuade one retailer in the state to agree by contract to abide by the prices suggested by the manufacturer, all other retailers in the

[39] For a discussion of the possible approaches to this problem by department stores, see Stuart U. Rich and Bernard Portis, "Clues for Action from Shopper Preferences," *Harvard Business Review*, March–April, 1963, and Walter Gross, "Strategies Used by Major Department Stores to Compete with Low-Margin Retailers," *Journal of Retailing*, Summer, 1964.

[40] An interesting account of how a bookstore successfully competed against discounters through stepped-up advertising and improved service is found in Harry W. Schwartz, "If Discounters Threaten, Don't Panic, Fight Back," *Publishers' Weekly*, March 30, 1964.

state are bound by that agreement, if it can be shown that they have received proper notification.

Under certain circumstances, a retailer is allowed to sell this merchandise at prices below the fair-trade prices established by a manufacturer. Thus, if the retailer removes the trademark, brand, or manufacturer's name from the product, if he is conducting a closing-out sale, or if the merchandise has deteriorated or has been damaged, he can usually mark down the price without getting into legal difficulty.

Enforcement of resale prices under fair-trade laws is the responsibility of the manufacturer; the states do not undertake the job of policing retail prices. When a manufacturer discovers that a retailer is violating these laws and wishes to prosecute him, he must file suit against him in an appropriate court of law in order to collect damages for injury sustained. He may also bring an action for an injunction that would prevent the violator from continuing to price the product in question below its fair-trade price.

Under resale price maintenance laws a manufacturer usually has the right to make use of legalized resale price maintenance if he so chooses, but he is not compelled to do so. However, in some states the manufacturer is required by law to make use of resale price maintenance for some products, usually liquor. Under compulsory fair trade the manufacturers or distributors are usually required to file resale prices with a state agency, and retailers who resell the products in question at prices less than those filed are violating the law. In such cases policing is sometimes done by the states.

A brief history of resale price maintenance laws   In 1911 the United States Supreme Court held that the Sherman Antitrust Act did not permit a manufacturer engaged in interstate commerce to contract with middlemen about resale prices.[41] However, in 1931 California enacted legislation that authorized resale price maintenance in that state, and other states soon followed suit. The legality of the laws and the nonsigner provisions in such laws were subsequently upheld by the United States Supreme Court in 1936.[42] In 1937 Congress made resale price maintenance lawful in interstate commerce by enacting the Miller-Tydings Act (an amendment to the Sherman Act), which

[41] *Dr. Miles Medical Company* v. *John D. Park and Sons Company,* 220 U.S. 373.
[42] *Old Dearborn Distributing Company* v. *Seagram Distillers Corporation,* 299 U.S. 183.

provides that, if a state has a resale price maintenance law, that law can be applied to shipments into that state from another state. Eventually, forty-six states enacted resale price maintenance laws.[43] The merchandise placed under fair-trade pricing by manufacturers includes a wide range of products. The leading products have been household appliances, liquor, cosmetics, books, drugs, and photographic equipment. However, probably less than 10 percent of all goods sold at the retail level has ever been under fair-trade pricing at any point in time.

The discounting revolution of the 1950's was made possible in part by resale price maintenance legislation. As we mentioned earlier, the existence of an established and often heavily advertised fair-trade price gave the discounters a base line from which to operate. When they sold merchandise at less than the established fair-trade prices, they could easily prove to customers that they were receiving genuine price reductions; customers could easily recognize and appreciate these reductions. At the same time, discounting helped to dilute the effectiveness of fair-trade legislation as a weapon of manufacturers. The proliferation of discounters and would-be discounters led to widespread price cutting on fair-traded products and greatly complicated the policing problem. In some cases, policing became virtually impossible. Policing also became much more expensive. Often the manufacturer had to be content with effective maintenance of the prices of only the larger retailers. Meanwhile, the discounters grew in importance and in purchasing power, and manufacturers found it increasingly difficult to avoid dealing with them. Finally, fair trade also encouraged the introduction of private labels over which the retailer himself had complete pricing control.

The advocates of resale price maintenance laws also began to encounter legal problems. In 1951 a supermarket operator in New Orleans won his argument that the nonsigner clauses were never specifically approved in the Miller-Tydings Act and hence could not be applied to goods in interstate commerce.[44] As a result of this decision, considerable price cutting subsequently took place in several large cities, but Congress promptly closed the loophole the following year by enacting the McGuire Act (an amendment to the Federal

---

[43] Alaska, Missouri, Texas, Vermont, and the District of Columbia have never had fair-trade laws.

[44] *Schwegmann Brothers* et al. v. *Calvert Distillers Corporation,* 341 U.S. 384.

Trade Commission Act), which specifically legalized the use of non-signer clauses in interstate commerce.

Since the passage of the McGuire Act, however, resale price maintenance has had considerable legal difficulty. A number of state courts have declared that the nonsigner clause violated the state constitutions. Several other state courts have gone further, holding that the state's entire resale price maintenance law was unconstitutional. In 1965 there were thirty-nine states with resale price maintenance laws in effect, but in only twenty was it constitutional to apply such laws to nonsigners.[45]

Because of the problems discussed above many manufacturers have given up trying to make use of resale price maintenance legislation. Those who try to control or influence retail prices without the aid of resale price maintenance laws do so by means of one of the several alternatives discussed in Chapter 6.

The advocates of resale price maintenance legislation continue to press their case. For several years there has been at least one bill in every session of Congress that seeks to legalize resale price maintenance in interstate commerce regardless of the provisions of the state laws. The most recent version of this is the "Quality Stabilization Bill," which was considered, but not passed, in recent sessions of Congress. This bill sought to provide that a manufacturer could vol-

[45] In 1965 states that did not have a resale price maintenance law in effect because such a law had never been enacted, or the law had been repealed, or the entire law had been held to be unconstitutional by state courts were Alabama, Alaska, Kansas, Missouri, Montana, Nebraska, Nevada, Texas, Utah, Vermont, and Wyoming. Those states in which the nonsigner clause had been declared constitutional by state courts or in which the constitutionality of the nonsigner clause had not yet been ruled on were Arizona, California, Connecticut, Delaware, Illinois, Maine, Maryland, Massachusetts, Mississippi, New Hampshire, New Jersey, New York, North Carolina, North Dakota, Rhode Island, South Dakota, Tennessee, and Wisconsin. In addition, Ohio's law of 1959 and Virginia's law of 1958 do not contain nonsigner clauses, but they apply to nonsigners through other means. Of the remaining nineteen states that still had resale price maintenance laws, the nonsigner clause had been held to be unconstitutional by state courts in eighteen, and in one (Hawaii) the nonsigner clause had been repealed. Some of the court decisions referred to here relative to resale price maintenance had been made by lower courts and could, therefore, be reversed by higher courts. This material was adapted from Commerce Clearing House, *Trade Regulation Reporter,* ¶ 6041. It is also interesting to note that the British Parliament recently enacted legislation that bars individual manufacturers from imposing minimum retail prices unless they get a specific exemption. See "No More Price-Fixing," *Business Week,* July 25, 1964, p. 86.

untarily require retailers to charge specified resale prices merely by notifying retailers of those prices.[46]

The pros and cons of resale price maintenance legislation Most of the support for resale price maintenance legislation in recent years has come from retailers, particularly small retailers. These retailers argue that, unless retail prices are controlled by manufacturers, large-scale retailers can underprice the smaller retailers and drive them out of business. Loss-leader pricing is particularly criticized by the smaller retailers. Furthermore, according to the small retailers, once the smaller retailers are eliminated, the large-scale retailers will take advantage of the situation by charging exorbitant prices.

Some wholesalers have also supported resale price maintenance because they are anxious to discourage the growth of large retail organizations, which tend to by-pass the independent wholesaler. Also, it is clear that their own fortune is tied in with that of the retailers who support fair trade, and hence they support it also.

Manufacturers who support resale price maintenance legislation do so for several reasons. Some are anxious to satisfy retailers who desire protection against price cutting by competitors. Others feel that price is a very important element in the purchase decision for their product and are therefore anxious to use price in their advertising with assurance that the prices quoted are actually used. A third reason is that some manufacturers believe that price cutting by retailers tends to cheapen their product in the eyes of the consumer and that this injures the reputation of the brand and the firm. Other manufacturers worry that price cutting by retailers may reduce retailer margins and that this may lead them to pressure manufacturers for lower prices, which would then reduce the margins earned by the manufacturers. Finally, many manufacturers believe that once some retailers cut the price of their product, perhaps as a loss leader, other retailers who do not cut prices will either not stock the product or will "put it under the counter," that is, they will not push the product or

---

[46] The title "Quality Stabilization Bill" is based on the idea that resale price maintenance protects the quality of a product by preventing the widespread price cutting that eventually results in lower margins for the manufacturer and reductions in the quality of the product. The possible impact of the enactment of the Quality Stabilization Bill on the Consumer Price Index is discussed in Jerome C. Darnell, "The Impact of Quality Stabilization," *Journal of Marketing Research*, August, 1965.

will avoid selling it because they do not want to match the low prices.[47]

The criticisms of resale price maintenance legislation are several, and they far outweigh any advantages it might offer. One problem is that resale price maintenance legislation goes beyond the prevention of unjust or unfair price competition—it prevents *all* price competition among retailers who carry the fair-traded product. Thus, fair trade endorses horizontal as well as vertical price fixing, in that all retailers who carry a given fair-traded product charge the same price. Although the retailers themselves do not actually fix this price, the effect is no different than if they had done so; such price fixing is generally considered unlawful under the antitrust laws.

Second, by providing large margins to retailers and by preventing price reductions, and because prices must provide adequate margins for both inefficient and efficient retailers, fair trade tends to yield artificially high prices. Hence, in the final analysis resale price maintenance legislation may work against the best interest of consumers. Although the evidence on this matter is not entirely conclusive, some studies report that prices in fair-trade states have been higher than in non-fair-trade states. On balance, it seems that the effect of fair trade is to maintain prices at a higher level than would be the case if the products were not fair-traded.[48]

Another criticism of fair trade is that it is unfair to those retailers who could price lower because of the cost advantages they enjoy. Retailers are not allowed to reap the benefits of the lower prices their cost differences permit them to assign to such products, and this also injures the consumer.

Fourth, price cutting by retailers may actually benefit a manufacturer by encouraging the sale of his product rather than damaging the reputation of the brand and the firm.

A fifth argument against resale price maintenance is that it tends to make retail prices somewhat inflexible since manufacturers usually do not make adjustments in fair-traded prices very often, and retailers are unable to make such adjustments themselves in order to meet changes in market or other conditions.

Lastly, resale price maintenance is unworkable. As we indicated

---

[47] The disadvantages a manufacturer encounters if he attempts to control resale prices charged by distributors are discussed in Chapter 6.

[48] Paul D. Converse, Harvey W. Huegy, and Robert V. Mitchell, *Elements of Marketing,* 7th ed. (Englewood Cliffs, N.J.: Prentice-Hall, 1965), p. 193.

earlier, the manufacturer has the responsibility for enforcing resale prices, yet evasion is so easy that many manufacturers have found it entirely too expensive to try to control retail prices and have given up the attempt. Aside from open price cutting, evasion can take such subtler forms as the granting of free goods or premiums to customers with purchases of the fair-traded product, the adjustment of prices through adjustment of trade-in allowances, or the provision of combination offers to customers.

In sum, the criticisms of resale price maintenance legislation are many and important. It is very difficult to justify such laws, particularly from the point of view of the consumer. From the point of view of the manufacturer, attempts to control resale prices also have their disadvantages, as we mentioned in Chapter 6, and the difficulties and expense of enforcement have added to these problems.

Large-scale retailers have generally opposed fair-trade legislation because it prevents them from taking advantage of their lower costs. They also resent the fact that manufacturers tend to enforce fair-trade prices against the larger retailers, but not against smaller retailers. Smaller retailers, on the other hand, have often supported resale price maintenance legislation on the grounds that it prevents the mass retailers from undercutting them in price. Nonetheless, for any retailer, large or small, fair-trade legislation does offer the assurance of an adequate, sometimes very liberal, gross margin on fair-traded products.

It should be noted, however, that the benefits of fair trade to the small retailer can be exaggerated. The large margins provided under fair trade may have the effect of encouraging the entry of new competitors. The existence of fair-trade pricing also encourages larger retailers to introduce private labels. Since such products are not subject to fair-trade laws, large retailers are free to charge low prices on such products. Furthermore, fair trade does not prevent price cutting on nonbranded merchandise or on branded merchandise that is not fair-traded and, as we indicated earlier, most products have not been placed under fair trade by their manufacturers. In addition, resale price maintenance legislation can do little for a retailer unless it is adequately enforced, and this is rarely possible.

It is also well to keep in mind that price is only one factor in attracting customers to retail institutions. Promotion, customer service, location, and product quality and assortment are important as well, and a small retailer can compete effectively on these grounds even though he operates at a price disadvantage on some of the merchandise he carries.

Another problem with resale price maintenance legislation for any retailer, large or small, is that it takes the pricing decision away from the retailer and gives it to the manufacturer. Even ignoring loss of pricing freedom, this means that prices are not properly adjusted to a particular retailer's costs, to the general nature of the market he serves, or to the degree of competition he faces. In short, by permitting manufacturers to fix prices at the retail level, resale price maintenance makes it impossible for retail prices to reflect local store and market conditions.

Given the many drawbacks of resale price maintenance legislation, it is perhaps fortunate that the number of effective resale price maintenance laws has been reduced. In general, fair trade seems to be declining in importance, and the only way it can be revived is through some sort of federal legislation. If it is revived, however, it will mean that manufacturers will face a difficult decision. On the one hand, they will have an opportunity of making general use of this device, and, on the other hand, many of their most important retailers, who account for substantial sales volumes, would rather operate without the restriction of fair-trade prices. Manufacturers will also be confronted with the almost insurmountable problem of how to enforce fair-trade prices.

UNFAIR PRACTICES ACTS

Another form of state legislation that deals with pricing is the legislation referred to as "unfair trade practices acts," "unfair sales acts," "minimum markup laws," and "minimum price laws." Beginning with California in 1935, a total of thirty-one states have enacted such laws. In 1964 there were twenty-seven states with unfair practices acts in effect [49] although, because of court interpretations, some of these were not enforceable.

The purpose of unfair practices acts is to prevent predatory price cutting that has the purpose or the effect of injuring or destroying competition. The acts require that retailers price at no less than a

[49] Lawrence E. Rudberg, "An Analysis and Appraisal of Unfair Sales Acts" (Unpublished Ph.D. dissertation, University of Minnesota, 1964).

certain minimum level, although they usually permit a retailer to meet the "legal" prices of a competitor. Furthermore, such laws usually exempt sales made under unusual circumstances, such as closing out or liquidation sales, sales of damaged or deteriorated goods, and sales made upon an order of a court. General unfair practices acts of this sort are mandatory and applicable to all retailers in a state. Over twenty states have similar laws that apply only to specific products such as dairy products, cigarettes, and liquor.

The minimum price a retailer can set under a general unfair practices act varies from one state to another. In some states the minimum is the invoice cost or replacement cost of the merchandise carried. In others it is the invoice cost or replacement cost plus some margin over invoice cost. Such a margin is often 6 per cent for retailers and 2 percent for wholesalers (where wholesalers are covered by such laws). In still other states the minimum is fixed at invoice or replacement cost plus a share of the retailer's operating costs, which are properly allocated to the merchandise in question.

There are many serious problems associated with trying to implement such legislation. For example, cost is not as easy to identify as the laws imply. This is obvious if the law provides for an allocation of operating expenses to a particular product. Such allocation is often extremely difficult. Frequently, the result is that "average" costs are used, and these, in turn, make pricing quite unrealistic from the point of both the retailer and the consumer. The problems of allocating are most serious in multiunit retail operations where some costs are common to all stores in the system.

Cost identification is also difficult when invoice or replacement cost is to be determined. Does invoice or replacement cost mean cost before or after discounts are deducted? How do free deals, combination offers, and advertising allowances received by the retailer from a supplier affect the determination? Should transportation charges be included or excluded in invoice cost?

A second major problem associated with unfair practices acts is that of policing and enforcement. Usually the state attorney general is responsible for the enforcement of these laws. Because of the vast number of retail stores and retail prices, however, it is clearly impossible for a state agency to police all retail prices. As a consequence, the enforcement agencies must rely primarily on complaints from injured parties. Once price cutters are detected, the problem of how to handle costs arises. Furthermore, most of these laws require that injury to competition, as well as price cutting, be shown. In addition, *intent* to injure or destroy competition must often be shown. This leads to thorny legal and economic questions. For example, Minnesota's unfair practices act requires that retailers take an 8 percent markup over invoice cost. However, the Minnesota Supreme Court has ruled that a price below that level, to be in violation of the law, must be accompanied by intent to injure a competitor or to destroy competition, and the burden is upon the state to prove the necessary intent.[50] As a consequence, the Minnesota law is largely unenforceable.

The enforcement problem is often complicated by the fact that retailers occasionally offer customers various premiums, free goods, combination offers, and trade-in allowances, which mean, in effect, that sales are made below cost, as defined in most unfair practices acts. Such below-cost sales are quite difficult to police. Another factor that reduces the effectiveness of unfair practices acts is that, unlike resale price maintenance laws, these acts can be applied only to intrastate commerce. Because of the problems of cost determination and enforcement noted above, unfair practices acts have generally proved ineffective in preventing significant price cutting at the retail level.

In addition to difficulties of implementation, unfair practices acts can be criticized because they have the effect of protecting *competitors* rather than protecting *competition*. If these laws were effective, they would prevent retailers from adjusting prices as they saw fit. This would protect their competitors from price competition and deprive consumers of the right to take advantage of low prices. Injury to competitors is to be expected in a competitive system and should not be condemned. "As a matter of fact, any other result indicates the existence of soft competition which might be the result of either sellers' market conditions or, indeed, collusion among vendors." [51]

In short it would seem that since unfair practices acts are generally unworkable, and since, if they were workable, they would hinder rather than promote competition, such laws should be repealed where they still exist.

---

[50] *State of Minnesota* v. *Applebaum Food Markets, Inc.,* 106 N.W. 2nd 896 (1960).

[51] Cassady, *op. cit.,* p. 239. See also his *Price Warfare in Business Competition,* Occasional Paper No. 11 (East Lansing, Mich.: Bureau of Business and Economic Research, Michigan State University, 1963), p. 74.

PRIVATE LABELS

Private labels (also termed private brands, middlemen brands, and distributor brands) are products that bear the trademark, brand, or label of a wholesaler or retailer, instead of the brand name of a manufacturer (manufacturers' brands). Many wholesalers and retailers who distribute consumer goods own one or more private labels; the use of private labels by distributors is increasing.

The product placed under a private label by a distributor is sometimes manufactured by the distributor himself, but more often it is manufactured by a separate manufacturing firm. The manufacturer may also have his own brands, in which case he is said to be engaging in "dual distribution," or he may manufacture only private labels for one or more distributors.

REASONS FOR INTRODUCING PRIVATE LABELS

There are several reasons a distributor might have for introducing a private label to the market. Often he can earn a higher gross margin on a private label than he can on manufacturers' brands, primarily because of lower landed cost. This has been particularly true in recent years, since discounting has reduced the margins retailers can earn on manufacturers' brands. Second, because the private label can be purchased only from the distributor who owns it, the distributor has some security against direct competition from other middlemen. Direct price comparisons are impossible, for example. Third, whatever advantages, such as customer good will, are associated with brand ownership accrue only to the distributor who owns the private label.

A distributor may also introduce a private label if he feels that manufacturers are not supplying the kind of merchandise he wants to sell under their own brand names, and that he can secure such merchandise only by designing it himself and having it produced under his own brand name. Furthermore, as we have mentioned earlier, efforts by manufacturers to control resale prices charged by distributors, perhaps through resale price maintenance laws, deprive the distributor of some pricing freedom, and this can be avoided if he introduces a private label, the price of which is entirely controlled by the distributor.

Finally, private labels are sometimes introduced because the distributor has been by-passed by manufacturers. Many wholesalers, in particular, have faced the problem of manufacturers by-passing them and selling directly to retailers or to final users. As a result, many of these wholesalers believe that in order to survive they must develop their own brands.

The conditions under which private branding can be profitable and the problems surrounding the introduction of private labels are beyond the scope of this book. However, it is interesting to note that the great expense involved in promoting a private label successfully, and the fact that small distributors cannot purchase in large enough quantities to give them any landed-cost advantage over what they would have with a manufacturer's brand, limit the use of private labels for the most part to large wholesalers and retailers.

Furthermore, although the introduction of a private label is sometimes caused by the fact that distributors have been by-passed by manufacturers, the introduction of a private label may itself cause manufacturers of the same generic product to retaliate by by-passing such distributors. Manufacturers can be alienated by the introduction of a private label that competes with their brands. To quote an executive of a large manufacturing firm:

> Roaming the seas of free enterprise, they (private branders) use the precious charts which our national brands have plotted. Muscling in under their price flag, they maraud the markets which . . . we . . . have developed with untold billions of dollars in product improvement and research. They free-load from our hard-won franchise—and drain from our costly advertising.[52]

The danger of being by-passed by manufacturers is a particularly important consideration for wholesalers. Retailers, particularly the larger ones, do not have the problem to the same degree because they cannot be dispensed with as easily.

---

[52] Edgar M. Bronfman, president of Joseph E. Seagram and Sons, as quoted by Leon Morse in "The Battle of the Brands," *Dun's Review and Modern Industry,* May, 1964, p. 100.

PRICING PRIVATE LABELS

In pricing a private label, consideration must be given to the prices of other private labels owned by direct competitors and the prices of competing manufacturers' brands carried by the distributor or other distributors. The principal advantage of having a private label is that it faces no direct price competition since no one else carries an identical product. This may mean that the distributor enjoys much more freedom in pricing than would otherwise be the case, and, depending upon the nature of the product, the degree of product differentiation, and other factors, the price charged by any one distributor for his private label may be more or less than that charged for competing private labels by other distributors. In general, however, the problem of pricing a private label in terms of prices on competing private labels is similar to that faced by a distributor on all the other products he carries.

As competitors of manufacturers' brands, private labels have both advantages and disadvantages. The basic advantage is that the conditions surrounding the point and time of sale of the product are under the control of the distributor. A retailer who owns a private label, for example, can adjust shelf facings, local advertising, and personal selling, if any, in favor of the private label. On the other hand, private labels are generally not highly differentiated from the brands of manufacturers in any favorable way since the usual procedure is for manufacturers to bring out new products and develop the markets for them and then for distributors to bring out similar products under private labels. Private label owners have not been noted for innovation. Indeed, they are often accused of copying products developed by manufacturers. There are some important exceptions, however.

In addition to the fact that private labels do not usually enjoy the benefits of favorable product differentiation, manufacturers' brands often have the benefit of large-scale advertising and a very favorable brand reputation, which a private label seldom has. Thus, it is said that private labels do not have the same degree of brand acceptance as competing manufacturers' brands. (Another related disadvantage of private labels is that the brands of manufacturers are often easier for salespeople to sell, and hence they may tend to push these brands at the expense of the private labels.) Although the problem of brand acceptance is apparently less serious than it has been in the past, it is still an important factor to consider when pricing a private label. To some extent this disadvantage may be offset by whatever customer good will the distributor enjoys.

In practice, private labels are ordinarily priced with reference to the prices of competing manufacturers' brands, and, because of the disadvantages noted above, it is generally impossible to price a private label above the prices of similar manufacturers' brands. Usually, private labels are priced somewhat below the prices of manufacturers' brands. This may not be true if the private label has become well known and widely accepted, or if buyers associate quality with price and the distributor purposely prices his private label high for this reason. Furthermore, as Cassady points out, a distributor should recognize that the good will enjoyed by his *firm* may justify the pricing of private labels above those of manufacturers' brands. He also warns that if customers associate quality with price a very low price may actually have the effect of decreasing the demand for a private label.[53]

Despite the fact that private labels are usually priced below the prices of competing manufacturers' brands, the gross margin earned on such private labels can be higher than that which the distributor receives on competing manufacturers' brands. This is one of the chief reasons that so many private labels have been introduced in recent years. However, it must be kept in mind that the large gross margin is not beneficial to the distributor unless an adequate volume of sales is achieved. The reason a distributor can earn a higher gross margin on these private labels despite the lower selling price is, of course, that the landed cost of these goods is often lower. Private-label merchandise can often be purchased at lower invoice cost than a similar manufacturer's brand. Manufacturers of merchandise made for private labels generally set relatively low prices on their products because there is less need for selling and promotion effort, or the product is being produced primarily to make use of excess capacity, or the distributor makes large quantity purchases, or the distributor has alternative sources of supply that enhance his bargaining power.

However, although the gross margin may be higher on private labels, the *net profit* earned may *not* be greater since the operating expenses are often higher for a private label because any promotion in connection with private labels must be done by the distributor. A

[53] Cassady, *Competition and Price Making in Food Retailing,* pp. 166–67.

lower gross margin and hence a lower net profit may result if private labels are used by distributors as price leaders. This has been a fairly common practice, particularly when resale price maintenance legislation was used more effectively by manufacturers than is presently the case. The fair-trade prices provided a well-known benchmark against which the low prices of the price leaders could be compared.

Selected References

Literature devoted specifically to pricing by wholesalers is somewhat sparse. However, the following general texts on wholesaling contain good accounts of the pricing process at the wholesale level: Theodore N. Beckman, Nathanael H. Engle, and Robert D. Buzzell, *Wholesaling,* 3rd ed. (New York: Ronald Press, 1959), Chapter 22, and Richard M. Hill, *Wholesaling Management* (Homewood, Ill.: Irwin, 1963), Chapter 7.

Suggestions for distribution-cost analysis by wholesalers are discussed by Charles H. Sevin in *Marketing Productivity Analysis* (New York: McGraw-Hill, 1965). See especially Chapter 2.

There is a considerable amount of published material on pricing by retailers. See William R. Davidson and Paul L. Brown, *Retailing Management,* 2nd ed. (New York: Ronald Press, 1960), Chapters 15 and 16, and Delbert J. Duncan and Charles F. Phillips, *Retailing Principles and Methods,* 6th ed. (Homewood, Ill.: Irwin, 1963), Chapters 16 and 17. An excellent article that discusses retail pricing is Oswald Knauth, "Considerations in the Setting of Retail Prices," *Journal of Marketing,* July, 1949. An alternative to the average percentage markup approach to retail pricing is offered in Gordon B. Cross, "A Scientific Approach to Retail Pricing," *Journal of Retailing,* Fall, 1959. See also Malcolm P. McNair and Eleanor G. May, "Pricing for Profit," *Harvard Business Review,* May–June, 1957, for criticisms of percentage of sales concepts in retailing. A fine book that is devoted to pricing in the supermarket industry and that also contains considerable material applicable to other kinds of retail pricing is Ralph Cassady, Jr., *Competition and Price Making in Food Retailing* (New York: Ronald Press, 1962). An empirical analysis of pricing by supermarkets is reported on in Bob R. Holdren, *The Structure of a Retail Market and the Market Behavior of Retail Units* (Englewood Cliffs, N.J.: Prentice-Hall, 1960), Chapter 4. Price warfare at the retail level is treated by Cassady in his *Price Warfare in Business Competition,* Occasional Paper No. 11 (East Lansing, Mich.: Bureau of Business and Economic Research, Michigan State University, 1963). Theories of retail pricing are discussed in some detail in Donald L. Shawver, *The Development of Theories of Retail Price Determination* (Urbana, Ill.: University of Illinois Press, 1956).

Distribution-cost analysis at the retail level is discussed in Sevin, *Marketing Productivity Analysis,* particularly Chapter 3 and pp. 63–70.

The development and future of discount houses has been the subject of numerous publications. Two of the best articles on the subject are Charles E. Silberman, "The Revolutionists of Retailing," *Fortune,* April, 1962, and William R. Davidson and Alton F. Doody, "The Future of Discounting," *Journal of Marketing,* January, 1963. Methods that can be used by conventional retailers (particularly department stores) to combat the discount house are discussed in Stuart U. Rich and Bernard Portis, "Clues for Action from Shopper Preferences," *Harvard Business Review,* March–April, 1963, and Walter Gross, "Strategies Used by Major Department Stores to Compete with Low-Margin Retailers," *Journal of Retailing,* Summer, 1964.

Resale price maintenance laws have received a great deal of attention in the literature and are usually discussed to some extent in general marketing texts. See, for example, Theodore N. Beckman and William R. Davidson, *Marketing,* 7th ed. (New York: Ronald Press, 1962), pp. 741–50. The pros and cons of resale price maintenance laws are discussed in House Committee on Small Business, *Fair Trade: The Problem and the Issues,* House Report No. 1292, 82nd Cong., 2nd sess. (Washington, D.C.: U.S. Government Printing Office, 1952), and in Jules Backman, *Price Practices and Price Policies* (New York: Ronald Press, 1953), pp. 418–37.

Unfair practices acts are sometimes given brief treatment in general marketing texts. A recent work on the subject is Lawrence E. Rudberg, "An Analysis and Appraisal of Unfair Sales Acts" (Unpublished Ph.D. dissertation, University of Minnesota, 1964).

8

OTHER PRICE POLICIES

AND CONCLUDING COMMENTS

In previous chapters we discussed a number of problems, factors, and questions relating to price policy and price procedure in general; we also examined some specific price policies. In this chapter, we will consider some additional price policies, a few of which were touched on briefly in other chapters, including cost-plus pricing, rate-of-return pricing, customary pricing, psychological pricing, promotional pricing, and the policy of using price discounts for quantity purchases or for other reasons. After the discussion of these various price policies, we will draw some conclusions concerning price policy and procedure in general.

COST-PLUS PRICING

In Chapter 2 we mentioned that many business firms practice cost-plus (or full-cost) pricing, which we defined as the attempt to establish prices that cover the estimated costs associated with each unit of the product or service sold. The costs used as a base for such pricing may be full costs or some estimate of average costs. For example, many firms attempt to determine "standard" cost per unit, or the estimated per-unit cost at a "standard" level of output, often expressed as some percentage of capacity.[1] Thus, levels varying from two-thirds to four-fifths of capacity of the actual volume of operations are commonly used as a standard in such calculations.[2] However, the costs used as a base for pricing can also be actual costs, costs in the most recent accounting period, or expected future costs. Distributors usually use invoice or landed cost as their base in pricing. Sometimes manufacturers merely use production cost as the guide and then add some arbitrary figure to cover all other costs and profits in arriving at a price.

In carrying out a cost-plus policy, a firm may demand a constant predetermined percentage markup over cost on each and every unit of product or service sold. Many believe that this fixed-margin approach is the most common method of pricing presently used by American business firms. However, a firm may also apply a flexible markup that always covers the designated costs but allows the margin over such costs to vary as demanded by the conditions surrounding the sale of each unit of product or service. This type of cost-plus pricing is said to be much less common than the constant-markup method. Nonetheless, as we indicated in Chapter 2, the popularity of cost-plus pricing in general, and the constant-markup method in particular, has probably been exaggerated.

Although there are administrative and procedural advantages in cost-plus pricing, deriving primarily from its relative simplicity, the method tends to ignore the demand, or market, side of the pricing problem and concentrates instead on the production, or seller's, side of the problem. This is a serious drawback. Actually, the extent to which demand and other market factors are ignored by this approach depends on the method used to determine the percentage markups. In some cases these factors are not considered at all, as when the price maker adds percentage markups that are "fair," "just," or "reasonable" in his opinion, or are "customary" in the industry or firm. In other cases, however, the price maker may take into account such factors as price elasticity of demand and competition in determining the markup to be added to costs. This constitutes at least some consideration of demand and other market factors, although the ability

---

[1] Examples of the use of standard costs are cited by A. D. H. Kaplan, Joel B. Dirlam, and Robert F. Lanzillotti in *Pricing in Big Business* (Washington, D.C.: Brookings Institution, 1958).

[2] Milton H. Spencer and Louis Siegelman, *Managerial Economics,* rev. ed. (Homewood, Ill.: Irwin, 1964), p. 372.

of the price maker to adjust prices in such situations is limited by the price floor of full costs, average costs, or some similar cost concept.

If a cost-plus approach is used, there is little question that the flexible-markup approach is superior to the fixed- or constant-markup approach in that it allows the price maker more discretion and permits him, within the limitation of the cost floor, to adjust prices to conform with whatever circumstances prevail, including market conditions.

RATE-OF-RETURN PRICING

When a company establishes as an objective the achievement of a given percentage rate of return on investment, or a specific total dollar return, this objective may also become a price policy. In a study of twenty large corporations made by Kaplan, Dirlam, and Lanzillotti [3] in 1958, it was found that many of the firms studied priced their products so as to achieve a target rate of return on investment. The only significant procedural difference between this approach and cost-plus pricing is that in this case the rate-of-return goal becomes the determinant of the markup to be added to costs.

The investment cost that is used as the base for target rate-of-return pricing can be the investment cost associated with specific products or groups of products, or a division, or an entire firm. The desired rate of return is in some sense an "average" figure in that the firm should not expect to achieve this rate of return every single year, but rather it should expect to earn this rate on the average over a period of years—perhaps the length of a business cycle.

The target rate of return may be what the management feels is a "fair," or "just," or "reasonable" return, in light of the risk involved, or it may simply be the rate that is customarily earned in the industry. Ideally, consideration should also be given to competition and to other market factors when setting the target rate of return.

Like the cost-plus approach, the rate-of-return approach tends to ignore demand and other market factors; it is not a market-oriented method of pricing. This, in turn, means that the prices that are se-

[3] *Op. cit.*

lected will not necessarily be acceptable to customers. Indeed, the study made by Kaplan, Dirlam, and Lanzillotti indicates that those firms that priced according to the rate-of-return approach often found that prices so determined had to be adjusted downward—or upward —in the market place because of competitive factors or changes in market conditions. To cope with this problem, the Aluminum Company of America, for example, adjusts rate-of-return pricing according to the nature of the product, the character of demand, the severity of competition, and the peculiarities of the market.[4] Furthermore, not only does target rate-of-return pricing tend to ignore market conditions, thereby acting as a damper on sales volume from time to time, but it also places a ceiling on profits in prosperous times by providing for a rigid markup over costs when a higher markup might be possible.

Because, in practice, a firm usually finds it impractical to use the prices selected by the target rate-of-return method, the method often does little more than provide a starting point from which pricing adjustments can be made. Even though the target rate of return may never be achieved, the use of the method at least will give the firm an idea of where it stands relative to its goal.[5]

CUSTOMARY PRICING

For some products and services there are customary prices; customers expect certain prices to be charged for them. In the consumer-goods market, for example, many convenience goods, such as chewing gum, soft drinks, and certain cosmetics, have customary prices. Sometimes this results from price lining since buyers become used to well-accepted price lines.

Where customary prices exist, it is difficult, if not impossible, for a seller to ignore them. It is usually impossible for a firm to sell products that are priced above the customary price since demand at such

---

[4] *Ibid.,* p. 31.

[5] To compare the actual rate of return with the target rate of return, one may employ rate-of-return analysis. For a description of the procedure involved in such an analysis, see Jules Backman, *Pricing: Policies and Practices* (New York: National Industrial Conference Board, 1961), pp. 40–41.

higher price levels is highly elastic. On the other hand, prices that are below the customary price will probably encourage only modest sales increases since demand at prices below the customary price tends to be inelastic. In other words, the demand curve for products of this sort tends to be kinked at the customary price, so that any price other than the customary price is not the best price.

In a sense, the existence of customary, or traditional, prices simplifies the pricing task. In effect, prices are determined by custom, and it is up to the firm to produce or purchase products or services that may be sold profitably at those prices. Clearly, this puts the emphasis on cost control.

Customary prices become troublesome during periods of rising costs because it then becomes increasingly difficult to keep costs low enough to offer the same product or service profitably at the customary prices. It may become necessary to reduce the quantity or quality offered in order to maintain a customary price during such periods.[6]

PSYCHOLOGICAL PRICING

Price has a psychological aspect to the extent that it influences customer reaction to the product. Some prices are preferable to others because they have more "appeal" to customers.[7] Customary prices are a good example of this. Sometimes a seller deliberately attempts to create an illusion about prices in the minds of buyers, and this may be termed *psychological pricing*.

In other chapters of this book, we have touched upon various forms of psychological pricing to some degree, including, for example, prestige pricing wherein an attempt is made to add prestige to a product or service by charging a very high price. Another form of psychological pricing is fictitious pricing in which consumers are led to believe that they are receiving bargains when, in fact, they are not. Bait pricing, wherein extremely low retail prices are quoted in adver-

---

[6] For example, manufacturers of candy bars in the early post–World War II period maintained the traditional $0.05 price but reduced the size of the bars.

[7] For an interesting discussion of "psychologically right" prices and how consumers and others perceive prices, see Alfred Oxenfeldt, David Miller, Abraham Shuchman, and Charles Winick, *Insights into Pricing* (Belmont, Calif.: Wadsworth, 1961), Chapter 4.

tisements and announcements as a lure, with the purpose of subsequently trading customers up to higher-price merchandise, also falls in this category.

ODD PRICES

A very common form of psychological pricing is called *odd pricing*. A product is said to carry an odd price if it is $0.19 instead of $0.20, $0.29 instead of $0.30, $4.95 instead of $5.00, $9.99 instead of $10.00, or $99.00 instead of $90.00.[8] Odd prices are used in all kinds of retailing operations, and also, although to a lesser extent, in wholesaling and in manufacturing.

Odd prices serve to create the illusion of low prices.[9] The supposition is that the buyer will believe a price of $9.95 to be much lower than one of $10.00. It is also meant to suggest that the price has been set as low as possible. However, sometimes such odd prices are actually arrived at by raising prices. Thus, a price of $0.29 may be the result of an adjustment upward from $0.24.

The seller who makes use of odd prices is really assuming that the demand curve for the product in question is jagged, as is shown in Figure 13. Such a curve reflects a situation in which sales are larger when price is expressed as an appropriate odd number than when it is expressed as an even number or some less satisfactory odd number. Indeed, this notion assumes that customers actually buy *less* when price is lowered from the appropriate odd price to the next lower even-numbered price, as from $0.19 to $0.18, or to some less satisfactory odd-numbered price, as from $0.19 to $0.17.

Odd prices have also been used on occasion to force retail sales clerks to make use of the cash register in order to make change for customers. Theoretically, this avoids the danger that some sales will not be rung up at all and the money paid for merchandise pocketed

[8] The term *odd prices* is sometimes also used to refer to prices that are just under a round number, whether ending in an odd or an even number. Thus, if the round number is $2.00, then $1.99, $1.98, $1.97, and $1.96 are all "odd" prices according to this definition.

[9] On the other hand, sometimes "even" prices are used deliberately to give the impression of high quality. Thus, certain fashion accessories are priced at even amounts such as $10.00 or $20.00.

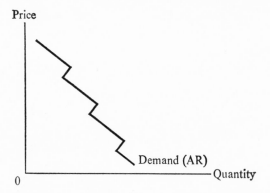

Figure 13   Odd Pricing

by the clerk. Another reason sometimes given for the use of odd prices is that it forces the customer to wait for change and this, in turn, permits him or her to look around and, perhaps, make an impulse purchase. To some extent, retailers also use odd prices out of custom.

Studies made of newspaper advertisements run by retailers indicate that the use of odd prices is quite widespread. For example, a study of food-store prices made in 1960 by Charles W. Hoyt Company showed that, next to prices of $0.10 and $1.00, the prices most frequently featured in the advertisements were those ending in odd numbers. The most strongly favored prices were those ending in 9 (such as $1.99), and the next most popular were those ending in 5 (such as $1.95).

Whether or not odd prices have the assumed psychological effect on consumers has never been adequately studied. It is entirely possible that odd prices repel some consumers just as they attract others. Also, where odd prices have been arrived at by making small reductions in price, as from $10.00 to $9.95, it should be kept in mind that, if odd prices do not have the desired psychological effect on customers, the small reductions in price required to achieve an odd price can cost the firm a good deal of money, particularly if sales volume is usually large.[10]

[10] It is clear that more research is needed to determine the value of odd pricing. Walter F. Kohn questions the effectiveness of odd pricing and suggests that the best retail prices are those that are the most convenient in terms of the coinage system. See "98 Cents or $1—Which Is Better Price Strategy?" *Printers' Ink,*

PROMOTIONAL PRICING

It was pointed out in Chapter 2 that whenever price plays its proper role in the marketing effort of a firm, it is helping to promote the product or service in question, even though this role may not be very obvious. The term *promotional pricing,* however, is used here to identify those situations in which the emphasis is on low prices as the major attraction of a product or service. Promotional pricing can take several forms, some of which have been discussed elsewhere in this book, such as leader pricing, bait pricing, and discounting as used by retailers. Other examples of promotional pricing that can be used by manufacturers and distributors include the use of temporary special sales, premiums, trading stamps, combination offers (two or more related or unrelated articles offered for one price), free deals (free goods given upon the purchase of a specified quantity of product), and trade-in allowances. Although some of the promotional-pricing methods listed above, such as the use of premiums, free goods, or trading stamps, do not involve actual reductions in price, the net effect is the same as a price reduction.

Promotional pricing is usually employed periodically to stimulate sales in slow periods, although some firms, particularly retail firms, use promotional pricing regularly. Some firms are continuously involved in some form of promotional pricing. The purpose of promotional pricing, which sometimes calls for prices that are below the usual cost floor, may be to build up sales volume in order to decrease costs per unit and eventually generate a profit at the low price.

The factors to consider in promotional pricing are the same as those to consider in any other approach to pricing. In this case some of the factors will be more important than others, of course, particularly the probable reaction of competitors since such pricing involves the risk of retaliation.

January 7, 1955, p. 30. See also Dik Warren Twedt, "Does the '9 Fixation' in Retail Pricing Really Promote Sales?" *Journal of Marketing,* October, 1965.

DISCOUNTS

For many firms the establishment of discount structures is an important part of price policy.[11] Regularly offered discounts of one kind or another are part of the pricing systems of most manufacturers and wholesalers even if such firms follow a one-price policy. As we noted in Chapters 6 and 7, discounts are entirely consistent with a one-price policy as long as all buyers who make their purchases under similar circumstances pay the same price. Unlike manufacturers and wholesalers, retailers usually do not make use of formal discount systems although they sometimes mark down merchandise for special reasons and provide discounts for certain groups such as employees and clergymen.

QUANTITY DISCOUNTS

One of the most common types of discounts is the quantity discount. This discount is granted for quantities purchased (measured in units or dollars), either in a single purchase (noncumulative quantity discount) or over a period of time such as a year (cumulative, deferred, or patronage quantity discount). The goods covered by the discount are usually of a single variety, although the discount system can allow for combining purchases of several different products. The latter method is sometimes used to boost sales on slow-moving products by tying them in with faster-moving products.

Noncumulative quantity discounts encourage larger orders at one time, and this benefits the seller in that it can lower his costs of selling, storage, order processing, delivery, and perhaps production. The cumulative quantity discount, on the other hand, does not necessarily offer these advantages to the seller since the individual orders may be quite small. However, cumulative discounts do tend to tie a customer to a seller for a period of time if the customer is anxious to get the discount. They may also help the seller plan production in the sense

---

[11] Discounts are reductions from the seller's "list" price granted by the seller to buyers.

that future orders may become more predictable because of the discount. Cumulative discounts are particularly suitable for perishable products because they cannot be purchased in large quantities at one time and stored, and for those products that distributors refuse to buy in large quantities at one time, such as refrigerators and other large home appliances, because of the large inventory costs involved.[12]

For the seller, the disadvantages of quantity discounts are that the savings made possible by large purchases may be overestimated and that they can lead to antagonism or ill will among smaller customers who cannot qualify for the larger discounts offered.

The practice of offering quantity discounts has broad social implications. It helps distributors and other purchasers achieve economies of scale, and these savings may, in turn, be passed on to ultimate users or consumers in the form of lower prices. In short, they permit the achievement of maximum efficiency in production and distribution. Often, however, such benefits are at the expense of smaller firms, which cannot take advantage of quantity purchases.

Managers who are considering the use of quantity discounts must determine:

1. The minimum quantity at which any discount is to be offered.
2. The number of "breaks," or additional discounts, to offer for progressively larger purchases.
3. The maximum quantity qualifying for any additional discount.
4. The actual amount of discount offered at each quantity level.[13]

The selection of the size of discounts and the quantities to which they are to apply should be based on a careful analysis of cost savings and any other advantages for the seller, buyers' habits with regard to size of purchase, and the advantages and disadvantages to buyers in purchasing in various quantities.

Legality of quantity discounts   Quantity discounts and other discounts have for many years been exposed to inquiry by the Federal Trade Commission under the Robinson-Patman Act, which attempts to prohibit unjust price discrimination.[14] In general, when a com-

[12] It should also be noted that sometimes a noncumulative or a cumulative quantity discount is offered merely to satisfy the wishes of very large buyers.
[13] John F. Crowther, "Rationale for Quantity Discounts," *Harvard Business Review,* March–April, 1964, p. 121. This article contains an interesting discussion of the idea that quantity discounts should be arrived at by balancing the extra costs to the buyer against the savings to the seller.
[14] See Chapter 4 for a discussion of the Robinson-Patman Act.

pany is accused by the Federal Trade Commission of injuring competition with its quantity discounts, noncumulative quantity discounts are theoretically lawful if they are offered to all competing buyers on the same basis and if they can be justified on a cost basis. To justify quantity discounts the firm must cite primarily costs of selling and physical distribution. However, since the cost defense has been successfully used in only a few cases, it can be concluded that, in practice, any quantity discount system that is likely to be charged with injury to competition can lead to legal difficulty. Cumulative quantity discounts are even more difficult to justify since there may be no directly measurable cost savings involved. In such a case, if injury to competition is claimed, it may be impossible for the firm to justify a cumulative quantity discount on a cost basis.

In addition to the cost defense, the other possible way to justify a quantity-discount system (noncumulative or cumulative) is to claim that a discount was offered to a buyer in good faith in order to meet an equally low price of a competitor. The good-faith defense, however, is seldom considered applicable to formal discount systems that are regularly used. Indeed, even if the discount offered is an isolated price adjustment, the uncertainties surrounding the interpretation of the good-faith clause make it unlikely that a quantity discount can be successfully defended on such grounds.

One further point, which was mentioned in Chapter 4, is that the mere fact that the same discount structure was offered to all competing buyers is not necessarily a defense against the charge of injury to competition since the Commission need only prove that there is a reasonable possibility that injury to competition may take place. In short, almost any quantity-discount system can be charged with injuring competition. This is particularly true if only a handful of large buyers qualify for the larger discounts offered.

TRADE OR FUNCTIONAL DISCOUNTS

Trade, or functional, discounts are those that are offered (usually by manufacturers although they are occasionally given by wholesalers, too) to buyers on the basis of their trade status or their position in the channel of distribution. Thus, a manufacturer of consumer goods may offer different discounts to wholesalers (say 50 percent off the list price) than to retailers (say 30 percent off the list price) with the understanding that the wholesaler would take a discount of 50 percent and pass on 30 percent to the retailer when selling to him.[15]

The justification for trade discounts is the fact that different distributors perform different functions in the marketing channel and should be compensated accordingly. Thus, wholesalers may provide storage facilities for a considerable period of time, extend credit to retailers, and provide personal salesmanship in moving a manufacturer's product through the channel to retail stores. Retailers do not provide any of these services; if wholesalers did not provide them, these functions would have to be performed by the manufacturer. Therefore, wholesalers often receive a larger discount (that is, they pay a lower net price) than do retailers.

Trade-discount structures should be established by the seller only after careful analysis of the functions that he would like distributors to perform for him, the costs of distributors, the discounts offered by competitors, the need to attract more or fewer distributors, the costs of selling to different kinds of distributors, and the opportunities for market segmentation (that is, whether discounts should be adjusted by trade channels used to reach different segments of the market).[16] To a great degree, however, trade discounts are determined by the margins that must be provided in order to secure the services of the various types of distributors used. In practice, industry custom is extremely important in determining trade-discount structures.

One serious problem that a firm often encounters in setting up a system of trade discounts is identifying the trade status of distributors. Many distributors are combinations of wholesale and retail operations, for example, and this complicates the identification task. Furthermore, there are many different kinds of wholesalers and many different kinds of retailers, all of whom perform different services and have different costs. It may be desirable to have the trade-discount structure reflect these differences if they can be identified and measured.

Legality of trade discounts   Although trade discounts are not specifically referred to in the Robinson-Patman Act, their legal status has always been in some doubt. It appears that such discounts are

[15] A variation of trade discounts as described above are adjustments made in prices through the use of discounts to differentiate between different kinds of industrial buyers, such as steel companies, the federal government, and fleet owners.

[16] Joel Dean, *Managerial Economics* (Englewood Cliffs, N.J.: Prentice-Hall, 1951), pp. 519–29.

lawful under the Act as long as they are offered on the same terms to all competing buyers of the same class and as long as the discounts granted do not exceed cost savings of the seller. This suggests that different discounts can in fact be granted to wholesalers than are granted to retailers without being considered a violation of the Act.[17] The problem arises when sellers attempt to distinguish between various kinds of retailers, such as chain-store companies, department stores, mail-order houses, and independent retailers, in their trade-discount structures or when they attempt to distinguish between different kinds of wholesalers, such as drop shippers and full-service wholesalers.[18] Since retailers may be in competition with one another regardless of these distinctions and since wholesalers of different types may compete with one another, it can be construed that competition is injured if different competing retailers or different competing wholesalers are charged different prices by means of trade discounts. However, although some discount systems that distinguished between retailers have encountered legal trouble, the present interpretation appears to be that different trade discounts may be granted to various trade groups without injuring competition and thus do not constitute a violation of the Robinson-Patman Act as long as they are offered equally to all buyers in a specific group.

CASH DISCOUNTS

Cash discounts are offered by many business firms, including some retailers. A cash discount is a reward for payment of invoices within a limited period of time, such as ten days. Although cash discounts vary greatly in terms of the amount of the discount and the time period involved, they are usually expressed on an invoice in terms such as "2/10, net 30 days," which mean that a 2-percent discount will be

[17] It has been proposed that the Robinson-Patman Act be amended to make mandatory the granting of functional discounts to force suppliers to maintain a price differential between their wholesale and retail customers so that a small retailer who buys from a wholesaler would be on "equal footing" with the large direct-buying retailer. See J. F. Barron, "Mandatory Functional Discounts: An Appraisal," *Journal of Business*, July, 1962.

[18] *Drop shippers* (or "desk jobbers") are wholesalers who place orders with suppliers but request that they be shipped directly to the retailer. Hence the drop shipper does not perform the wholesale warehouse function. A full-service wholesaler, on the other hand, performs all of the usual functions of wholesaling, including buying, warehousing, financing, risk taking, and others.

given the buyer if payment is received within 10 days and that the full amount of the invoice must be paid within 30 days of the date of purchase.

Cash discounts are used to encourage prompt payment of invoices and thereby keep the seller's cash turning over as rapidly as possible. Cash discounts also tend to reduce credit risks and the cost of collection of invoices since, if buyers are rewarded for prompt payment, there will be fewer overdue invoices, as a rule. In short, this discount is more a financial tool than a marketing tool. Here again the primary reason for cash discounts is sometimes merely industry custom.

According to Richard H. Buskirk, the wisdom of cash discounts is often questioned by executives of firms that are adequately financed. They point out that it is much cheaper for a firm to borrow money from a bank than to offer cash discounts. Second, many sales executives are critical of large buyers who do not pay within the discount period but take the discount, nevertheless. Of course, it is perfectly legal and justifiable to rebill these firms for the discounts they took, but this is a nuisance that can otherwise be avoided.[19]

The amount of the cash discount is determined by a number of factors including industry practice, the competitive situation, and economic conditions. In practice, however, the most important determinant seems to be industry practice.

Cash discounts tend to be taken regularly by buyers because they usually represent a relatively significant saving. Terms of 2/10, net 30 permit the buyer to deduct 2 percent from the total amount payable if the invoice is paid within 10 days. This means that the seller is willing to pay the buyer an interest rate of 36 percent expressed on an annual basis if the buyer will allow him to use the money 20 days sooner.[20] If cash discounts are generally taken, then the "real" price of the product is the price *less* the discount, and this may require that the seller adjust his list prices upward.

Legality of cash discounts   Cash discounts are lawful under the Robinson-Patman Act provided they are offered under the same terms to all competing buyers. There has been little legal difficulty with such discounts.

---

[19] *Principles of Marketing* (New York: Holt, Rinehart and Winston, 1961), p. 421.

[20] Assuming a 360-day year, there are 18 periods of 20 days in the year. Thus, 18 periods at 2 percent represents an interest rate of 36 percent per annum $\left(\dfrac{360}{20} \times 2 = 36 \right)$.

PROMOTIONAL ALLOWANCES

A promotional allowance given by a seller to distributors in return for local advertising, window displays, or other promotion on behalf of the seller's product is also a form of discount. Promotional allowances may be in the form of a percentage reduction in the price (on future purchases) or an outright cash payment. Although promotional allowances do represent a type of price reduction, the decision to use these allowances as a marketing tool is not a pricing decision.

Legality of promotional allowances Since promotional allowances are price reductions, they are subject to prosecution under the Robinson-Patman Act if they are discriminatory and tend to lessen competition or promote monopoly. In fact, one of the reasons for the enactment of the Act in the first place was the common practice of granting promotional allowances to distributors who did not engage in any promotional work in return. As we pointed out in Chapter 4, the policy of the Federal Trade Commission has been that promotional allowances must be offered on proportionally equal terms to all competing buyers. This means that all competing buyers must be informed of the availability of the program, that payment made to buyers must be in relation to the value of the services performed by them, and that the seller is obliged to see that the promotional work paid for is actually done.[21]

---

[21] In addition to the four kinds of discounts discussed here, there are several others. Vaile, Grether, and Cox state that "special" discounts are occasionally given for accepting trade-ins, providing installation and repair service, processing, cartage, financing, prepayment, warehousing during slack periods, and stocking a complete line. "Bargaining" discounts are given simply to attract business. See Roland S. Vaile, E. T. Grether, and Reavis Cox, *Marketing in the American Economy* (New York: Ronald Press, 1952), pp. 395–96. Another kind of discount is a seasonal discount given to a buyer for taking delivery in other than a normal delivery period.

The existence of secret bargaining discounts means that published or quoted prices are not the actual prices being used. They are, in effect, departures from a one-price policy. The prevalence of such discounts is difficult to estimate, although they are probably more important in highly competitive industries than in others and during a recession or depression period.

There are also concessions to buyers that do not affect prices or discounts as such, as when a manufacturer furnishes free local advertising for a retailer, or when a seller alters the date of an invoice to make it possible for a buyer to qualify for a cash discount beyond the normal discount period.

CONCLUSIONS

In preceding chapters we have discussed some of the basic types of pricing problems faced by the marketing executive, the kinds of pricing decisions he must make, and the manner in which pricing problems are, and should be, handled.

We mentioned in earlier chapters that the factors that affect pricing decisions are both internal and external to the firm. The internal factors—pricing objectives, organization for pricing, the role price plays in the marketing program, the characteristics of the product or service being offered to the market, and costs—are controllable, in the sense that the firm itself can determine the nature of these factors and their influence on pricing. In contrast, the external factors, which include legal considerations, the nature of competition, the kinds of buyers, the price elasticity of demand, and others, are largely beyond the control of the firm and as a body represent the uncontrollable "environment" within which pricing decisions must be made. These considerations may be expressed diagrammatically as in Figure 14.

The price maker must take into consideration both the controllable internal and the uncontrollable external factors when developing price policies and procedures. The various kinds of pricing problems that confront the firm, such as the pricing of a product line, the pricing of a new product, or the selection of distributor margins, determine what decisions must be made concerning price policies and procedure. Some possible pricing problems are listed in the lower part of Figure 14.

Accomplishing these tasks in a logical, systematic fashion in order to solve the pricing problems faced by the firm and to arrive at the optimal price policy(s) and prices is not easy.[22] Since the characteristics and pricing problems of business firms differ considerably, it is

[22] Alfred R. Oxenfeldt has set forth a step-by-step approach to pricing called the "multi-stage" approach. See his "Multi-Stage Approach to Pricing," *Harvard Business Review,* July–August, 1960, and *Pricing for Marketing Executives* (San Francisco: Wadsworth, 1961), pp. 72–76. Another kind of approach to pricing is discussed by Francis S. Doody in "Pricing for Profit—A Case for Discussion," *Boston University Business Review,* Winter, 1963–64.

Figure 14   Internal and External Considerations in Pricing

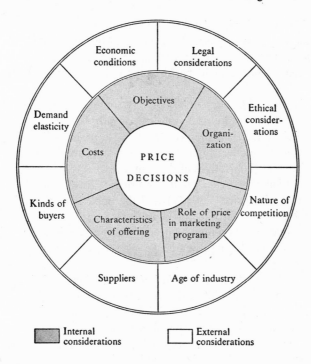

DECISIONS CONCERNING PRICE POLICY AND PROCEDURE
MUST BE MADE IN CONNECTION WITH THE
FOLLOWING KINDS OF PRICING PROBLEMS:

- Determination of the Level of Prices
- One-Price Policy Versus Varying Prices
- Pricing to Achieve Market Segmentation
- Product-Line Pricing
- Pricing Replacement Parts
- Pricing New Products
- Pricing Older Products
- Determination of Distributor Margins
- Control of Prices Charged by Distributors
- Provision for Protection Against Price Declines
- Determination of Geographic Pricing Policy
- Determination of Margins
- Determination of Markdowns
- Pricing Private Labels

not possible to set forth a detailed, universally applicable approach to pricing that any firm can use. However, from the preceding discussion in this book it should be clear that in developing price policies and specific prices a firm should perform the following general tasks.

1. *Define the objectives of pricing.* A sound approach to pricing requires that the overall objectives of the firm be articulated as clearly as possible since they are the proper guides to pricing. In order to be meaningful and effective, price policy and procedure must be consistent with the overall objectives of the firm.

2. *Determine the organization for pricing.* Responsibility for the establishment of a price policy(s) and the implementation of such a policy(s) must be clearly assigned. It is also necessary to determine what kind of cooperation may be needed from others in the firm, such as sales people, marketing research people, company economists, and accountants.

3. *Determine and collect the kind of information needed.* The kind of information needed will be determined by the relative importance of the various internal and external factors shown in Figure 14. The sources of such information vary widely from firm to firm and include company records, company personnel, outside consultants, research studies done in the field, suppliers, and buyers.

4. *Assign a role to price in the marketing program.* In developing a price policy it is necessary to determine what role price is to play in the marketing effort of the firm and how price is to fit in with the other elements in the marketing mix. Price may be a neutral, moderately neutral, moderately active, or an active instrument in the marketing program. In some cases, price will play an active role, as when a firm decides to stress low prices; in other cases, it will play a comparatively neutral role, as when a firm decides to match the prices of a price leader.

THE ROLE OF JUDGMENT IN PRICING

Products *can* be priced purely on the basis of intuition or the "feel of the market," without *any* examination of the pricing factors discussed in this book or any attempt to employ a systematic approach to arrive at a price policy or a price. A firm that prices by intuition does not necessarily have a poor pricing program, but the chances are good that the firm does not have the best possible program.

Nonetheless, it cannot be denied that judgment must play a key role in pricing. It is usually impossible to take all the information that could possibly influence a pricing decision, quantify it, and feed it into a machine or a formula and come up with *the* most desirable price policy or price.[23] Much of this information simply is not of the proper nature to be handled in such a manner. Furthermore, even if it were, one cannot assume that all the information desirable for pricing is available or that, when available, it is always accurate. For example, the true nature of price elasticity of demand for a product is seldom known. Furthermore, the probable reactions of competitors to price changes are often quite uncertain. This is illustrated by the difficulties encountered in trying to construct normative pricing models. According to one writer:

> Pricing is more an art than a science. It is the result of an attempt to balance factors to which no precise weight can be attached. The problem is not mathematical, but rather one of estimating the effects of various marketing policies upon sales—both in the near and distant future. Because of variations in a thousand and one factors, what is good policy for one company may be unworkable for another.[24]

Like other decision makers in marketing, price makers must operate with imperfect knowledge and under conditions of uncertainty. Although pricing is to some degree an art, not a science, and although judgment is a necessary part of the pricing process, this judgment should be an *informed* judgment, not merely a hunch. The points discussed in this text can help the price maker approach his task in an organized and systematic manner with proper consideration given to the objectives of the firm, the organization required for pricing, the kind of information required as a basis for pricing decisions, and the role price is to play in the marketing program.

[23] The main appeal of formulas is that they simplify pricing by minimizing the need for judgment. In a survey conducted among sales executives of firms of various sizes and kinds, it was found that 35 percent of the firms used a combination of a pricing formula—such as cost plus desired profit—and competitive prices, while 27 percent depended primarily on a formula, and 18 percent relied mainly on competitive prices. The rest relied mainly on other methods, such as estimates of what the traffic will bear (8 percent), field tests (8 percent), market surveys of consumer reactions (2 percent), and market surveys of distributor opinions (2 percent). See "Pricing Techniques and Practices Today: A Survey," *Management Review,* May, 1957.

[24] N. K. Dhalla, "The Art of Product Pricing," *Management Review,* June, 1964, p. 65.

Selected References

References on the relationship between costs and pricing are found in Chapter 2.

Rate-of-return pricing is discussed in Jules Backman, *Pricing: Policies and Practices* (New York: National Industrial Conference Board, 1961), pp. 40–44 and in Milton H. Spencer and Louis Siegelman, *Managerial Economics*, rev. ed. (Homewood, Ill.: Irwin, 1964), pp. 368–69.

Discounts of various kinds are commented on in general marketing textbooks such as E. Jerome McCarthy, *Basic Marketing: A Managerial Approach*, rev. ed. (Homewood, Ill.: Irwin, 1964), pp. 738–47. A good account of different kinds of discounts is found in Joel Dean, *Managerial Economics* (Englewood Cliffs, N.J.: Prentice-Hall, 1951), pp. 517–48. For a discussion of methods to use in determining quantity discounts, see John F. Crowther, "Rationale for Quantity Discounts," *Harvard Business Review,* March–April, 1964.

The legality of different kinds of discounts is discussed in the literature on the Robinson-Patman Act referred to in Chapter 4. See especially Corwin D. Edwards, *The Price Discrimination Law* (Washington, D.C.: Brookings Institution, 1959), particularly Chapters 7, 8, 9, and 10; Herbert W. Taggart, *Cost Justification,* Michigan Business Studies, Vol. 14, No. 3 (Ann Arbor, Mich.: Bureau of Business Research, University of Michigan, 1959); Donald F. Fennelly, "On the Judging of Mince Pies," *Harvard Business Review,* November–December, 1964; and Robert A. Lynn, "Is the Cost Defense Workable?" *Journal of Marketing,* January, 1965.

INDEX

A 6
B 7
C 8
D 9
E 0
F 1
G 2
H 3
I 4
J 5